ITALO SVEVO

ITALO SVEVO

Naomi Lebowitz

RUTGERS UNIVERSITY PRESS
NEW BRUNSWICK, NEW JERSEY

Library of Congress Cataloging in Publication Data
Lebowitz, Naomi.
    Italo Svevo.

    Bibliography: p.
    Includes index.
    1. Schmitz, Ettore, 1861–1928—Criticism and
interpretation. I. Title.
PQ4841.C482Z718   853'.8   77-12011
ISBN 0-8135-0848-7

To my twin,
una burla riuscita

Contents

Prefatory Note

The standard edition of Svevo's work in Italian is the four-volume edition of Bruno Maier (Milan: dall'Oglio, 1966–69) :

1. Epistolario

2. Romanzi (*Una vita, Senilità, La coscienza di Zeno*)

3. Racconti, Saggi, Pagine sparse

4. Commedie

The letters and essays in vols. 1 and 3, as well as some of the sketches and minor short stories in vol. 3, have not been translated. The translations from these texts are all mine and will be referred to in the book as OO (Opera omnia) followed by the volume number. The titles of untranslated texts will be referred to in Italian. The novels and major short stories have all been translated into English and will be referred to in the following editions:

Confessions of Zeno, trans. Beryl de Zoete (New York: Vintage paperback, 1958) .

As a Man Grows Older, trans. Beryl de Zoete (Harmondsworth, England: Penguin paperback edition, 1965) .

Short Sentimental Journey and Other Stories, trans. Beryl de Zoete, S. Collison-Morley, Ben Johnson (Berkeley, Calif.: University of California Press, English translation and copyright 1967 by Martin Secker & Warburg Limited) .

Further Confessions of Zeno (a collection of sketches about an older Zeno, which Svevo was working on when he died), trans. and collected by Ben Johnson and P. N. Furbank (Berkeley, Calif.: University of California Press, English translation and copyright 1969 by Martin Secker & Warburg Ltd.).

A Life, trans. Archibald Colquhoun (New York: Knopf, 1973).

These will be the editions used for citation and they will appear in the text as:

Confessions of Zeno (**CZ**)

As a Man Grows Older (AMGO)

Short Sentimental Journey and Other Stories:

"The Hoax" (H)

"The Story of the Nice Old Man and the Pretty Girl" (NOM)

"Generous Wine" (GW)

"Argo and His Master" (A)

"Short Sentimental Journey" (SSJ)

The large number of critical articles and books used will be cited in my translations and referred to by the Italian titles in the notes. This is true, as well, of the French and the German.

Acknowledgments

I would like to thank the John Simon Guggenheim Memorial Foundation for a fellowship which allowed me to start work on this book. I am grateful to Egon Schwarz for his help on the Hapsburg background, and to Margaret Israel for editorial help with the translation from the Italian. To the Interlibrary Loan Department of Washington University's Olin Library I owe a great debt. Their indefatigable detective work allowed me to be an armchair scholar. I am grateful for the encouragement of Iris Murdoch and John Bayley throughout this project, and for that of my best editor, my husband. Thanks, too, are due Leanna Boysko for profitable suggestions during the preparation of this manuscript.

Also, permission to quote from the following published works is gratefully acknowledged. AS A MAN GROWS OLDER by Italo Svevo, translated by Beryl de Zoete. This translation first published by Putnam, 1932; published by Secker & Warburg 1962, where the work appears as Volume 2 in the Uniform Edition; published in Penguin Books, 1965; reprinted by permission of G. P. Putnam's Sons and Martin Secker & Warburg Limited. CONFESSIONS OF ZENO by Italo Svevo, translated by Beryl de Zoete; copyright 1930 and renewed 1958 by Alfred A. Knopf, Inc.; reprinted by permission of Alfred A. Knopf, Inc. FURTHER CONFESSIONS OF ZENO by Italo Svevo, translated by Ben Johnson and P. N. Furbank; copyright © 1969 by Martin Secker & Warburg Limited; reprinted by permission of the University of California Press; also reprinted by permission of Martin Secker & Warburg Limited, where the work appears as Vol-

ume 5 in the Uniform Edition. A LIFE by Italo Svevo, translated by
Archibald Colquhoun; copyright 1963 by Martin Secker & War-
burg Limited; published 1973 by Alfred A. Knopf, Inc.; reprinted
by permission of Alfred A. Knopf, Inc.; also reprinted by permission
of Martin Secker & Warburg Limited, where the work appears as
Volume 3 in the Uniform Edition. SHORT SENTIMENTAL JOURNEY
AND OTHER STORIES by Italo Svevo, translated by Beryl de Zoete,
L. Collison-Morley and Ben Johnson; copyright © 1967 by Martin
Secker & Warburg Limited; reprinted by permission of the University of California Press; also reprinted by permission of Martin
Secker & Warburg Limited, where the work appears as Volume 4
in the Uniform Edition.

ITALO SVEVO

Introduction

THE CULTURAL MELODRAMA of Italo Svevo's "case" has been well documented.[1] It is satisfying to witness a writer with very little of the kind of belief in his own talent that carried Joyce through his years of disappointment, suddenly achieving, at the end of his life, the recognition so longed for and so long denied by circumstance, situation, and character. We like to see a man schooled in unsentimental self-irony become in his joy a "bambino di 64 anni"[2] after a daily sublimating and soothing of literary ambition with the help of business, marriage, cigarette daydreams, the violin, and scribbling. Following his death, Svevo's place in cultural history was assured even if it could not be adequately described.

The case of Svevo seemed predestined to be an international one. Not only could he be honored as a father of modern Italian narrative literature but he would also have to be seen as a brother of the great masters of modern fiction. He was championed by Joyce, enthusiastically received in 1925 by the French literary world, and simultaneously discovered by Eugenio Montale. The Italian poet, struggling against conservative resistance to the impurity of the Triestine's language, the irregularity of his narrative rhythms, and his queer analytic humor, gave Svevo to the young Italian writers associated

1. The only biography of Italo Svevo in English is that of P. N. Furbank, *Italo Svevo: The Man and the Writer* (Berkeley and Los Angeles, Calif., 1966), a good introduction to Svevo's life and literature. See also the critical introduction of Brian Moloney, *Italo Svevo: A Critical Introduction* (Edinburgh, 1974), which is particularly good on the cultural situation of Svevo's Trieste.
2. Svevo uses this term ("a 64 year old baby") to describe his feelings about his late fame in a letter to one of his French discoverers, Valéry Larbaud, 15 September 1925, OO, 1: 764.

with the magazines *Solaria* and *Il Convegno,* who were eager to claim
a father for a new Italian literature that could take its place next
to the narrative literature coming out of Europe, England, and
America—that of Proust, Joyce, Kafka, Mann, D. H. Lawrence, and
Faulkner.

What had appeared a biographical curse, a literary life in Trieste,
a city with an Austrian head and an Italian heart, comes to be seen
as a cosmopolitan advantage, for geographical alienation was an
emblematic climate for the homeless, weightless, bourgeois, superfluous man relentlessly portrayed in modern literature as politically
useless, socially decadent, and psychologically anxious. Svevo's situation at the center of a paralyzed and weary world on the brink of war
has made him a favorite subject of Marxist, Freudian, and Existentialist critics. Like Trieste, he is open on all sides to every cultural
influence that shaped the modern novel—to the self-irony of Austria's
literary Jew and to his psychoanalysis; to the Slavic preference for the
insulted and the injured; to the cramped dreams of France's post-
Napoleonic heroes doomed to live out bourgeois monarchies; to the
pathologists dissecting the old morality, Schopenhauer, Nietzsche,
and Ibsen; to a new Italian fiction waiting for wider recognition, that
of Tozzi, Cantoni, and Pirandello; and, as an older man, to the
beginnings of a Triestine tradition in Stuparich, Slataper, and Saba.
This exposure makes him available to a variety of critical disposi-
tions. Yet, despite all that would raise Svevo to a high degree of
historical representation, the undeniable fact is that he is a writer
who did not seize the world he read or traveled in, but played with it,
casually subordinating it to the interests of his amiable temperament.
Having nothing of the nature of a revolutionary, he is one of the
most original writers of modern fiction.

Lina Galli's description of Svevo's uniqueness in his own city helps
to confirm his imperviousness to domination by his time and place.
Noting the distance between him and the rhetoric of the irredentist
years, the rhetoric of "liberation literature,"[3] the historian of Trieste
reminds us that not even in *As a Man Grows Older,* which takes
place in the Trieste of the end of the century, can one trace the
presence of this political sentiment:

    3. Lina Galli, "Svevo and Irredentism," trans. Camilla Rudolph, *Modern Fiction
Studies,* Svevo issue (Spring 1972) , p. 115.

He described the city as if it did not burn with hot political problems. He never wrote a line concerning the Risorgimento myth.[4]

The public Svevo lived an exemplary life of bourgeois liberalism. He
was educated in Germany, trained in banking and business, wrote for
an irredentist newspaper, was a responsible head of a bourgeois
household. But the private life, hidden behind the smoke of
"l'ultima sigaretta,"[5] examined the depths of its own soul with
humor and perception, then paid for its publication. It would be
difficult to refute Lina Galli's contention that the political struggle
was, for this life, "contingent, temporary, and did not touch deeply
the human essence."

The international world embraced by Musil, Mann, Proust, and
Joyce produced atmospheres vastly different from the ambience of
Svevo's novels, in every case intellectually more imposing, literarily
more aggressive, wider in physical and mental geography, loftier in
irony, bolder in the mixture of tones and styles, and more confident
in visions that play with notions of cultural, social, and verbal orders
high enough to stave off anarchies. The peculiar and unique texture
of Svevian intimacy and spontaneity, the sly and relaxed presence of
the author in the major work, the characteristic humor, both auda-
cious and touching—all seem dwarfed in the midst of such sweeping
energy. Yet the Svevo of *As a Man Grows Older, Confessions of Zeno*,
and the late fiction breaks bread at this banquet of kings. This is not
primarily because of the breadth of his case, but by virtue of the
nature, provincial and parochial, of his humane and ironic temperament.[6] In the Svevo issue of *Solaria* (1929), Ilya Ehrenburg describes a dinner given by French admirers to honor Svevo and other
contemporary writers. Joyce is present and Jules Romains presides.
Through the speeches and flattering devotions, the natural embar-
rassments between writers flung together at such an affair, the artifice
of literary roles assumed, Ehrenburg notes the irresistible presence of
the Svevian irony and tolerance hiding behind the habitual screen of
cigarette smoke of a sexagenarian baby, delighted and bewildered by

4. Ibid., p. 116.
5. This is the phrase ("the last cigarette!") used by Svevo in his letters to his wife
and by Zeno to indicate the resolution to quit smoking, a hope that never came to pass.
6. See Lowry Nelson, Jr., "A Survey of Svevo," *Italian Quarterly* 3, no. 10 (Summer
1959), p. 5: "In most things Svevo was far from 'international.' It would be closer to
the truth to call him parochial."

the rhetoric of professional literary company. It is this understated presence that makes the case.

Because the nature of Svevo's literary temperament as it comes into his best fiction is the predominant reason he continues to be read, I am reversing the usual order between historical placement and the description of his literary voice. The readers of Svevo have for so long been distracted by discussions and reviews of his case that I think it important to begin with the Svevo who would continue to be amazed at being designated a revolutionary force in modern Italian literature and a modern master. The first chapters will attempt to translate this Svevo largely through his major, last period, in which added confidence allowed a more lenient atmosphere to his irony. They refer to his contemporary Freud, who, as Svevo admits, touched his later work significantly, and to Montaigne who, absent from Svevo's articles and letters, illuminates and helps to describe Svevo's spirit by the public example of the form and tone of his *Essais*. Following an examination of the development of Svevo's fiction, the second half of the book will review the cultural atmosphere in which Svevo worked. Of course, the case and the temperament cannot be neatly separated in many instances, but by subordinating as much as possible to the fiction the arguments on language and influence surrounding Svevo, I hope to emphasize the man who can be read before he is studied.

PART I:
THE PRESENCE

Chapter 1

The Lyric Zeno

IN HIS OWN VERSION OF THE EUCHARIST, Montaigne, reveling in the identification of his body with his book, calls them *consubstantial*,[1] and the term economically describes the impression we have that the form and the subject of the *Essais* consume each other. Indeed, when Montaigne speaks of the pleasure of tasting himself, we are witnesses to the most commodious cannibalism on record. We are not curious about Montaigne's life because his book uses it up completely. So sated are we with his spirit that his biography seems almost to belong to someone else. Though all literature is to some extent consubstantial with its author, we recognize from time to time a thoroughness of assimilation that allures us by its intensity. It is difficult to describe the reasons for our belief that we have met in such a piece of literature the whole man, to account for the absence of suspicion that the confession or the fiction is engaged in special pleading. We know, by contrast, that while the presence of Rousseau is strong in the *Confessions*, it forces upon the reader the task of adjustment that sends us to biography and history, to the testimony of others, because we are likely to resist the absolution that is demanded. Fiction, screened through character and invention, is susceptible to similar distortions of the spirit that feeds it. In a recent review of Sybille Bedford's biography of Aldous Huxley, Martin Green registers his disturbance at the disparity between the nice person pictured at the dinner table and his ruthless presence in the novels. "How can we account for this

1. *The Complete Essays of Montaigne*, trans. Donald M. Frame (Stanford, Calif., 1958), 2: 504: "I have no more made my book than my book has made me—a book consubstantial with its author, concerned with my own self, an integral part of my life."

difference?" he asks. Green offers us a choice: "Either the life was insincere or the imaginative vision was." The reviewer generalizes:

> There just are men whose imaginative or intellectual life is vitiated by some fatal inauthenticity, and struggle as they may with all the instruments of the intellectual and the moral lives to cauterise the infection, it is always there.[2]

Since the attempt to measure biography against the fictive presence is likely to prove unsettling, it remains important to insist that a perversion of spirit must first be felt in the literature itself before we seek its definition outside it. For it is not a question of whether Montaigne was really this kind of a man or that. It is a question of how persuasive his *Essais* are in convincing us in themselves that we see him as he sees himself.

Henry James has given us the term *saturation,* which serves fiction in a way analogous to that in which *consubstantial* serves confession. In his central essay, "The Lesson of Balzac," he speaks of the quantity and intensity of life that are the sign of Balzac's art and that convince us that "his spirit somehow paid for its knowledge."[3] The novelist vulnerable to his fictions cannot contrive his presence. Whatever the faults of Balzac, his moral sops to the reader, his awkward intrusions, and his heavy-handed metaphors and digressions, they are faults of method rather than spirit and do not vitiate his presence:

> When saturation fails no other presence really avails; as when, on the other hand, it operates, no failure of method fatally interferes.[4]

A rich saturation between the felt life of the author and its presence in the novel guarantees the liberation of character, atmosphere, and reader from imposed responses. Paradoxically, the more fully these are possessed, the more spontaneously they exhibit themselves. For all the power of Zola's novels, they too often force themselves upon us by their breadth and energy rather than by the penetration that derives from the possession of the subject by the spirit. James imagines Zola as acting in the Dreyfus affair like a man "with arrears of personal history to make up,"[5] a history left over from the novels.

2. "Huxley's Fatal Flaw," *The Guardian,* November 10, 1973, p. 23.
3. Henry James, *The Future of the Novel,* ed. Leon Edel (New York, 1956), p. 114.
4. Ibid., p. 115.
5. Ibid., p. 166.

The unwillingness or inability to give oneself wholly to this translation is seen as aesthetic faithlessness by D. H. Lawrence, who pounces
upon perversions between intention and effect in *Studies in Classical
American Literature,* in his long essay on Hardy and elsewhere.

An admittedly unsophisticated standard of response draws us to
works that reflect an author's personality, presence, and temperament, particularly to those we happen to like. This impulse is fully
credited by E. M. W. Tillyard in his appealing debate with C. S.
Lewis. Lewis's contrary position is familiar to modern criticism:

> We must go to books for that which books can give us—to be in-
> terested, delighted, or amused, to be made merry or to be made
> wise. But for the proper pleasure of personality, that is, for love,
> we must go where it can be found—to our homes or our common
> rooms, to railway carriages and public houses.[6]

While honoring Lewis's qualifications, Tillyard is unwilling to admit
that such distinctions can be so neatly made. Can we avoid the feeling that, since Tennyson "came to trust his unconscious too little
and . . . tried to check it rather than to follow its frightening
vagaries," the result is that "Tennyson did not make a very good job
of himself and we tend to shrink from his personality?"[7] Can this
response ever be irrelevant to our evaluation of literature's worth?
Tillyard's arguments ally themselves with the prejudices of James
and Lawrence for a literature that does not hoard, but spends the
consciousness behind it. The quality and quantity of saturation between the body and the book are still a major measure of value and
motive to response.

No impression has been more frequently affirmed by Svevo's readers than that of the fullness of the author's participation in the atmosphere of his fiction. As with James's Balzac, it is the sign of his
appeal. The poet Eugenio Montale was the first to talk of the
thoroughness and spontaneity of Svevo's entrance into his fiction as
saturazione, a term that inevitably recalls that of James:

> I have met many famous writers, both foreign and Italian, and al-
> most always, even when I have not been disappointed, I have had to
> distinguish between the man and the writer: in all these cases, the
> scale went down on one side or the other, but at any rate the scale

6. E. M. W. Tillyard and C. S. Lewis, *The Personal Heresy* (London, 1939), p. 69.
7. Ibid., p. 81.

dipped. Not in the case of Svevo: in him one felt a presence that was all of a piece.[8]

The impression of "un solo blocco" derives particularly from an atmosphere that came into full flower in *Confessions of Zeno* and after. But it had gradually accumulated through earlier fiction the gestures, motifs, and tones that had assumed, by the very fact of Svevo's participation in them, such an independent life of their own that in the last fiction they live almost without the help of character itself. Noting the resemblance between the atmosphere emanating from Svevo and that surrounding his characters, between his whims and their whims, his attitudes and theirs, Montale reads from the book back to life: "In Italo Svevo everything . . . was Svevian from head to toe."[9] By the time of Zeno it had become Svevo's second nature not to hold back from the world of his fiction any part of his spirit that would make the reader feel an unused portion reserved for the life. With the creation of Zeno's consciousness and the opening up of a universe wide enough to house the bourgeois salon, the crazy constellations of Mother Nature, and the double time of desire and duty, Svevo walks with Zeno into a world of rationalization so expansive that it makes analysis and affection socially compatible, entirely absorbing the Svevian temperament.

If Zeno, in his struggle to exercise independence, may occasionally falter, he has been licensed with qualities that both create and endure life on the Svevian planet—humor, self-irony, a consciousness both analytical and moral, and a temper susceptible to the neutral lyricism of the universe that resists all human control. The atmosphere that is large enough to hold both Zeno and his creator is a climate that takes on the full color of Svevo's own consciousness. It spreads through three zones, each distinctive and each jealous of the other's exclusive hegemony. The bourgeois order, its chronology, manners, and morals, constitutes the most conventional narrative zone. Its characteristic rhythm depends upon Zeno's resolutions to be good, resolutions that "bridge the gulf between [a] gloomy present

8. The comments of Montale on Svevo are collected in Eugenio Montale, *Lettere Italo Svevo: con gli scritti di Montale su Svevo* (Bari, 1966). The term *saturazione* was used in an article in the Svevo issue of *Solaria* of 1929, p. 125 of the *Lettere*. The second comment, *Lettere*, p. 152, comes from a lecture of 1963.

9. Montale, "Poesia e società," dal *Corriere d'informazione, Lettere,* 21 February, 1946, pp. 131–132.

and the bright future" (CZ, 244). Motives and the unchronological workings of the mind are the subject and matter of the second zone, which eases some of the constrictions of the first, while the third, which represents the loftiest and most expansive perspective, is the zone of lyric humor, of comic objectivity beamed from the eyes of space. This view gives us philosophies of life and Mother Nature's plots that are as unpredictable and devious as psychoanalytic discovery. Zeno occupies all these zones. The movement that passes him from one to the next in a constant series of oscillations is Svevo's comic rhythm of life's dilettante who can neither be dominated by systems of salvation nor reconciled to a world that refuses to imagine them.

Many readers have attempted to organize the Svevian perspective by isolating Zeno in one or another of these spheres of influence. Some psychoanalytic critics have seen in his fantasies, rationalizations, defenses, lies, and thirst for absolution the signs of evasion of knowledge of the self gained from therapy. In this view Svevo may either be superior to these tricks or show his own trembling hand by sharing with Zeno a fear of the ultimate truths about the personality. After the aging Zeno, in the section called "Umbertino" of *Further Confessions of Zeno* (FCZ, 73), has a nightmare based upon a fantasy "conceived in that little blond head of Umbertino's" in which the grandfather's body has been severed from his head, he sighs: "One ought not to have to live a life in which such monstrous things can be imagined." The psychoanalytic critic, spotting a castration anxiety, seizes upon this statement as an evasive Svevian rationalization.[10] But this is a distortion of the Svevian spirit as it spans both a younger and an older Zeno, a spirit that chooses to open anxieties to common philosophies, refusing to close upon the restrictive clinical designation. Those who accept as the ultimate summation of Zeno's personality the diagnosis of Dr. S., who frames the confession and concludes that Zeno has an Oedipus complex, distort the presence that binds Zeno to Svevo. The point is not that he has an Oedipus complex, but that he cannot be defined by it. If Zeno's flippant attacks on the psychoanalyst exhibit a defensive choreography, or, as the analyst hints to the reader, one of negative transference, it is a dance that

10. See, for example, Paula Robison, "Svevo: Secrets of the Confessional," *Literature and Psychology* 20, n. 3 (1970): 101–14.

spins Svevo out to a larger universe where all Oedipal lovers can delight in the "special genius and freedom"[11] of each other, including Svevo and Zeno. Predictably, the Zeno through which Svevo "made such a good job of himself," has aroused hostility in the hearts of psychoanalytic critics. Intent upon severing Zeno's head from his Svevian body, some, overestimating the danger of Zeno's lies and fantasies, assume that Svevo was prompted to expose Zeno[12] rather than to live in him.

By forcing Zeno to socialize his sickness, by refusing to let him nurture a privileged isolation, Svevo turns exposure to sympathy. If Zeno's rationalizations compromise bourgeois morality and protect desire, they unaccountably support the social order that benefits from their humor. They are always in the service of Zeno's crazy diplomacy that strengthens the bonds with other characters and with the reader. Zeno's benevolent consciousness does not convert itself into the hysterical self-righteousness of the underground man, into any lasting and paralytic self-justification. Instead, it keeps him open to the surprises of a world without solutions, without victories, a world in which confession is forced to submit to the leaven of a conversation[13] that cannot take too seriously claims of innocence and demands for absolution. It seems to me a grave misreading to assume that the younger Zeno, in his deployment of lies and improvisations, of evasions and "mauvaise foi," is engaged merely in defensive actions against judgment. Again and again he eludes the protective custody of his rationalizations to mingle with the bourgeois crowd that laughs at them, stimulating him to climaxes of perception, intuition, and shared affections. It is for the spirit of his lies that Augusta loves him, and by that spirit he wins her:

> It was long afterwards that Augusta told me that none of them had believed my stories to be true. Augusta liked them all the more on that account for, as my invention, they seemed to her to belong to me more than if fate had actually inflicted them on me. (CZ, 75)

11. James, "The Lesson of Balzac," *Future of the Novel,* p. 116. The phrase is used to describe the way Balzac knows his characters and respects their independence by first loving them.

12. See James's distinction between Thackeray and his Becky and Balzac and his Valérie as a distinction between a prompting to exposure in the first case and to love in the second, in ibid.

13. See Pietro Citati, "Il violino di Svevo," *Il tè del capellaio matto* (Milan, 1972), p. 163.

The hypotheses of self-analysis inevitably suffer qualification by experience. After Guido's marriage, Zeno's devotion to him seems, by his own estimation, to be a symptom of his disease, a public display of his indifference (an inversion of his hostility) to losing Ada. But it might also be, he muses, a manifestation of great benevolence (CZ, 248). And if neither of these motives can remain decisive when his aid to Guido backfires, a strong affection born of daily contact neutralizes Ada's harsh judgment of him after Guido's death (CZ, 248–49).

A consciousness whimsical enough to chase the truth down the devious paths plotted by Mother Nature is at the same time too dependent to have it at the price of sacrificing or compromising affection. By opening up the Malfenti salon to a world without moral security in which mutations of intention and effect are the rule, Zeno's mind and its humor check the superiority of the impersonal and systematic diagnosis of Dr. S. They move us into a fuller and more flexible reality. Svevo and Zeno cohabit worlds unpremeditated and uncategorical, conscious and unconscious, moral and amoral, suffused by the spontaneous acceptance of the inability of the human heart to purge itself of confusion and surprise as long as it needs sympathy. Rationalizations and improvisations, provisional analyses, and the making and breaking of resolutions carry with them values that make Dr. S.'s certainties too flat for Svevo's novel, though they are by no means canceled. Nothing is canceled in the Svevian universe—no thought, no perception, no story, no influence. If, as John Freccero claims,[14] Dr. S. spots for us the subterfuges of self-rationalization or self-justification that render Zeno's novel a deliberate travesty of the conversion process deriving from Christian confession, the acrobatics of absolution have never quite persuaded Zeno himself, even when moved to frequent fits of self-pity, to isolate himself in comic inauthenticity. Zeno's basic interest is not in refuting the doctor's analysis. This is evidenced by the broadness of his defensive play against him, by the farcical nature of his accusation that the doctor himself has the complexes he ascribes to others, and by the hyperbolic claim for an independent cure childishly trumpeted. What he is interested in doing is in staving off a description that

14. John Freccero, "Zeno's Last Cigarette," *Modern Language Notes* 77 (1962) : 3–23. Reprinted in *From Verismo to Experimentalism: Essays on the Modern Italian Novel,* ed. Sergio Pacifici (Bloomington, Ind., 1969), pp. 35–60.

threatens to rid him of spontaneous desires, for if these lead him into adulteries, they also impel him to love the maternal tenderness of Augusta and to resolve, like a child, to be better with an energy and happiness born of his sickness. Zeno flinches, like Svevo, though more awkwardly, from any menace to the mystery of his personality, which, by whatever means, has procured him all that he really wants. He shrinks, like the novelist, from the definition that might put an end to surprise. If he acts out Svevo's amorous fantasies, he also lives out his marital devotion, his kindness, his humor. By making the lyric smiles of Augusta (despite her limitations of consciousness brought on by a fatal condition of health) a more powerful influence than the psychoanalyst's diagnosis, by making her impervious to the doctor's analysis, Svevo creates a force and a face that prize the confession's sociability over its truth. Zeno avers:

> I could not have borne it if . . . my conduct had obliged her to repress a single one of those tender smiles of hers, which seemed to me the kindest and most final judgment that anyone could pass on me. (CZ, 235–36)

Between the motherhood of Augusta and that of Mother Nature, it would be difficult to imagine Zeno's taking his "conversion" as anything but a daily adjustment.

Zeno's improvising of the past as an evasion of the psychoanalytic discovery reflects the positive preference of the novelist himself to remain halfway between memory and invention. The novelist is in important ways competitive with Dr. S., for, while exploiting psychoanalytic recognitions of repetition, he is intent upon rescuing faces and personalities from retreat into archetypal patterns. Unfortunately for the doctor, he has to live in the novelist's world, where his mode of getting at truths will not often be able to display itself to good advantage. The novel's improvisations honor the ultimate mystery of personality with an entirely unsentimental tolerance, and it is the novelist's resistance to clinical summations allowed the analyst, never rejection, that motivates the Jamesian action of penetration into the subject by loving him before knowing him. In a moving entry of 1896 in the "Diario per la fidanzata," that unique document in which he comes to terms with the joys and doubts of his own coming marriage, Svevo speaks of his fear that his deep concern and jealousy in relation to Livia might prejudice the tolerance that had always been the trait he most cherished, an imperious obligation, as he calls it:

> It was a major quality of my character up to now to allow to the characters and dispositions around me the full freedom to develop and display themselves according to their own nature. Any interference on my part in these exhibitions would have seemed to me a crime.[15]

Since fiction is the form designed to exhibit these characters in the presence of their curious and interested creator, it is no wonder that so many readers have felt that the novel for Svevo was a necessary and instinctive choice of genre, that it was the most natural medium for his temperament as a writer.[16]

It is well to remember this attitude of Svevo when confronted by the controversial hypothesis of Giacomo Debenedetti, who theorizes that Svevo's reluctance to dominate the reader by his form and characters is a symptom of Svevo's failure to master himself.[17] By this flaw he falls considerably short of giants like Tolstoy, whose major characters take us in with such power that their consciousness elevates us immediately to a shared universality. It is Debenedetti's contention that the reader is stopped short, even with Zeno, of the kind of identity that sweeps us into the novel to embrace the destiny of fictional heroes. We certainly feel the reticence that Debenedetti so subtly describes, yet we also feel that it is this very quality that is the major source of the appeal that draws us to Svevo's work, and that it has something to do with a beneficent desire to leave the reader alone. Even the abortive momentum of the narrative, which jerks us from episode to episode, when fingered by Debenedetti as further evidence of Svevo's need to retreat from custody of his ma-

15. Svevo, OO, 3: 785.
16. See, for example, the emphatic insistence of one of Svevo's best critics, Giacomo Debenedetti, "Svevo e Schmitz," *Saggi critici*, n.s. (Milan, 1955), p. 56: "Il romanzo fa parte del suo temperamento di scrittore." For his discussion of the historical consequences of this attitude, see pt. 2, chap. 4 of this book. See also Antonio Testa, *Italo Svevo* (Ravenna, 1968), p. 61: ". . . nel romanzo Svevo è impegnato e nelle opere teatrale semplicemente si diverte."
17. Debenedetti, "Svevo e Schmitz," p. 93. For an interesting parallel to this argument see Edmund Wilson, "A Dissenting Opinion on Kafka," *Kafka*, ed. Ronald Gray (Twentieth Century Views), (Englewood Cliffs, N.J., 1965), pp. 91–7.

terial, can be appreciated as a testimony to the independent life of
the mind, whose secret workings keep cause from complacently predicting effect. Svevo's reticence, seen as psychological and narrative
tolerance, is the very essence of his original and attractive temperament and is one more indication of the way in which he turned his
nonheroic qualities into the humor that wins us to his world.

Taking his measure from the God who stands back from the world
with "curiosity, never with wrath,"[18] the novelist places himself between Mother Nature and his characters, alternately anxious and
amused, sympathetic and ironic in the face of his own creation. Under these eyes Zeno never abuses his freedom. He is held to the world
by the very oddity that seems to distance him from it, for his mixed
time takes account of both the actors and their watchers. John
Freccero feels that "by the act of making his own experience (which
he cannot understand) into a *story* (which he understands for
having invented it), Zeno rationalizes away the history of his own
freedom and, with the miracle of the lie, becomes his own God,
seeking to justify, at least in the world of fiction, the flesh and blood
reality from which he has abstracted himself."[19] But he cannot
justify reality by the miracle of a lie while he stands in the middle of
the Svevian universe of parallel forces, uncooperative enough to
allow comedy and cooperative enough to permit the survival of the
social order. Nor does he want to be his own God, for his apparent
abstraction does not, finally, function as evasion, nor are his lies
transvaluations. He is thoroughly suffused by an atmosphere and a
time that makes contradictory demands, and his rationalizations test
the possibility of reconciliation. A larger humor at the end of the
novel, shared by Svevo and Zeno, finds a philosophy that tolerates lies
without exonerating them. Life itself is superior to its analysis, as it is
to our literatures. Zeno's stories, no less spontaneous and unpredictable than his life, reflect life's irregular lurching; they remain vul-

18. This is a favorite idea of Svevo. See SSJ, 220:

if the Lord God had created us merely to see us as He wished, there would have
been no point in the creation. No, He created us, and then stepped back to examine
us—with curiosity, never with wrath.

and an entry in "Pagine di diario e sparse," OO, 3: 848–49:

I don't think God, after having created us, could have intended to punish or reward
us according to what we do here on earth. He is looking at us with curiosity because
if he had known everything that he made, and if his experiment had not reserved a
surprise for him, he would have no need to create us.

19. Freccero, "Zeno's Last Cigarette," p. 5.

nerable to new interpretations, reaching the window from which
Svevo's presence watches, but no higher.

This spacing has been largely neglected by critics of *Confessions of
Zeno* who, with Montale, assume that the noise and rhythm of
searching introspection and tunneling analysis, in part at least, dim
the novel's music and poetry.[20] While the pervasive lyricism bathing
Angiolina and transforming her to a symbolic light in *As a Man
Grows Older* has been noted, the gradual expansion of the poetry of
the amoral universe throughout *Confessions of Zeno* has not been
commented upon. Readers have been too eager simply to accuse
Zeno of the modern disease of intellectual analysis that interrupts the
natural rhythms of the universe and calls attention to the weightless-
ness and lack of integration in modern man. And it is clear that
Zeno's compulsive improvisations are directly related to his guilt incessantly parsed. Not for him the innocent song of the drunken
musician in "The Old Man" (FCZ, 21), which is always the same
and which elicits these words from Zeno: "Far be it from him to
consider improvising." We have been so distracted by Zeno's psychological antics that it is difficult to identify the presence of a mind—
too pervasive to be overlooked in novels like *Fathers and Sons* and
A Passage to India—that welcomes the indifferent poetry of nature
and provides a powerful counterforce to civilization's ideological and
moral debates. Yet Svevo uses that very mind to receive the waves of
a beautiful and fluid universe that soothes not only his own disease
but that of the psychoanalyst as well. Though sublimated in an atmosphere dominated by puncturing anecdotes and analyses, the lyric
mind in *Confessions of Zeno* that is present from the beginning
paradoxically swells in the last sections on business and psychoanalysis. The dissolution of moral anxiety by such an extension of consciousness protects self-analysis from the fatal narcissism we habitually anticipate in modern literature.

As we might expect, the space that hosts nature is never allowed to
drift off from the spheres of the bourgeois and psychoanalytic orders
and is invariably colored by a humor drawn from them. In one of the
most memorable scenes in the novel, just after Zeno's sudden and
almost unconscious proposal to Augusta, which has filled him with

20. Montale, *Lettere*, 3 March 1926, p. 15. See also Debenedetti, "Svevo e Schmitz,"
p. 93.

resentment against the fortunate Guido, Zeno and Guido walk together. Guido, a student of the misogynistic theories of Weininger,[21] is busy sprinkling about negative comments on women. Suddenly the moon dips into the novel, with features remarkably similar to those women. Zeno refers to a poet's metaphor about a kiss in the moon and then comments: "How sweet that kiss seemed in the moon of our dark nights, when compared with the injustice done me by Guido" (CZ, 130). At once the time is suspended that had encased so many successive minutes of jealousy and anxiety. But it is important to note that Svevo does not allow Zeno to leap to the moon for absolution without carrying with him the Malfenti women he had just left behind, along with the womanhood maligned by Guido. The sweet kiss is the same as that by which Augusta will wash away Zeno's guilts in marriage and that has to be renewed again and again. Guido makes a joke about the woman's face in the moon and then stretches himself out on a wall. In an act of aggressive exorcism, Zeno prays for his fall. The fantasy of pushing Guido, who had "stolen" Ada from him, off the wall is dissolved by "an idea . . . which seemed important enough to be compared to the great moon climbing up the sky and sweeping it clean" (CZ, 131). If, meditates Zeno, I have proposed to Augusta merely to have a good night's sleep, how could I sleep having killed Guido? The poetry of space is domesticated by the rejection of a fantasy on grounds that show us it was never seriously entertained, if furiously felt. Zeno's neurotic body pains, relieved by the fantasy, must now be faked to cover it up. The fantasy joins the climbing moon with the kneeling clown, bringing into play the indifferent, the unconscious, and the conscious spheres in which Zeno lives.

In a later chapter, "A Business Partnership," the walk, like most scenes in the novel, is recapitulated. Zeno has, at this point, changed positions with a fading Guido and is now the stronger, a repetition of his competition with his father. The scene on the night of the engagement is recalled, the kiss on the moon. To Guido's lament about the difference between the moon's eternal love and the earth's transitory kisses, Zeno, perhaps remembering his own envy of the moon kiss, says: "Kissing is above all, movement" (CZ, 298), a spontaneous

---

21. Otto Weininger, author of *Geschlecht und Charakter* (1930), was a radical and extremely controversial student of the mind in the Vienna of Freud. He committed suicide at an early age.

reply that nicely brings together man's motions with the movement of the universe, taking away from the sky its advantage of eternity and easing the pain of mortality. The comment is a deliberate effort to reconcile Guido to his disappointments in business and to free his scapegoat marriage, to stave off the envy of the kissing on the moon, which "did not produce twins." It is this effort of mediation between man and the moon that precipitously leads to the climactic recognition of the novel: "Life," blurts out Zeno, "is neither good nor bad; it is original" (CZ, 299). It hangs characteristically halfway between an indifferent universe and the moral world that commands us to be good. The aphorism does not sanction immorality, but assumes that the will buys goodness at the price of pain. It is crucial that the recognition should have come upon Zeno almost by accident, like a truth bubbling up from the unconscious at moments in which a present situation abruptly recalls analogies from the past. This scene corrects an earlier one in which Zeno was in a different position. Jealousy and anxiety are soothed by the influence of the moon on the mind, as if it were, in fact, the tide. When Zeno has been raised by his perception to the eye level of Mother Nature, he makes of Guido's unhappiness a general existential situation of man who has wandered into a fantastic universe by mistake. Guido's case then touches his own, and that of the other characters in the novel, for the Svevian blend of generosity and cynicism envelops them all. The famous ending of the novel is even now anticipated, and its spasm of apocalyptic despair grows naturally out of Zeno's easy passage between spheres. Only if the presence of the moon and its magnetism are forgotten will it seem to rise from an arbitrary and atypical fit of prophetic gloom:

> I felt as if I were seeing life for the first time, with all its gaseous, liquid, and solid bodies. If I had talked about it to someone who was strange to it, and therefore deprived of an ordinary common sense, he would have remained gasping at the thought of the huge, purposeless structure. He would have asked: "But how could you endure it?" And if he inquired about everything in detail, from the heavenly bodies hung up in the sky which can be seen but not touched, to the mystery that surrounds death, he would certainly have exclaimed: "Very original!" (CZ, 299)

With a marvelous touch that entirely individualizes him, Zeno does not correct Guido's assumption that he had read the aphorism somewhere, so that it might seem more impressive. This personal idiosyncrasy brings the moon down into a sublunary world in which the moral and psychiatric tides wash together in the heart of the child. As Guido reenacts the first scene on the wall, the doubt of Zeno's childhood and the childhood of man—"Am I good or bad?"—is resurrected. There is no way to hide the jostling between worlds which, if they can correct each other, also compete, discomfiting consciousness. If recapitulation reminds us that responses can develop and change, it also tells us that we are incurable: "Was ever anything so original as life? It is extraordinary that the doubt which it had imposed on the child in so puerile a form should still remain unsolved by the grown-up person, even after he had lived half his life" (CZ, 300). The meditation leads to the determination to stand by Guido in his emotional agony, and with the recognition that such a decision may really be a correction of feelings of resentment (comically illustrated by Zeno's mistake in following the wrong funeral cortège), Zeno draws together, by a metaphor, the worlds of resolution and perception. One is neither good nor bad, but "goodness is the light that in brief flashes illuminates the darkness of human soul" (CZ, 302). The will to goodness, the recognition of motive, and the moon as it comes in and out of the clouds thread together the lyric and the analytic consciousness.

If we accept Zeno's conciliatory definition of kissing as movement, perhaps we could say that the spheres of perception merely flash in and out of each others' territories like comets, like pecks on the cheek. As Guido goes toward ruin, his house, like the patient's mind, flickers between light and dark and adopts the same coloration as that surrounding the death of Zeno's father. From his armchair a semi-conscious father had gazed fixedly at the stars through the window, unable to say what he found there, and Zeno remarks: "During his whole life he had probably never gazed into the distance for so long on end" (CZ, 50). The active man, entirely absorbed with the business of the world and living in one time alone, is not normally vulnerable to such a large influence. But his son's consciousness is crossed by many constellations. Zeno accepts an invitation to go fishing with Guido on an evening in which Zeno is driven from the house by his baby's screams. The scene opens into "one of those transparent nights that calm and tranquilize the spirit" (CZ, 271). The moral will begins to relax: "The vast and tranquil beauty of the night brought me peace; I did not even feel the need of making resolutions." As Zeno dangles his bait, he imagines an underwater sentience:

> In the darkness I could just see the hook through the tail of my crab, which seemed to be moving the upper part of its body to and fro. It was a gentle motion and seemed to express meditation rather than bodily agony. Perhaps what produces pain in larger bodies may, in very little ones, be so refined that it is experienced merely as a fresh sensation, a stimulus to thought. (CZ, 273)

Such a fabulous ascription of human sensation to a smaller animal world has the advantage, often used by Svevo, of checking the self-pity latent in psychological perceptions with semicomic reminders of our place on the Darwinian scale of beings. The starry sky and the mildly sensitized ocean frame human anxiety, preventing it from crowding the scene. The same light and darkness quiver under water, in the mind and in the sky around death's bait. The flight toward death of a hooked silver fish gleaming in the dark water seems to Zeno like a surfacing cry from the underworld as death simplifies in one grand stroke a various life. The imagined cry is that of the dying father and, lest we become lulled by lyric analogies, we hear the actual scream of Guido's mistress, Carmen, squeezed in the dark by Guido (CZ, 274–75). When later Guido once again takes Zeno fishing on a moonlit night, Zeno observes:

> The moon's rays must have penetrated to the bottom of the sea, lighting up all the wiles of the fisherman for the fishes big and small, so that they only nibbled at the bait but never let the hook come near them. (CZ, 328)

For Guido, baiting the instrument of his own death with questions about chemical poisons, the light is melancholy. There is no fortunate face in the moon and no place for argument in such a scene, in which words are drowned by sea and sky. Zeno plays upon Guido's sigh by agreeing, in a display of sympathy meant to silence his complaints, that the light was certainly "sad because it lit up this sad world and also because it prevented us from fishing." Typically, Zeno has cut through the pretense of sentimental philosophical simplification with this practical reminder, seconded by his yawn in the moon's face. He mentally checks Guido's humorless self-pity by once again drawing from the heartless biology of Mother Nature. De-fusing Guido's self-absorption by generalizing on the inevitability of unhappiness, Zeno thinks cynically of the world of parasites preying on life's booty and giving way to what, in turn, consumes them. The pitiless restitution of nature's balance recalls Zeno's office fables stimulated by his habit of competition with Guido. Man's parasitic hooking of the crab and the fleas' parasitic living on man yield a comic equilibrium. Zeno mocks the thinking of the dying sea creatures that life could be without its hooks. Mother Nature continually experiments with her parasites, compelling the mixture of hook and meat. If this is hardly comforting, at least she keeps us from believing in hymns of higher purpose that cradle us in a complacency that ignores accidents of humor. The designs of psychological parasitism, by which sons prey on fathers and fathers on sons, by which Guido sinks and Zeno rises, prove that Mother Nature's experiments are not just biological. And it is no accident that the major business of the novel is speculation, for the stock market might easily be one of Mother Nature's most delightful tricks. Zeno's strength, in relation to those who live by one time alone, lies in his ability to absorb these experiments without dying of them, without organizing them by an imposed system of order, and without using them as a license for moral indifference or philosophical nihilism.

Only death frees man from consciousness of this experimentation. In a touching diary entry, Svevo reverses with a tone of ironic self-magnification a favorite Proustian idea: "And thinking that when I die, my doubt, my struggles with myself and with others, all my curiosity and all my passion will die with me, I really think that the world will be much simplified by my death."[22] Death of another, here, allows to the living a spasmodic return to innocence before it starts up the doubts, guilts, struggles, and passions that gnaw at the liver. Zeno's dead, "innocent" brother-in-law, Guido, seems to shed a new light, "suddenly refracted as though it had passed through a prism" (CZ, 351). Death has purified the light that had flickered on Guido, on the wall, in the boat, the light that had cast up its own shadows of self-pity, doubt, and envy. There are no answers to Ada's accusation that Zeno had always hated Guido, but his tears, protestations of innocence, the same he had shed for his father, reflect the spectrum of mixed motives that hold the shadow of Ada's judgment

22. Svevo, "Documenti umani," OO, 3: 835–36.

and the peace of Guido's face together. Neither the earth's kisses nor its tears are pure. The light is purified only in the pictures from the past that Zeno half invents, half remembers.

It is difficult for readers not to insist upon the self-deception of a character who invents and organizes his free associations and then interprets them as victories over the psychoanalyst. The pictures evoked by his desires clearly reveal as much about the mind as its "true" dreams. But while Zeno manipulates the light and shadows of the past, he is standing by Svevo's side absorbing the prejudice of the novelist in the face of Dr. S.'s interpretation. At the same time, the psychoanalyst is not merely flattened. Zeno admits to his own illegitimate doctoring, and all his adjustment of the past cannot obscure the patterns of his compulsions and desires, for if Augusta can read behind the lies, so can Doctor S. While Zeno is desperately scrabbling to relive one day of innocence from the past, the doctor is willing to grant him days of innocence in the present. If the doctor's diagnosis is restrictive in relation to the novelist's, his plea for a "reeducation" (CZ, 373) that would allow Zeno to realize that an Oedipus complex is no crime, no moral breach, no cause for remorse, is generous enough to prevent death from caricature. Zeno's resistance to the absolution so long sought is not frivolous, however willful and adolescent his rebellion might seem. His deepest fear derives from the suspicion that his sickness is what unites him to other men, that his guilt is an inevitable concomitant of love. His own analysis takes on the sudden forms of his whims. Zeno the scribbler wriggles away not from the truth uncovered by the analysis, but from what he jealously imagines to be a solution to his personality. This is evident in his final response from his villa at Lucinico. The resolutions have been dutifully reinstated, and the desires bloom in the air of contemplation: "I have never known life without desire, and illusions sprang up afresh for me after every shipwreck of my hopes" (CZ, 382). He is talking specifically of his dream of women, released by the beauty of the air and the landscape from moral doubt. But it is clear that this capacity to dream is the innocence that enables a man to see that life is merely original.

The instinct to neutralize the doctor's "cure" is the same that provokes the middle-aged Zeno to unsentimental meditation, in the novel's introduction, on the future of the newborn baby about to enter the checkered world. Both Svevo and Zeno refer to themselves, at various moments of provisional absolution, as "neo-nato,"[23] a state that is renewed continually because it continually dies. The irony inherent in this process, still strong in the middle-aged man, chastises the notion of the innocent babe who grows into sin and despair: "Perhaps the passing moments may be pure; not so the long centuries that went into your making" (CZ, 4). The imagined baby is partly Zeno himself, squirming even in the cradle from the mysterious forces that change discovery into disease and suffering. When Zeno evokes the vision of a childhood drenched in sun, we know it will bring its own shadow:

> The sun! The sun! dazzling sunlight! From the picture of what I thought to be my youth, so much sun streamed out that it was hard for me not to believe in it. Our dining-room in the afternoon. My father has come home and is sitting on the sofa beside my mother, who is printing initials in indelible ink on a lot of white linen scattered all over the table at which she is sitting. (CZ, 371)

The set scene might help to explain the long history of Zeno's guilt, but we have been warned that such pure light belongs only to the dead. Soon the light is blotted out by the ink knocked over by the child and the vision fades with the threat of paternal punishment. It is important to note here the Svevian resistance to a melodrama of lost beatitude. When the scene dies, with it fades its pretense to an Ur-scene of sin. Seeking safety in a vision of the past, the dreamer now relishes the safety of the present in which he is merely old (CZ, 372). The one-sided image of the brother joyfully at home while he is "condemned eternally to go to school" (CZ, 369) has been lifted out of history to the status of metaphor by its perpetual repetition, and as a metaphor it arouses emotions as deep as any specific and single moment of passion. But when the vision is corrected by the recognition that the brother envied his going more than he did the brother's staying, the tyrannical sentimentality of dreams of innocence is exposed as well as the emotional displacement of their content.

When the doctor's diagnosis is proportionate to Zeno's illustration,

23. For a typical confession of Svevo, see entry of February 1896 in *Diario per la fidanzata*, OO, 3: 791:

After having telephoned you [his wife] my conscience feels as pure as that of a newborn babe.

like the recognition early in the novel of the relation between cigarette smoking and Zeno's relation to his father, psychoanalysis seems
a sufficient perspective. When, however, the letter of the official interpretation falls short of the spirit of the novel, we realize how much
we need other worlds and spaces. The most glaring reduction is the
analysis Zeno reports of the motives behind his marriage. Dr. S. is
said to have indicated that Zeno hated Augusta's father, a double of
his own, and that he married a daughter of his, then betrayed her, to
dishonor him. Zeno laughs defensively and mocks the doctor's air of
"Christopher Columbus discovering America" (CZ, 376). We have,
in the novel, a scene that tends to support this view. After displeasing
Giovanni and feeling forced to retract, for the sake of Guido's visit-
ing father, Zeno feels justified in going to his mistress's house:

> I did not actually go off intending to betray Augusta. But I felt
> justified in doing exactly as I liked now, in the light of day. (CZ,
> 178)

Yet the novel has been colored by Augusta's blushes, the torch lit in
Zeno's honor (CZ, 134), which fade into smiles. It is a rosy indulgence that hangs in the air of every scene. Wordless, it has no trouble
spreading beyond the range of psychoanalytic argument. Augusta
cannot be used up as a displaced target for Zeno, intent upon
avenging his hatred for her father. Such a picture simply does not
reflect the spirit we have read in the attraction, and we refuse to give
up the comic spontaneity of the courtship. What of the Mother Nature who, in one of her finest experiments, makes Zeno propose to a
woman he actually, but unwittingly, loves? Her affection opens space
beyond the psychoanalyst's book, as does the humor of Zeno that
makes his desires "normal": "All the same," he drolly says of the
analyst, "I think he must be the only person in the world who,
hearing that I wanted to go to bed with two lovely women, must rack
his brain to try and find a reason for it!" (CZ, 376). This is not by
any means a retort that is allowed to stand without qualification, nor
does it justify Zeno's adultery, but it does manage to make the
doctor's diagnosis a little uncomfortable in a larger space. At the
same time, the picture of competing mistresses in the expansive landscape of Lucinico contributes to the rhythm of comic humiliation
that blocks self-justification. Limbs, gestures, voices more perfect still

(CZ, 382) are not easy to argue with, and neither is Augusta. Humor, necessarily absent from the doctor's therapeutic tone, is a double agent for revelation and defense.

If we are sensitive to the space and air cohabited by Svevo and Zeno, a universe of humor mediating between times, tones, and orders, the last terrible vision is not so disturbing. The acceptance of sickness, which from one perspective might seem psychological cowardice, from a wider one becomes a heroic refusal of cures. The domination of space and time by myths of philosophy and science is to Svevo a humorless horror unfit to be compared to the experiments of Mother Nature, which keep man at his proper measure. Zeno's visionary bespectacled man, to whom the restraints of guilt have become irrelevant, leads us straight to destruction. Although he inevitably exhibits some of his symptoms, Zeno is not to be equated with this mastermind, for his guilts, desires, and dreams are the children of his flesh and blood. His sickness refuses transcendence by will. The earth, returned "to its nebulous state" and "wandering through the sky, free at last from parasites and disease" (CZ, 398), has winked at Zeno all through the novel. The space that is an obsessive term in the last part of the novel does not tempt him to conquering dreams. The voice that registers the comic claim that confession lies in the Tuscan tongue is the same one that refuses to blame the doctor "for regarding life as a manifestation of disease" (CZ, 397). Zeno's resistance to recovery begins with a personal boast, a typical blend of faked naiveté and the enthusiasm of victory. But as he thanks God, on seeing Teresina, that he is not yet cured, having stopped treatment just in time (CZ, 384), it soon expands into a persuasive philosophy. Svevo and Zeno are united in blaming the doctor only for assuming that the illness that pitches life on the fever chart between "crises and periods of quiescence . . . daily improvements and setbacks" can be cured (CZ, 397). Who will cure us, asks Zeno, when man has consumed the air and space that humble his predictions?

The final vision is, in the best Svevian tradition, set between historical time and the time of consciousness. Svevo saw in the realization of the myth of domination of the technical man both a willed historical climax of modern civilization and a natural evolution of a perpetual illusory hope. Freud had much the same sense:

They seem to have observed that this newly-won power over space and time, this subjugation of the forces of nature, which is the fulfillment of a longing that goes back thousands of years, has not increased the amount of pleasurable satisfaction which they may expect from life and has not made them feel happier.[24]

Readers of *Confessions of Zeno* have been bothered by the apparent relentless cynicism of the final apocalyptic vision, which assumes the guise of prophecy. But Svevo habitually demonstrated that he has the Freudian lack of desire or courage to "rise up . . . as a prophet."[25] As the terrible picture of the end of the earth dwarfs the psychological perspective ("We need something more than psychoanalysis to help us"; CZ, 398), it ironically haunts Zeno's happy ending, which requires a return of the whole manuscript from the psychoanalyst for rewriting (CZ, 397) and its extinction with the world's end. The Svevian process of the neutralizing of one level of discourse and vision by another remains intact. Once Zeno has accepted the impossibility of cure and the war reinforces the personal verdict with its ageless pestilence, he is free to make himself available to luck. To conceive of a Zeno unaware of the irony of treating this luck, tainted with the breath of immorality, as the climactic illustration of his health is to miss the final juggling of grammars. First we have the personal justification. Freed by the war from the inherited hierarchy of business ("Austria had released me from my two tyrants"; FCZ, 133), Zeno picks an awkward moment in history to prove himself the equal, for the time being, of his father, Giovanni, and Olivi. The psychiatric victory as usual takes precedence over the historical realization. We get the same comedy of humiliation by disproportion to which we are accustomed. Zeno himself takes particular pleasure in his business luck because with it he can chastise the doctor, yet another bourgeois father. The man who succeeds in seeing that life is original may delight in the originality of the success but not be taken in by it. His vulnerability to this adolescent desire for vengeance against paternal authority is the very basis of his capacity to envisage the death of a world obsessed by systematic cures. But history leads

24. Sigmund Freud, "Civilization and Its Discontents," *The Complete Psychological Works of Sigmund Freud,* Standard edition, trans. James Strachey and Anna Freud (London 1961), 21: 87–8.
25. Ibid., p. 145.

him to a wider sense of cause and effect. Zeno's horror at the war and the recognition of absurdity in his response actually spares him from the charge so often leveled at him of historical insensitivity. As the supermen of cures eat up space and destroy men (and war is waged in the name of an ultimate cure), Zeno and his creator keep an ecological humor that prevents apocalypse from determining personal history. Earth would be healthy, but man is its disease. The disease is not just his desire for cure, but the imposition of it upon others. Zeno seeks—and with the self-irony that assumes its impossibility—only to cure himself. This desire looks selfish in time of war, but from the perspective of Mother Nature, the comedy is a kind of queer heroism. This is a humor that speculates, like Mother Nature, with bourgeois currency. *Not* to be an amateur in a world of professional destroyers would be indecent. The last terrible vision, in isolation, may make us wonder, like old Zeno, why we should live in a world in which we can imagine such nightmares; conjoined to the domesticated anecdotes and analyses in the novel, such nightmares may darken life, like the spilled ink of Zeno's remembered childhood scene, but the moon and the sun climb to the next day and night.

Chapter 2
Between Freud and Montaigne

An analytical writer, he is, nevertheless, a great generalizer as well, inferential and ahistorical: he ultimately describes not the specimen, but the pattern, the human condition itself.[1]

HAPSBURG TRIESTE had natural access to Viennese culture, and Svevo, with Umberto Saba, was one of the literary figures most responsible for introducing Freud into Italy. For various reasons, which I shall note in the second part of the book, Svevo's interest was by no means typical of his society. But his hybrid culture, his passion for daydreaming and introspection, and his fluency in German made him particularly open to Austrian psychoanalytic currents. Svevo acknowledges in his short autobiographical sketch his reading of early Freud, an acquaintance that stirred him deeply in the period just preceding the writing of *Confessions of Zeno*. He actually undertook the translation, with his nephew, of *The Interpretation of Dreams*.[2] He was proud of what he assumed to be psychoanalytic ideas and structures in his novel and sent a copy to Freud and one to Edoardo Weiss, a prominent Triestine psychoanalyst, a friend of Freud's, and Svevo's personal friend. When Weiss told him that his book had nothing to do with psychoanalytic theory, and when Freud failed to acknowledge the novel, he was disappointed, for he had fantasized a response from the great Austrian doctor: "It would have been a great

1. Geno Pampaloni, "Italo Svevo," *Storia della letteratura italiana,* ed. Emilio Cecchi and Natalino Sapegno (Milan, 1969) , 9: 503.
2. See Svevo's "Profilo autobiografico," OO, 3: 807, and "Soggiorno londinese," OO, 3: 686.

day if Freud had telegraphed me: 'Thank you for having introduced psychoanalysis into Italian culture.' "[3] What would Svevo not have given to have received Freud's testimonial to Arthur Schnitzler:

> Your determinism and your scepticism—what people call pessimism— your deep grasp of the truths of the unconscious and of the bio- logical nature of man, the way you take to pieces the social con- ventions of our society, and the extent to which your thoughts are preoccupied with the polarity of love and death; all that moves me with an uncanny feeling of familiarity. So the impression has been borne in on me that you know through intuition—really from a delicate self-observation—everything that I have discovered in other people by laborious work. Indeed, I believe that fundamentally you are an explorer of the depths.[4]

Dream as Svevo might of getting such a response from Freud, it was not forthcoming. Yet a revolutionary role was ultimately ascribed to him by the young writers associated with the magazines *Il Convegno* and *Solaria*. Characteristically, Svevo turned his defense in the face of disappointment into affirmative recognitions about the novel. If novelists merely toy with the great philosophies instead of expounding and developing them, if they falsify and distort them in the process of absorption, they also humanize them: "Le falsifi- chiamo ma le umanizziamo."[5] He associates this attitude with a tem- peramental scepticism about the therapeutic value of psychoanalysis, admitting his love of his own sickness, his "autodifesa."[6] He never abandons this conviction, but neither does he sacrifice his fascination

3. Svevo, OO, 3: 807.
4. See Ernest Jones, *Life and Work of Sigmund Freud* (New York, 1953), 3: 443–44. The letter cited is dated 14 May, 1922.
5. Svevo, "Soggiorno londinese," OO, 3: 686. Cf. letter of Umberto Saba to Giovanni Comisso, 1 September, 1929, in Sutor, Mario, ed., *Saba/Svevo/Comisso* (lettere inedite) (Padua, 1968), p. 25:

> Psychoanalysis is a great thing, but it is not art, nor can it, by itself, become art. It can, after much effort, bring facts, or better, repressed feelings to consciousness and therefore give to a man's consciousness a greater extension in depth; if that man is an artist, his art can be affected by this process.

In a letter to Valerio Jahier, 1 February, 1928, OO, 1: 863, Svevo speaks of his suspicion that too rigid an application of Schopenhauerian theory might have harmed *Una vita*.
6. See Svevo, "Soggiorno londinese," OO, 3: 688:

> I was healthy, or, at least, I loved my sickness (if sickness it is) enough to want to protect myself thoroughly in the spirit of self-defense.

And see also the important letter of 1927 to Valerio Jahier, OO, 1:857–60.

with the psychoanalytic process. He was perhaps the first to consider Freud more valuable for novelists than for patients.[7] From this double attitude of scepticism (attributed to the evidence of a disastrous therapy undergone by a brother-in-law) and interest emerges the illegitimate but productive self-analysis admitted to by Svevo in a letter to Valerio Jahier.[8] Dr. S., according to Svevo, had no model and had the grave disadvantage of playing second fiddle to a real patient.

By remaining a dilettante of systems, the novelist can plunder without being captured. He has a great advantage over philosophers of "cure" by transvaluation or therapy. By sponsoring the impossibility of being cured of life he lets us keep what is best about us. It is this vital infection that makes us immune to the hopes of supermen: "We become a living protest against the ridiculous conception of the superman as it has been foisted on us, particularly on us Italians."[9] Freud himself was, of course, hardly a propagator of perfect cures ("I do not think our cures can compete with Lourdes"[10]) , but the mere hope of cure set up in the minds of neurotics torn by tension and anxiety seemed a dangerous and cruel expectation to Svevo who had himself spent a lifetime wondering with considerable irony, both in and out of his novels, if there were such a thing as perfect moral health.[11] The value of Freud to the novel is not that of a saving priest, but of giving to the details of experience a proper emphasis.[12] It is not the meaning of Zeno's mistake at Guido's funeral that interests us so much as the demonstration that such lapses lend a comic air of accident to the most serious of life's moments. The novelist delights in the full description of the mistake, now become, by the attention paid it, as important to the narrative as the death itself.

---

7. Letter to Valerio Jahier, 10 December 1927, OO, 1: 857.
8. Ibid., p. 858.
9. Ibid., 27 December, 1927, OO, 1: 859–60.
10. "Explanations, Applications and Orientations," Standard ed., (1964) , 80: 152.
11. Svevo, "Profilo autobiografico," OO, 3: 807.
12. See Lionel Trilling, *Sincerity and Authenticity* (Cambridge, Mass., 1972) , pp. 156–57:

> Freud, in insisting upon the essential immitigability of the human condition as determined by the nature of the mind, had the intention of sustaining the authenticity of human existence that formerly had been ratified by God. It was his purpose to keep all things from becoming "weightless". . . . He was intent upon rescuing from religion one element, the imperative actuality which religion attributed to life.

Zeno's absence from the funeral is judged with a mixture of reproach and indulgence, for his frantic game of speculation to save Guido's honor has been, in part, successful. The harshest judgment comes from Ada who, displacing her own guilt at not having adequately loved Guido, accuses Zeno of having hated him. We support Zeno's sense of distortion in this judgment, even if we cannot concede him the innocence he desires. The distracted Zeno, riding with a broker in a cab to the wrong funeral, totally absorbed in his stock market speculations, has been painted for us with Svevo's ironic gaiety in a beguiling way that lets us enjoy the Freudian lapse without fretting about its meaning:

> Our cab was still following the procession, which seemed to be going on to the Greek cemetery.
> "Was Guido a Greek Catholic?" he asked in surprise. And the procession was, in fact, passing the Catholic cemetery and proceeding toward one of the others, Jewish, Greek, Protestant, or Serbian.
> "Can he have been a Protestant!" I wondered. But I at once remembered having gone to his marriage in the Catholic Church. (CZ, 355)

We know Zeno's motives are not pure, but we are placated by the further knowledge that they are largely goodwilled. If they are prompted by guilt, they are also stimulated by a desire to change the childish need to be good to a paternal sense of responsibility. That is how the novelist wants to leave it, with a tone of comic indulgence that does not eliminate pain. The authority of such an experience and its effects would be hard to imagine without Freud, but more for the conviction that perfect moral health is impossible than for any therapeutic recognition.

The interest and weight of the anecdote lie, then, in the fullness with which it is experienced by the characters, not in a superior Freudian analysis. For this reason, the following generalization seems to me particularly misleading when applied to *Confessions of Zeno*, perverting, as well, our sense of the earlier fiction:

> One must be in some sense a Freudian in reading Svevo in order to detect, beneath the innocent and witty exterior, the unconscious cruelty and desire of the characters, their near total ignorance of their motives, and above all the family romance which occupies so

many if not all of them and keeps them from confronting the real issues of their lives.[13]

What one needs rather to detect is the quality of the surface texture where rationalizations and every variety of mental adjustment are worked out and forged into instruments of sociability. The symptoms of conflict between the external and internal life are incessantly displayed and periodically analyzed, but the novels of Svevo are more interested in how they are used than in their derivation. Admitting that we all start as children with distinctively different parents, by the time we are in the middle of our lives and of Zeno's, we all share the same sickness. Of this we have varying degrees of consciousness, and varying need for that consciousness, which in the best modern tradition is both a curse and a blessing. The intention of putting poor, blind, struggling, dim fools upon the scene and condemning them for their "family romances"[14] would seem to Svevo as sentimental as that which stimulates the heroics of transcendental cures. The real issues of the lives presented are those which concern the survival of affection between the claims of conscience and consciousness, and this unglamorous task keeps motivation in its place. When motives are revealed by Dr. S., like those which stem from Zeno's unresolved Oedipal conflict, the spontaneity and interest of the scene are threatened rather than deepened. The open-ended play of a comic surface against depths of psychological and existential despairs is not to be seen as evidence of ignorance, evasion, and repression that affords the reader clues by which to analyze lives with the help of Freudian categories. The bursting forth of envy, resentment, and self-pity into a world that refuses them the dignity of tragic magnitude is a necessary chastening of the pretense of the special case, binding one family romance to another. No complex is allowed to stand in isolation, blooming egoistically apart from the social comedy that receives it and acts upon it. The Freudian patterns of family romance and displaced judgments are themselves subject to the comic view that confuses motives and intentions. The momentum of Svevian fiction pushes us through and beyond psychoanalytic

13. Paula Robison, "Senilità: The Secret of Svevo's Weeping Madonna," *Italian Quarterly* (Winter 1971) , p. 84.
14. The phrase is the title of Freud's essay of 1909 on the manifestations of the Oedipal relationship in the growing child. See his "A Special Type of Object Choice Made by Men," *Psychology of Love,* Standard ed. (1957) , 11: 171–72, 171 n. 2.

therapy, at least as it is undergone by Zeno. It prods unconscious feelings forward to a social manifestation where they join our limited perceptions of them. Motives never achieve the priority to which they aspire in therapy. Svevo works it so that we, whether Freudian or non-Freudian readers, do not desire to go deeper than the level at which impulse tests itself in behavior. We see clearly how Svevo, as a novelist, hangs between the nineteenth and twentieth centuries, for like the nineteenth-century novelist, he is less interested in motives than in moral education, but like the twentieth century-novelist, he knows that moral education is made irregular and unpredictable by the invasions of the unconscious. The Freud who binds psychoanalytic process to its social and moral manifestations is one whom Svevo could cherish. Svevo's passion for making Zeno's hostilities compatible with love, as in his relations with his "fathers," would embrace Freud's simultaneously hard and consoling paradox:

> It might be said that we owe the fairest flowering of our love to the reaction against the hostile impulse which we sense within us.[15]

One is inevitably tempted to exaggerate the contrast between motives and their social realizations if one insists upon being a Freudian reader in a world that refuses to rest upon Freudian perceptions alone. To speak, for example, of an innocent exterior and unconscious cruelty, to speak of nearly total ignorance of motives as if that were some kind of fatal condemnation, is to distort both the Svevian tone and the Svevian hierarchy of values. The surface is no more innocent than what lies beneath it; cruelty is constantly tempered by a humor that falls democratically on everyone; and ignorance of Freudian insights does not seem so important an issue when we see how Zeno subordinates them to a larger view that, unsentimental and unconsoling as it is, diminishes, without denying, the significance of Dr. S.'s diagnosis. Ada's accusation is given more assent by the reader than is the psychoanalyst's revelations, not because it is more true, but because the response it stimulates yields a reality still filled with confusion and surprise, unsolved equations and doubts, the reality that Svevo inhabits. Because Ada has more body than the psychoanalyst, because she is a richer personality on her own and in relation to Zeno, and because her judgment is colored by her needs, her words have far more interest and value for us than do his.

15. Freud, "Our Attitude Towards Death," Standard ed. (1964), 23: 299.

If Zeno cannot have Ada's body through courtship, he marries her
sickness, so imperative is the desire to keep faith with all those he has
been bound to. And, in fact, the metamorphosis that Zeno works that
makes of her sickness a metaphor for life itself is a great and touching
hymn of love. Her body, fashioned from Freud's dream of his friend
Otto, his face brown and his eyes protruding from Basedow's disease,[16] is a literal manifestation of Zeno's imaginary disease. It speaks
with the authority of genuine illness that Zeno often longs for as a
release from hypochondria, a longing whimsically and momentarily
fulfilled at the end of the novel when urinalysis replaces psychoanalysis. The disease ravages Ada's beauty and allows her to join Zeno's
dying father in privileged reproach to Zeno's innocence. To clinch
this identification, when Ada leaves with her children for Buenos
Aires after Guido's death, tears fill Zeno's eyes and he experiences the
same regret that shook him after his father's death: "Never again
should I be able to prove to her that I was innocent" (CZ, 365). The
claim does not separate him from his father and from Ada as we
imagine it might. On the contrary, it is a way of keeping alive by the
rite of advocacy a relationship suffering physical absence. In his consciousness, Zeno will go on pleading his case with both his father and
Ada, not merely in hope of justification but also as a way of overcoming the limitations of linear time. Zeno's reaction to Ada's decline is complicated by pride in Augusta's health, compassion, some
satisfaction in his change of role from rejected lover to brother, and
even some black humor, but these responses are all dependent upon
a dread of isolation that modern sickness imposes upon its victims.
His personal neurosis must share the burden of Freud's awareness
that Western culture has a shaky hold on large and binding beliefs,
and that private hypochondrias have limped pathetically to the
fore.[17] Zeno works desperately to save Ada from going into oblivion,
and *not* merely to prove his innocence, but to preserve his desire.
Intent on making his own hypochondrias companionable by his
clowning throughout the book, now he must keep Ada's loss of
beauty from melodramatic withdrawal. This is one cause of his
humor, even of his gesture of mugging her distorted features, to the
amusement of Augusta who understands his meaning. By making of
Ada's disease a synecdoche for life itself, one that precipitates and

16. Freud, "Interpretation of Dreams," Standard ed. (1953) 4: 269.
17. See Philip Rieff, *Freud: The Mind of the Moralist* (New York, 1961), p. 317.

tames even the last horrible vision, he turns the tables on the fate that would cut her out of the herd. Life finds a purgatorial ledge between a goiter on one end and a dropsy on the other (CZ, 287). Zeno himself assumes her illness through hypochondriacal devotion: "I too suffered from a very slight form of her disease and it took me some while to get rid of it; for a long time I thought too much about Basedow" (CZ, 287). The expansion of Ada's case into a general metaphor of our design is Zeno's most touching tribute to his first love. Ardently, compulsively, Zeno pushes confession to the purposes of conversation and reminds us of Montaigne's plea for a charity that would allow the body to complain in sickness, for that complaint is a kind of conversation.[18] As analysis paradoxically becomes a spur to improvisation, so real and imagined diseases, self-centered like analysis in most of its modern forms, become a social and philosophical base.

Ultimately, it is difficult to understand why so many critics have ascribed to Zeno the standard traits of the modern anti-hero, narcissism, mediocrity, and self-deception.[19] Only if we ignore the uses to which Zeno puts his sickness can we look upon him, as one reader does, as "a parody of the Schopenhaurian investigation of the 'thing in itself,' because the solipsist hero can never arrive at a full understanding of the true and peculiar nature of an external object."[20] Zeno, like his creator, never for any length of time achieves ascetic peace and poised wisdom. He has fused the alternating views of man described by Schopenhauer:

> The life of every individual, if we survey it as a whole and in general, and only lay stress upon its most significant features, is really always a tragedy, but gone through in detail, it has the character of a comedy. For the deeds and vexations of the day, the restless irritation of every hour, are all through chance, which is ever bent upon some jest, scenes of a comedy.[21]

The novelist refuses to divorce the most significant features of life from the compulsive details of daily gesture, and this is precisely what Svevo found most valuable in Freud. Even the tragic elevation

18. Montaigne, *Complete Essays*, 2: 37, p. 576.
19. See, for example, Lee Jacobs, "Zeno's Sickness Unto Death," *Italian Quarterly* (Spring, 1968) : 58.
20. Ibid.
21. Arthur Schopenhauer, "The World as Will and Idea," *The Philosophy of Schopenhauer*, ed. Irwin Edman (New York, 1928) , p. 265.

of the novel's ending, which pictures the world provisionally only as Idea, freed from the parasites of Will, has been countered immediately before by Zeno's boast of business success (CZ, 397–98).

The influence of Freud upon Svevo in the composition of *Confessions of Zeno* is everywhere manifest. Zeno's first-person resistance to the psychoanalyst, who encourages the act of remembering, generates an ironic tension which could make the author's own presence more immediate than in his earlier novels in which delicate intrusions by conditional, half-hearted sharing of the scene kept him from stretching out to his full length. The contest between Zeno and Svevo on the one hand, and the psychoanalyst on the other, over the meaning of a form that emphasizes the simultaneity of past and present, unconscious and conscious, anecdote and crisis, comedy and tragedy is managed by a rich and securely directed irony. Those who consider Zeno an unreliable narrator instead of a partner in Svevo's maturest vision have felt uncomfortable with this irony, which seems to complement the authority of the doctor's diagnosis and to mock Zeno's resistance. Dr. S., however, is confined by the therapy to a sober role, one not made more winning by his sarcasm, nor more dignified by his judgments flippantly condensed by his patient. He is allowed a few compassionate recommendations by his novelist, the comic and unorthodox vengeance of publishing his patient's sickness. Zeno, on the other hand, is taken through Svevo's full universe of thought. He seems to exist almost as a scapegoat for Svevo's skepticism about the therapeutic process so that the larger Freud, the moralist and the philosopher of the mind and its culture, could be freed of this function. Svevo did not seem to recognize the Freud cautious of cure, especially one who could say, some time after Svevo's death, to be sure: "I have never been a therapeutic enthusiast."[22] For it is the Freud who deemphasizes distinctions between neurosis and normality ("Our patients tell us nothing that we might not also hear from healthy people"[23]), who assumes that if we are cured of our fantasies, we cannot be of reality, who is closest to Svevo and his hero. We certainly can imagine Svevo's applauding Freud's early celebrated promise to a patient:

22. Freud, "Explanations, Applications and Orientations," Standard ed. (1964), 22: 151. See also his "Analysis Terminable and Interminable" (1964), 23: 211–53.
23. Freud, "Creative Writing and Day-Dreaming" (1908), Standard ed. (1959), 9: 146.

No doubt fate would find it easier than I do to relieve you of your illness. But you will be able to convince yourself that much will be gained if we succeed in transforming your hysterical misery into common unhappiness.[24]

The Freud who recognizes that the "physician is not to be a fanatic about health and therapy" is one not often emphasized. Of the psychoanalyst facing an exceptional case he writes:

It is not his business to restrict himself in every situation in life to being a fanatic in favour of health; he knows that there is not only neurotic misery in the world but irremovable suffering as well, that necessity may even require of a person to sacrifice his health; and he learns that a sacrifice of this kind made by a single person can prevent immeasurable unhappiness for many others. If we may say, then, that whenever a neurotic is faced by a conflict he takes flight in illness, yet we must allow that in some cases that flight is fully justified, and a physician who has recognized how the situation lies will silently and solicitously withdraw.[25]

Zeno does not qualify for such an extreme retreat, nor does he ever really seriously take flight into illness, but the reminder that some neuroses might be the most socially tolerable solution to a psychic

---

24. Freud, "Studies in Hysteria," with Breuer (1895) , Standard ed. (1955) , 2: 305.

25. Philip Rieff does emphasize this Freud. See Rieff, *Freud*, p. 68. The cited passage comes from "The Common Neurotic State," Standard ed. (1963), 16: 382. This qualification is stated elsewhere in Freud, particularly in passages exhorting the psychoanalyst to do what he can in the face of odds. See, for example his "Future Prospects of Psychoanalysis" (1910) , Standard ed. (1957) , 11: 150:

Let us remember, however, that our attitude to life ought not to be that of a fanatic for hygiene or therapy. We must admit that the ideal prevention of neurotic illnesses which we have in mind would not be of advantage to every individual. A good number of those who now take flight into illness would not, under the conditions we have assumed, support the conflict but would rapidly succumb or would cause a mischief greater than their own neurotic illness.

Neuroses have in fact their biological functions as a protective contrivance and they have their social justification; the gain from illness they provide is not always a purely subjective one.

See also Jones, 2: 447 for Freud's comment to Ferenczi in 1910 that complexes are never entirely renounced, merely displaced or exchanged, and another admission, again to Ferenczi in 1911:

One should not try to eradicate one's complexes, but come to terms with them; they are the legitimate guiding forces of one's behavior in the world. (Jones, *Freud*, 2: 452) .

See also Paul Roazen, *Freud and His Followers* (New York, 1974) and Russell Jacoby, *Social Amnesia* (Boston, 1975) for further comments on Freud's skepticism about therapy.

problem might make the Freudian reader less eager to separate him from Svevo. By making Zeno's symptoms socially tolerable, and even desirable, Svevo diminishes the uniqueness of his neurosis, so that beyond gaining from his illness, a suspicious and dangerous game to Freud, he can become a philosopher of sickness and an advocate of reality.

The series of calamities that gradually eroded the early, secure foundation of Svevo's childhood gave the novelist a premature understanding of "real unavoidable suffering." His resigned temperament—he always, as his wife attests, expected the worst and was prepared to meet a new sorrow at any moment[26]—took in the bankruptcy and premature degeneration of his father, the subsequent reluctant life of a bank clerk, the early death of his devoted brother Elio that was succeeded by other family deaths, and, to top it off, the almost complete critical neglect of his first two books and the death of his friend the young painter Umberto Veruda. What his wife called the "track of ineffaceable melancholy"[27] that furrowed his life did not prevent a satisfying marriage and enjoyment of a belated public recognition, but Svevo's obsessions with jealousy, old age, sickness, death, and the hoaxes of Mother Nature attest to the omnipresence of the ghosts of his early suffering, his "frogs," as he called them. What one critic terms his "pessimismo bonario,"[28] his good-natured pessimism, a lifelong mood he shared with Freud,[29] seemed to inspire in his young admirers "a confidence in life which he himself did not feel."[30] A defensive wit, the habitual use of self-irony as a means of adjustment to continual disappointment, has led some critics to identify his humor as particularly Jewish, but one must be skeptical about ascribing it to his heritage, as one would, too, Freud's partiality to Jewish humor. Svevo's refusal to take too seriously a "Jewish destiny," which again links him with Freud, might be interpreted as a psychological cowardice, like his attitudes toward therapy, but Furbank sanely reminds us that there was, in fact, little anti-Semitism in Trieste in Svevo's youth that might have encouraged a more intense identification, and little pressure from his

26. Livia Veneziani Svevo, *Vita di mio marito,* ed. A. Pittoni (Trieste, 1958) , p. 96.
27. Ibid., p. 28.
28. Debenedetti, "Svevo e Schmitz," p. 66.
29. See Jones, *Freud,* 2: 413.
30. Letizia Svevo Fonda Savio, "A Daughter's Tribute," *Modern Fiction Studies,* Svevo Issue, p. 98.

family.[31] Nothing could be more typical of Svevo's broad spirit in regard to any identification than the quip reported by Sergio Solmi in the 1929 Svevo edition of *Solaria* concerning his Jewishness: "It isn't race that makes a Jew, it's life."[32] It is probably safer to say that, indifferent to a strong formal identification, Svevo, like Freud, saw himself as a psychological Jew. Debenedetti, whose assumptions about Svevo's evasion of his Jewish heritage remain tenuous and highly questionable, reports a conversation with Svevo in which the novelist, speaking of Kafka, admits that being Jewish is not a comfortable situation.[33] A sense of personal oppression made sociable by an acute but gentle self-irony, a passion for introspection and a simultaneous sense of the absurdity of life's logic constantly surprised by fantasy and desire, are the psychological traits commonly attributed to the Jewish sensibility by those who see in Svevo's humor the kind of defensive wit that Freud enjoyed. A generous pessimism that recognizes the subversion of moral order in the heart of a bourgeois who nevertheless pays tenacious homage to that order, leads Svevo's temper quite naturally into alliance with that of the father of psychoanalysis.

Sharing with Freud an enjoyment of a standard bourgeois marriage, which the wife regulates,[34] the novelist retreats into the study from which he dreams and scribbles, while the doctor diagnoses and tests hypotheses about scribblings and dreamings. From these sanctuaries, Freud and Svevo could, in the words of Philip Rieff, safely "invade the whole rotten empire of the family, without running the ultimate risk of cutting [themselves] off from the devout practice of its creed."[35] The "Diario per la fidanzata" and the letters, as well as the fiction of Svevo persuade us to adopt Rieff's description of Freud for the novelist: "No more compulsively moral man ever has explored the compulsiveness of morality."[36] If such a situation fostered

---

31. Furbank, *Italo Svevo,* p. 98. Furbank's correction of Debenedetti's thesis that Svevo's heroes reflect the self-hate of the Jew described by Weininger is an important one. If self-hatred leads to self-examination, the self-love that Svevo recommends to Cyril Ducker in a letter of 1927 (OO, 1: 837), as a means to sincerity, leads to self-acceptance, and it is this strain that is strongest in Svevo's nature.

32. Sergio Solmi, "Ricordi di Svevo," in "Omaggio a Italo Svevo," *Solaria* (March-April 1929), p. 71.

33. Debenedetti, "Lettere a Carocci intorno a 'Svevo e Schmitz," *Saggi critici,* n.s., p. 97.

34. See Rieff, *Freud,* p. xvi.

35. Ibid., p. xvi.

36. Ibid., p. xvi.

the split between the affectionate and sensual feelings that Freud traces beyond the bounds of modern civilization to its totemic origins,[37] but that is emblematic of the unnatural divorce plaguing the twentieth-century bourgeois husband, it also allowed him the means of enduring it. Balzac refers to the need for both a mistress and a wife in post-Napoleonic society as the "quest of that mysterious hermaphrodite, that rare work, which most often turns out to be a work in two volumes,"[38] and both Freud and Svevo exorcised that need by analyzing its process in the lives of others.[39] "In only very few people of culture," notes Freud, "are the two strains of tenderness and sensuality duly fused into one."[40] The "Diario per la fidanzata," impelled by jealousy and anxiety about such a bifurcated sentiment, reveals the tension that is eased by the comic expression of Zeno's adultery. In a rare instance in which Svevo puts responsibility for his sickness on the century, he writes to his wife: "I will always love you as much as the fin de siècle allows me to and not otherwise."[41] More typical is his lament over his affective inferiority to Livia: "Oh! if I could become like you with your simplicity of expression I would not even need to become healthy and strong."[42] By these confessions he consigns the high consciousness of his own modern symptoms to the care of his household Lares. All the ailments of bourgeois civilization in decline, diagnosed by Christian and existentialist, by Freud and the Marxists, the religion of health

37. See Freud, Postscript to "Group Psychology and the Analysis of the Ego," Standard ed. (1955), 18: 141, in which Freud hypothesizes that as a result of totemic exogamy, "a wedge was driven in between a man's affectionate and sensual feelings, one still firmly fixed in his erotic life today."

38. Honoré de Balzac, *La Cousine Bette,* trans. Marion A. Crawford (Baltimore, Md.: Penguin, 1965), pp. 288–89.

39. Svevo's letters attest to a constant fidelity. See, for example, one to his wife from Plymouth, England, 1901, OO, 1: 305:

Here, I would have the opportunity at every step to betray you and I feel so pure, so removed from all desire that I could not imagine that you are made differently. I look at the women, as I look at them in Trieste, and that's all. Last night I dreamed I had betrayed you and I felt such sorrow at not being able to tell you all about it and pain in the understanding that our relationship would necessarily have to change that in my dream I wept over it. You understand from this that you too can be reassured by this.

40. Freud, "On the Universal Tendency to Debasement in the Sphere of Love," Standard ed. (1957), 11: 85.

41. Svevo, entry in *Diario per la fidanzata,* 3 February 1896, OO, 3: 784.

42. Ibid. Aware of the infantile nature of his "senility," Svevo calls himself "un piccolo delinquente," OO, 1:210–11 and laments his affective split between the tender brother and the jealous husband, which seems to confirm Freud's assumption in n. 37.

and its hell of hypochondrias, the sense of political uselessness, of social superfluity—all these and the guilts brought on by that "quest of that mysterious hermaphrodite," can be kept at bay by the "dolce confessore," the real Livia and the fictional Augusta.[43]

The professional confessor of the new secular world, the psychoanalyst, is relegated, like the adulterer, to the fantasy of the study. He finds his place in the fiction of a compulsively moral dreamer. Svevo likes to picture himself as a dreamer escaping bourgeois responsibilities in a cloud of cigarette smoke, but always within the bourgeois order:

> My habit of dreaming is really what gives me my almost continual serenity. Otherwise, I also would live like our Marco* in the midst of the continual harshness of a reality that deprives him of sleep and of the will to live.[44]

This habit might seem familiar to readers of the nineteenth-century novel, one manifested in the decadent post-Napoleonic heroes frustrated by bourgeois monarchies. But Svevo's dreamer, in fiction as in life, does not often have the luxury of attributing inertia to a general cultural climate. "Senilità" is not diluted into a fin de siècle condition. The Svevian interest sharpens to the specific psychiatric tension, not only between the hero and others, but between the hero's rational and irrational life. Svevo supports the claim that after Freud it is impossible to think of dreams and fantasies as innocent, just as it is impossible to write novels innocently.[45] If the artist is so inconsolable in the face of public neglect, writes the poet Saba, it is because

43. Ibid., OO, 3: 786–87.
* Svevo's brother-in-law.
44. Letter to his wife, 5 December 1903, OO, 1: 376.
45. See Alain Robbe-Grillet, "Zeno's Sick Conscience," *For a New Novel*, trans. Richard Howard (New York, 1965), pp. 89–94. It seems to me that Robbe-Grillet makes just the right emphasis when he lowers the Svevian scene from high complaint to low:

> Sick time, sick language, sick libido, sick body, sick life, sick conscience. . . . We must not, of course, see in these some vague allegory of original sin, or any other metaphysical lamentation. It is a question of everyday life and of direct experience of the world. What Italo Svevo tells us in his way is that in our modern society nothing is any longer *natural*. Nor is there even any reason to be upset about it. We can be quite happy, talk, make love, do business, wage war, write novels; but nothing of all this will any longer be done without thinking about it, the way one breathes. Under our gaze, the simple gesture of holding out our hand becomes bizarre, clumsy; the words we hear ourselves speaking suddenly sound false; the time of our minds is no longer that of the clocks; and the style of a novel, in its turn, can no longer be innocent. (pp. 93–4)

the work of art is *always* a confession and desires absolution. Success denied is equivalent to absolution denied.[46] Like art and wit the dream of both day and night has the psychic usefulness of elaborate protection and the psychic economy of exorcism, and though it was always so, the modern dreamer cannot pretend to be ignorant of the dream's vocabulary. Since Svevo constantly referred to his dreaming as the activity of a dilettante, we might suspect that the dreaming is a way of preserving delusions of grandeur, of prolonging the period of latency.[47] The hero of "The Hoax," Mario Samigli, an early pen name of Svevo's, is described at the beginning of this superb novella as a man of sixty with a novel now long in the past, still picturing, in the state of inertia, a glorious future that absolves him "from the painful task of destroying a long-cherished illusion." Svevo adds in ironic sympathy: "So, in a sense, he triumphed over fate" (H, 11). Neither in his fiction, where his characters continually fall short of significant literary activity, nor in his picture of himself, does Svevo ever boldly distinguish, like Flaubert, between daydreaming and art. Freud's hypothesis that art softens the egoism of the daydreamer's fantasies by "changes and disguises" putting us in a position to appreciate and "enjoy our own daydreams without reproach or shame"[48] might be accepted by Svevo, but he consciously mutes the distinction, soft-pedals the transformation.

More compelling to Svevo are the Freudian interest in the relationship between the man who dreams and the man who works and the emphasis upon the closeness of day to night dreaming.[49] The refusal of the novelist to separate dramatically the dreamed life from the waking life distances his characters from the Romantic victim and visionary, from prophetic Josephs predicting feasts and famines, from gigantic Fausts whose dreams overcome tragedy and illusion. Ironically comparing his own dreams of becoming an industrial

---

46. Umberto Saba, *Prose* (Milan, 1964), p. 290.

47. See section 2 of the excellent three-part article by André Bouissy, "Les fondements idéologiques de l'oeuvre d'Italo Svevo," *Revue des études italiennes* 12, (October-December 1966): 350–73.

48. Freud, "Creative Writers and Day-Dreaming," (1908) Standard ed. (1959), 9: 143–66.

49. Ibid., pp. 148–49, and "The Paths to Symptom Formation," Standard ed. 16: 373:

   A night-dream is at bottom nothing other than a day-dream that has been made utilizable owing to the liberation of the instinctual impulses at night, and that has been distorted by the form assumed by mental activity at night.

genius of beneficent discoveries and activities and Faust's plans for saving land from the sea, Svevo ends a paragraph in a letter to his wife by admitting: "It is not activity that makes me so alive, it is dreams."[50] The dreamer who creates novels and the industrialist who translates them live in a cultivated oxymoronic twinship. In the life and literature of Svevo neither role is given license to soar untainted by fantasy or the paint factory. Half of Svevo lives in Giulio, the indolent hero of one of Svevo's Murano stories, "In Serenella," who is called by his industrious brothers "an eternal dreamer,"[51] but even his dreaming in exile is checked by the presence of the active life in others. Similarly, Enrico Gaia, Mario's enemy in "The Hoax," is described as a commercial traveler who has strangled the poet in himself, which then is reincarnated in the jokester, whereas Mario, in the long indolence left over from his small job had continued to live on a literature of apology, on dreams and fables. In each case, Svevo prevents full success and satisfaction for one half of his image by haunting it with the other. After success, long delayed, in his literary life, Svevo looks back and laughs with a tolerance tinged with cynicism at those who, unable to call him a great writer, called him a great businessman.[52] He himself felt more comfortable during his long climb to literary fame with a defensive role of the dilettante commuting between the violin and the factory.[53] One term of his existence always chastises or invades the other. He writes to his wife:

> You know that in spite of my serious effort to become in the shortest possible time a good businessman and a good industrialist, in fact I have only the intention. I remain in the face of the new purpose the old dreamer. When I foresee a piece of business, I at least have had the practical sense to think and dream of it in the forms and terms in which it presents itself. Oh, I go so far into it that the business itself soon becomes a misfortune but the stimulation for dreams so powerful as to procure me a distraction that some day will topple me into a paint basin.[54]

By demoting his literature to the daydream and his industry to anticipation, he diminishes the rift between life and art, and by good-

50. Svevo, 6 June 1900, OO, 1: 196.
51. Svevo, OO, 3: 362.
52. Svevo, "Soggiorno londinese," OO, 3: 689.
53. Svevo, "Profilo autobiografico," OO, 3: 806.
54. Svevo, 6 June 1900, 1: 195.

natured self-irony he pacifies ambition in either direction. Mario Ricciardi suggests that this habit of Svevo was his modest way of closing the gap between art and society that had so tortured the great European novelists Proust, Mann, and Joyce,[55] and certainly, if this was not a conscious program, it corresponds to our impression of a literature that ardently avoids historical and cultural categories of dialectical opposition. The refusal to sequester fantasy from reality, dream from waking, may function as a cultural reconciliation, but the simultaneity of mixed times and levels of experience was a basic recognition of Svevo's complex, antirevolutionary and unsentimental temperament. In an essay on Joyce, Svevo notes the contrast between his two dreamers, Stephen, the artist, whose active dreams adorn the life he has and despises with the well-chosen word and the colorful image, with Bloom, whose dreams are mere fantasies and to whom he gives the title "il fantastico pratico," the practical fantastic.[56] It is easy to see why critics have assumed that Svevo was an important model for Bloom, for his temperament is that of the gentle dilettante of life whose daydreams fall short of art and whose business lives on anticipation. The oxymoronic title that Svevo gives to Bloom seems perfectly suited for Svevo's image of himself.

The true dreamer, says Svevo, always leads a double life, and, in a vision that reverses Freud's direction in which art organizes the day-dream, Svevo likes to picture the daydream as wasting and disorganizing the observed. In an essay entitled "Echi mondani" he talks amusingly, in terms of quantity, of the diminution in territory and time covered in daydreaming and fantasy when they surface onto the page:

> Dreams may be bold and ingenious, but they will leave a dispro-portionately small trace in comparison to their volume; a world might have been dreamed, and a cloud traced, a whole tragedy, an epic, and a verse put down. The dreamer is never commensurate with his waking self because the dream carries us far away and not in straight lines, whereas the waking person, consistent with him-self, moves in a space that is more symmetrical and restricted.[57]

---

55. Mario Ricciardi, *L'educazione del personaggio nella narrativa di Italo Svevo* (Palermo, 1972), pp. 24–7.
56. Svevo, "Scritti su Joyce," OO, 3: 722, 743.
57. Svevo, OO, 3: 621–2.

It is both rich and disconcerting to see the two times in one consciousness, in Flaubert the dreamer, for example, whom Svevo pictures as a smoker, drawing out the long luxury of procreation for *Salammbô* after Flaubert the observer had shaken the world with his *Madame Bovary*. The elongation of contemplation and the multiplication of the objects of the observed world allow inviting possibilities but not really genetic transformations. In his notebooks Svevo writes that reality is the reality of one woman, while the dream is the reality of many women, better, sweeter, more willing.[58] Even more telling is the passage in "The Story of the Nice Old Man and the Pretty Girl," in which the old man, after dreams deeper and more frustrating than mere fantasy, muses:

> He knew now that he loved the girl of the bright-colored old clothes and loved her as a daughter. She had been his in fact, as she had been in his dream, or rather in two dreams. In both dreams, remarked the old man to himself, not being aware that dreams occur at night and are completed by day, there had been great suffering, which was perhaps the cause of the illness with which he was seized, the suffering of compassion. (NOM, 114)

The reality of such visions scares the old man into superstitions of morality, an amusing overreaction to the responsibilities that begin in dreams.

In an essay called "Del Sentimento in arte," Svevo speaks of the superior accessibility of the dreamer to the appreciation of art. The dreamer's sensitivity allows him to arrive at an understanding that short-circuits long critical study. With characteristic humor, he notes that the source of this sensitivity is a megalomania that translates the viewer into the creator and fantasizes an identity between them. It is this interest that lends energy to perception.[59] Svevo does not attribute a primary energy to the dreamer, for the fantasy is parasitic upon a life already lived. In noting the resistance of Joyce to the psychoanalytic thought that surrounded him, Svevo describes the genius that rejects whatever impedes or competes with his own thought.[60] Svevo himself identified rather with the parasitic dreamer, coming from the underside of art, receptive to the most

58. Svevo, "Pagine di diario sparse," OO, 3: 842.
59. Svevo, OO, 3: 673.
60. Svevo, "Scritti su Joyce," OO, 3: 725.

delicate of intellectual pressures and dominated by none, least of all personal myths. If his sensitive observer rises to the level of creator, it is by a secondary megalomania, one that is checked by humor.

Like the Svevian dream with its easy access to waking, the Svevian wit seems to hang between two worlds, refusing the glamor of melodramatic exorcism and correction. In speaking of the question of Svevo's Jewish identity, we noted the self-reflective nature of the novelist's wit as a trait that can be compared to that of Freud's Jew who, finding it socially difficult to express directly his criticism or aggression in a hostile atmosphere, is compelled to resort to indirection.[61] This kind of humor is identified by Freud as a form of tendentious wit that uses the self, or a composite personality, as a nationality with which one can identify, as a target for the release of "the intended criticism of the inner resistance."[62] On the way to a larger humor, Zeno relieves his hostilities primarily through wit, and wit, like the scribbling of the confessions themselves, the dreams and fables in the novel, can be used to lend an air of innocence to his compulsions. Like other defensive agents, it guards against the criticism of reason.[63] Because, according to Freud, "reason, critical judgment, suppression . . . are the forces against which it fights in succession,"[64] wit is never purposeless. Freud's famous definition of the process of tendentious jokes as an economy in psychic expenditure of inhibitions or suppressions, an alleviation from the pressure of reason,[65] relates it to both dreams and art. Svevo must have been delighted with the metaphors of economy and expenditure, for the novelist's attraction to the civilizing terms of the debit and credit system of physiology and psychology, as well as of the universe of that comic Darwinian, Mother Nature, is a way of keeping the artist and the industrialist together. The man who saw the stock market as one of the most accurate metaphors for life sees eye to eye with Freud in his description of the workings of wit:

> I may perhaps venture on a comparison between psychical economy and a business enterprise. So long as the turnover in the business is

61. Freud, "Jokes and Their Relation to the Unconscious," Standard ed. (1960), 13: 142.
62. Ibid., p. 111.
63. Freud, "Humor," Standard ed. (1961), 21.
64. Freud, "Jokes," p. 137.
65. Ibid., p. 119.

very small, the important thing is that outlay in general shall be kept low and administrative costs restricted to the minimum.[66]

The economy effected in the mind of the listener is of primary interest to both Freud and the producer of wit. Wit is necessarily social, and for this reason it is a favorite tactic of Zeno, who refuses to be isolated by his neurosis. The presence of the receiver of wit is an important one in every scene of *Confessions of Zeno,* and it is that presence which allows Zeno's wit to function as a social benefit while it poses as a social disaster. "Laughter arises," conjectures Freud, "if a quota of psychical energy which has earlier been used for the cathexis of particular psychical paths has become unusable, so that it can find free discharge."[67] The "indestructible persistence of psychical processes"[68] is caught by Guido when he says to Zeno: "Your fable is a criticism of me" (CZ, 280). But the hearer who laughs has "saved on psychical expenditure and his pleasure corresponds to this economy."[69] Even Zeno's desire for innocence is spared an exclusive narcissism by the social nature of wit, which procures an attractive moment of absolution:

> For the euphoria which we endeavour to reach by this means is nothing other than the mood of a period of life in which we were accustomed to deal with our psychical work in general with a small expenditure of energy—the mood of our childhood, when we were ignorant of the comic, when we were incapable of jokes and when we had no need of humor to make us feel happy in our life.[70]

The desire to recapture through wit a childhood mood may, if intense enough, give to the personality childlike forms. One of the most often-noted characteristics of both Svevo and Zeno is the presence of that child, amidst so much senility of spirit, in the willingness to be surprised by the world of others and to improvise on its material. The devious paths of defense and rationalizations that Zeno trods is a long trek to innocence, especially since it has no end, but when the goal itself is accepted as part of the journey, the child momentarily comes to the fore. The child that Saba saw in the

66. Ibid., pp. 156–7.
67. Ibid., p. 147.
68. Ibid., p. 148.
69. Ibid., p. 149.
70. Ibid., p. 236.

naturalness of Svevo's curiosity[71] is the same that Jacques Boulanger senses in the humor he gives to Zeno:

> He had a way of seeing things and himself that was charming: I am thinking especially of his humor. It is not a humor in any way imposed by the author, but spontaneous, involuntary, that the author hardly expresses but which seems, instead, to rise out of the disposition of the events.[72]

It is an irresistible temptation to call Svevo himself a good child:

> He is not one of those who plunge into a mystical delirium at the mention of the words "life" or "the absurd," nor one who wishes to force life into moral frames, nor one who works himself into an anger of invective, or of irony; but he belongs to those who refuse to take things tragically and who play quietly in their corner, as it suits well-behaved children of really critical minds who know how to draw a kind of pleasure out of their troubles.[73]

Umberto Saba labors his definition of the poet in order to distinguish the childlike aspect from more deliberate temperaments. Though Svevo would not appreciate the title, having an innate resistance to the poet's literary self-consciousness, he certainly qualifies for Saba's definition:

> What, basically, is a poet, a true poet? I have already defined it elsewhere: he is a little boy who wonders at the things that happen to him as an adult.[74]

It is no accident that Svevo saw himself in his favorite image as a little boy in the body of an old man, called upon to bear sudden fame.

The childlike wit of both Svevo and Zeno achieves a kind of innocence that cannot be had by the deliberate search for perfect moral health. As a "little neurotic delinquent"[75] delighting, as Saba describes him in his *Scorciatoie,* like a spiteful child over a steak which, at the end of the war, would probably be the only one eaten in the city,[76] Svevo could not have perfect health but, with Zeno, he could

71. Saba, *Prose,* pp. 269–70.
72. Jacques Boulanger, "Sur Zeno," *Solaria,* Svevo issue, p. 16.
73. Ibid.
74. Saba, *Prose,* pp. 737–38.
75. Svevo, Letter to his wife, 17 June 1900, OO, 1: 210.
76. Saba, *Prose,* p. 269.

find another kind of innocence through the humor that expands, beyond wit, into an attitude toward life. Nothing could more closely match the nature of Svevo's mature vision than Freud's moving tribute to humor:

> Its fending off of the possibility of suffering places it among the great series of methods which the human mind has constructed in order to evade the compulsion to suffer—a series which begins with neurosis and culminates in madness and which includes intoxication, self absorption and ecstasy. Thanks to this connection, humour possesses a dignity which is wholly lacking, for instance, in jokes, for jokes either serve simply to obtain a yield of pleasure or place the yield of pleasure that has been obtained in the service of aggression.[77]

The major meaning of humor, writes Freud, is expressed by this tone: "Look! here is the world, which seems so dangerous! It is nothing but a game for children—just worth making a jest about."[78] Recognizing that this is comfort for the intimidated ego, rather than cure, Freud projects a touching and intriguing hypothesis that this humor might be wielded by a superego that promotes it:

> And finally, if the super-ego tries by means of humour to console the ego and protect it from suffering, this does not conflict with its origin in the parental agency.[79]

The child in Zeno might, through this consolation, at least have found the kind and absolving parent he looked for in his father.

This defense prompts another version of Freud's psychic doubling in the superego's function offered by Svevo's contemporary, Pirandello: his famous description of the true humorist as one who simultaneously feels and criticizes.[80] The critic punctures all forms of idealizing myths and abstract systems of belief devised by the supermen of cures by allowing digression that distracts. In *Confessions of Zeno*, the wings of incipient rhapsodies of self-justification are clipped and flutter, in a bathetic movement, from theory to anecdote. The humorist's faith in life is at best provisional, moved by curiosity and the willingness to see it through. Psychoanalysis was, for

77. Freud, "Humour," 21: 163.
78. Ibid., p. 166.
79. Ibid.
80. Luigi Pirandello, "Alberto Cantoni: Un critico fantastico," *Saggi, poesie et scritti vari* (Milan, 1960), pp. 365–87.

Svevo, a means of knowing himself, but was always qualified by the understanding that every kind of knowledge about the self is partial and temporary, always subject to convenient amnesias and the adjustments of experience. The constant downdraught that accompanies all of Svevo's enthusiasms pulls together the dreamer and the businessman, the artist and the critic, the child and the old man. In distinguishing Freud from Marx, Philip Rieff speaks of the absence in Freud of the religious temper, an absence Freud himself certainly knew of, and calls him a "statesman of the inner life, aiming at shrewd compromises with the human condition, not at its basic transformation."[81] Though Svevo gave more credence than Freud to the mysterious nature of the hoaxes and accidents for which we are not always responsible, he too might be considered a psychic diplomat. If Freud's therapy is one that, unlike the old religions, cannot be "a therapy of belief, but one which instructs us how to live without belief,"[82] it embraces Svevo's cynical compassion. Rieff calls this an "ethic of honesty," one that does not bypass traditional ethical ideals but recognizes the need for a more efficient and realistic compromise with them.[83] The reality that Freud turns us to—the inevitable and painful struggle between culture and instinct, particularly acute in the middle classes—and his hope of mitigating rather than curing such a tension, are the same reality and hope that Zeno enacts on a personal level and ultimately views from a more general perspective with his author. In his essay "A Weltanschauung" Freud sees in Marxism the religious structure of exclusion and claims for psychoanalysis no world view of its own.[84] This is certainly a more Svevian posture than that ascetic retreat of the novelist's cherished Schopenhauer.

When Thomas Mann speaks in "Freud und die Zukunft" of the relation between literature and psychology as one based upon a mutual passion for truth, a mutual willingness to accept the bittersweet complexities of such a passion,[85] he ascribes to both a kind of

---

81. Rieff, *Freud*, p. xx.
82. Ibid., p. 334.
83. Ibid., p. 338, 346.
84. Freud, "A Weltanschauung," Standard ed. (1964), 23: 158–82.
85. Thomas Mann, *Adel des Geistes* (Frankfurt, 1959), pp. 498–99:
    Die Liebe für *Wahrheit* erstens, ein Wahrheitissinn, eine Empfindlichkeit und Empfänglichkeit für diese Reize und Bitterkeiten.
The essay is translated as "Freud and the Future," *Essays of Three Decades*, trans. H. T. Lowe-Porter (New York, 1948), pp. 411–28.

moral imperative to understand and accept the generative value of disease. He credits Nietzsche with the "morally conditioned love of truth as *psychology*,"[86] but it is in Schopenhauer that Mann first encountered, like Svevo, "the dauntless zeal for truth that stands for the moral aspect of the psychology of the unconscious."[87] The laying of the bridge between the perceptions of psychiatry and those of the novel would have interested Svevo enormously, and it seems almost uncanny how intimately these reflections of Mann, who had his own literature in mind, apply to Svevo's own understanding of the relationship between psychiatry and his literature, though the Italian novelist would have felt uncomfortable with the lofty insistence of such a high rhetorical speculation. Joyce, who was fascinated by the way in which smoking dominates Zeno and by the treatment of time in his novel,[88] surprised Svevo by countering the latter's interest in psychoanalysis with the statement: "Well, if we need it, let us keep to confession."[89] Such rebellious bravado, so typical of Joyce's resistance to intellectual domination, reveals by contrast the vulnerability to influences that Svevo entertained without jealousy for his originality. Svevo did not seem threatened by psychoanalysis's competition with the novel. The order, or disorder, of psychoanalytic confession richly complemented Svevo's desire, in his last work, to make the novel's structure less self-conscious and deliberate—less literary, in effect. While Joyce was consciously busy at his revolution, Svevo was only trying to find a way to make his fiction seem more sincere. Svevo had neither the need nor the desire to impose, like Joyce, fierce chains upon his own inspiration in order to free it.[90] The use of psychoanalysis as a containing system, against which an imprisoned fiction, in its desire for freedom, would relentlessly break, would not suit Svevo's porous temperament. The form it gave him, the dreams, the lapses, the slips of tongue and the limps of body—all these could be played out casually without recourse to parody in his open comedy. The vision it gave him, which he first seized in Schopenhauer, of the necessary shift of view from the rigid categories of good and bad to a term like *original,* a shift made

86. Ibid., p. 413.
87. Ibid., p. 415.
88. Harry Levin, ed., "Carteggio inedito; Italo Svevo e James Joyce," introduction Harry Levin, *Inventario* 2 (1949) : 120.
89. Svevo, "Scritti su Joyce," OO, 3: 725.
90. Ibid., p. 717.

without moral trauma by figures as disparate as Montaigne and Freud, did not paralyze the good bourgeois.

One of Freud's most perceptive readers sees his science as the completion of the circle started by Montaigne's humanism. Philip Rieff asserts:

> It continues the strategic retreat of knowing men from a civilization of public authority to a civilized inspection of the private life. With Montaigne begins the modern distrust of civilization; in Freud that distrust found its theoretician.[91]

And Nietzsche, by pairing Montaigne with Schopenhauer, points him toward Freud:

> I only know a single author that I can rank with Schopenhauer or even above him, in the matter of honesty, and that is Montaigne.[92]

Svevo's climactic aphorism on life's originality, which he gives to Zeno; the nature and form of his final adjustment to life as a disease, itself a kind of health; and so much about his spirit and the configuration of his fiction reflect the *Essais* that they can profitably be considered as an illuminating parallel to Svevo's mature work. From a static position of retirement from the busy world, "en pleine oisiveté"[93] Montaigne and the old Zeno contemplate their lives through a disordered and mixed time. Old age, complains Zeno, "pushes me into the shadows and robs me of the role of leading actor" (FCZ, 29). Now, his role is to provide a background for others and to recapture his youth (a task burlesqued by a rejuvenation operation) with the pen. He recalls another time, that of *Confessions of Zeno,* in which he wrote to become sincere. So here now is modern man, his body scientifically updated, an incomplete Freudian therapy in the past, protesting the ills of old age to prepare for resignation, and witnessing the tragicomic disequilibriums of his children. From the times and estate of Montaigne, we have lost class, composure, and the secure moral and rhetorical example of the ancients, yet the juxtaposing of the temper of the meditations of Zeno with that of the *Essais* does not appear a travesty of historical and rhetorical decline. The Svevian adoption of an antiliterary posture

91. Rieff, *Freud*, p. 72.
92. Friedrich Nietzsche, "Thoughts Out of Season," *The Philosophy of Nietzsche,* trans. Oscar Levy, ed. Geoffrey Clive (New York, 1965) , 2: 334.
93. Montaigne, "Of Idleness," *Essays*, 1: 21.

and the attendant projection of sincerity fails to radiate the confidence needed to serve as a prescriptive recommendation for the
education of the young man. It does for Montaigne.[94] But the demotion of literature to life by giving it the body's digestive system,
shape, and sicknesses limits in both writers its possibilities of transvaluation, lends it the odors of our mortality:

> Here you have, a little more decently, some excrements of an aged
> mind, now hard, now loose, and always undigested. (3: 9, 721)

If the body's domination, in an age that features health as a new
religion, is neurotic in Zeno while it seems robust in the *Essais*, a
kidney stone insistently weighs down the end of Montaigne's confessions, as psychoanalysis and urinalysis weigh down the end of Zeno's.
The body's ills keep the subject from supercelestial cures and salva-
tions and help him to accept the metaphor that binds sickness to life.
Emerson's comment that the *Essais* seems a book less written than
any others, that its language is the language of "conversation transferred to a book," and that its words would bleed if they were cut[95]
honors the identification of the book and the body in a way that
would most please Montaigne, dedicated as he was to the notion of
the consubstantiality of his words and his body:

> In this case we go hand in hand and at the same pace, my book and
> I. In other cases one may commend or blame the work apart from
> the workman; not so here; he who touches the one, touches the
> other. (3: 2, 611–12)

When all the arguments over the irregularities of Svevo's language
died down, the acceptance came in the form of compliments to a
style that was what Emerson called Montaigne's "vascular and
alive"[96] in a way that reflected the physiological twitches of modern
neurosis. Without slighting the enormous differences between a
secure style of studied nonchalance and what Svevo called his
"dialetuccio," a self-conscious obstacle before it became a blessing,
there is obviously a striking similarity in the humor of the two
writers that makes of the body's contradictions of spirit a saving
form.

94. See Montaigne, "Of the Education of Children," *Essays*, 1: 106–31.
95. Ralph Waldo Emerson, "Montaigne," *Representative Men*, The Portable Emerson, ed. Mark van Doren (New York, 1946), p. 501.
96. Ibid.

The temperamental persuasions of the two writers move in the same direction, though we cannot miss the changes wrought by the passage of space and time. We feel that Montaigne makes a controlled appeal when he argues in his essay on the education of the young that words must follow the feelings and that dialect might express thoughts more spontaneously than the king's French, while the protest of Zeno: "We lie with every word we speak in the Tuscan tongue" (CZ, 368) is bent by irony. Montaigne's closeness to the medieval topos of humility[97] and his natural familiarity with the ancients make him relaxed about the relationship between rhetoric and sincerity. When Svevo, on the other hand, criticizes a writer by calling him "a man who writes too well to be sincere,"[98] we feel how anxious the question has become for the modern writer,[99] to say nothing of Svevo's personal literary complexes. If both writers are suspicious of the relation between the labored literary effect and sincerity, Svevo's anxiety can push him to a Rousseauesque fantasy parallel to the last vision in Zeno, which suggests the relief of the heart no longer hindered by the obstacle of language:

> Perhaps when we finally are released from space and time we will know each other so intimately that we will have a direct path to sincerity. We will speak with familiarity to each other and laugh at each other in turn as we deserve. Literature which now, unfortunately, is so intimate a part of our soul, will finally perish and we will see each other immediately and deeply.[100]

But as a novelist delighting in the mysteries of the human personality, he adds this deflation: "Gruesome prospect." Montaigne is not apprehensive about working through words to effects of unmediated confession. He confidently aims for a style by which the material makes its own divisions:

> It shows well enough where it changes, where it concludes, where it begins, where it resumes, without my interlacing it with words,

97. See Montaigne, *Essays*, 2: 503–06, and the interesting book of Charles Lapp, *The Aesthetics of Negligence: La Fontaine's Contes* (Cambridge, Mass., 1971) .

98. Svevo, "Pagine sparse," OO, 3: 820.

99. This change, so visible in the passage between the confessions of Montaigne and those of Rousseau, is perceptively traced by Lionel Trilling, *Sincerity and Authenticity* (Cambridge, Mass, 1973) . David Perkins concentrates upon Wordsworth as a reflector of the change in *Wordsworth and the Poetry of Sincerity* (Cambridge, Mass., 1964) , and the best study on this subject concerning Rousseau is that of Jean Starobinski, *Jean-Jacques Rousseau: la transparence et l'obstacle* (Paris, 1971) .

100. Svevo, "Pagine sparse," OO, 3: 829.

with links and seams introduced for the benefit of weak or heedless ears, and without glosses on myself. (3: 9, 761)

The modern adjustment in which Svevo participated is described by Sartre in his criticism of Mauriac's closed classical form. Dostoevski, Conrad, and Faulkner are praised for having known how "to use . . . resistance to words, which is the source of endless misunderstandings and involuntary revelations, and thereby to make of dialogue 'the fictional moment,' the time when the sense of duration is richest."[101] The subsequent deemphasis on plot, a muting that is an attribute of the desire for authenticity, is in Svevo reinforced by the psychoanalytic structure by which spontaneous images and anecdotes, uncushioned syntax, and transition come to have great value for the reflection of sincerity. The same advantages are gained by Montaigne's insistence that "it is not my deeds that I write down; it is myself, it is my essence" (2: 6, 274), but without the tension that accompanies the modern subversion of traditional form. Public attitudes and ancient examples are quite comfortable in Montaigne's body:

> Every movement reveals us. That same mind of Caesar's which shows itself in ordering and directing the battle of Pharsalia, shows itself also in arranging idle and amorous affairs. (1: 50, 219)

His own variability serves as an example rather than a symptom of rebellion:

> We are all patchwork, and so shapeless and diverse in composition that each bit, each moment, plays its own game. And there is as much difference between us and ourselves as between us and others. (2: 1, 244)

The inconsistency that testifies to a consciousness of mixed times is taken by Montaigne as a natural phenomenon, whereas for the modern hyperconscious and compulsive man, such contradictions stimulate withdrawals, the heroism of transvaluation, or brave new literary declarations of independence from the ancients.

The modern version of Montaigne's erasing of the line between public and private confession is the impulsive attempt of Zeno to ingratiate his sickness into bourgeois strongholds of traditional

---

101. "François Mauriac and Freedom," *Literary Essays*, trans. A. Michelson (New York, 1938), p. 21.

health, giving it public form in improvisation and anecdote. The self-conscious and self-pitying attempts to gain acceptance and absolution, such as the false confession to Augusta that elicits a "povero Cosini,"[102] are cited as examples of bad faith, but for all the distance between Montaigne and Svevo, this criticism might be tempered by remembering an assumption common to them both, that the display of one's sickness and debility, when it derives from the passion for health and rejects transvaluations, missions of conversion, and self-glorification, serves as a common denominator by which to bind men together. The comic desperation of Zeno's performance and the modern vocabulary of guilt and anxiety tempt us to place Zeno in the tradition of Rousseau and the underground man. His confessions arouse suspicion. But the reader is not bullied into the role of witness, and Zeno's confessions have a purpose beyond self-exoneration and personal therapy. They ultimately allow access to mankind as well as to the mistress. The journey, if a neurotic and comic version of Montaigne's, is still not a parody.

The whirling rhythms of compulsion and Mother Nature's hoaxes spin us, in unexpected ways, into the orbit of Montaigne's secular deity, the inner and outer wind of our nature and of the universe, the wind that clears the way for sincerity. Where there is motion, there is truth:

> Every day a new fancy, and our humors shift with the shifts in the weather. Our ordinary practice is to follow the inclinations of our appetite, to the left, to the right, uphill and down, as the wind of circumstance carries us. (2: 1, 240)

Montaigne gives the classical precedence by which to lend dignity to Zeno's justification of the natural motion of life on the line between the hyperactive Basedow's disease and a depleting dropsy:

> I still believe that at whatsoever particular spot of the universe one settles down one ends by becoming poisoned; it is essential to keep moving. Life has its poisons, but counter-poisons too which balance them. It is only by moving about that one can avoid the first and profit by the second. (CZ, 287)

---

102. See OO, 1: 889. In one of Svevo's last known letters, in which Svevo describes himself as uttering to his grandson: "Povero Schmitz," he reports his grandson as correcting him: "Beato Schmitz."

What looks like health is only a provisional suspension of movement between diseases. The relentless present tense and horizontal trajectory of both the *Essais* and *Confessions of Zeno* stubbornly renounce the more impressive curves and climaxes of sacred ascents, apocalypses, and conversions, and it is altogether fitting that with this tendency, true health is measured by disease, not in terms of contrast, but of inclusions. If we look for a moment at Montaigne's essay on his accident, centrally placed in the *Essais,* as an illustration of how this form becomes, in fact, a philosophy, it will be easier to see how in Svevo's novel the same process softens and widens the psychoanalytic influence.

Lightly parodying the Christian Fall and Resurrection, the soul, clinging to the body, experiences a secular version of incarnation and consubstantiality. Montaigne has fallen to the ground in an imitation of death, but the soul and body can neither consume each other nor struggle in debate. Accident refuses to take on the meaning that conversion might lend it. The simultaneity in space, time, and substance of death and life, body and soul, is never resolved by the ascendancy of one term. The pairs are doomed to mixed time. The physical hangs on the neck of the metaphysical (3: 13, 412). The correspondence between inner and outer weather permits simulations of death by which the mind can incorporate it, but not transcend it. We dance on Zeno's line while death occurs again and again with no more finality than Zeno's resolutions. Accident is for Rousseau Providence, its passive reception the way to exoneration, each fall in the *Confessions* an ejection from Eden precipitated by a hostile world and therefore a cause for celebration and justification. Rousseau's uniqueness, his innocence, is assured by this interpretation that persistently separates him from his contemporaries. The time of Montaigne, by contrast, plays between past and present, psychological and linear time, art and life in such a way that one term cannot take advantage over the other, necessitating conversation with the world. The closest we get in either Svevo or Montaigne to a consolation for falls is "that sociable wisdom," which the philosopher recommends (3: 13, 857) and which honors the originality of life while merely assuming as natural our compulsions to be good or bad.

The anxiety about originality, a modern disease that plagues Rousseau, is another manifestation of the desire to protest against surprises that come "au passage" (3: 2, 611). Montaigne likes rather to call himself a plagiarist, giving him common ground with the reader and ascribing to the world the role of original artist. Svevo's comment on originality in "Del sentimento in arte," in which he restricts it to the confines of the artless temperament without special privilege or pretense, vulnerable to the winds of body and mind,[103] and the conventional effects of Zeno's antics are evidence of Svevo's classicism, which allows the world that laughs at us immunity from our claims. In his last great essay, "Of Experience," Montaigne reminds us that the wind does not fret about its lack of stability, but loves its own proper qualities, its own functions. That wind, which has blown through the essays overturning the controls of body and mind, their semblance of order and consistency, now becomes a friend in the same way that Svevo's Mother Nature, outwitting Zeno by hoaxes and accidents, becomes a friend to all but the bespectacled technicians of destruction. Softening again the line between the zones of our consciousness, Svevo, in one of his most interesting diary entries, subjects the imagination, eager to rise above the vagaries of our immediate perspective, to the same unpredictable set of rules by which reality is run:

> One ought to believe in the reality of one's own imagination. But one must not interfere, by any force, to regulate it, for then it will become an incredible God which is missing in nature.[104]

"The imagination," writes Svevo, "is less monotonous than reality only because creatures move through it who originate in reality but are isolated from our desire and passion."[105] Disease and death, the unconscious and its dreams, the imagination, are all checked in their descents and flights. Montaigne's great admirer and Svevo's contemporary, André Gide, cherished the philosopher's belief that the important thing is not to be cured, but to live with one's diseases.[106] If an anxious concentration on personal neurosis has displaced a classical view of man's common ills, a comforting sense of identity between what is natural to man and what is good for him, Svevo is still intent on pushing beyond the bounds of private therapy to a

103. Svevo, "Del sentimento in arte," OO, 3: 672.
104. Svevo, "Pagine di diario e sparse," OO, 831.
105. Ibid., pp. 831–32.
106. This Montaignesque motto is ascribed, in *Corydon, Oeuvres complètes*, 9 (Paris, 1932–39), to l'abbé Galiani.

vision that is public enough to gather in all men in a common existential illness, life. Exposure to the trinity of modern determinisms, Darwin, Marx, Freud, pinioned the wings of the Romantic imagination, but Svevo drew from them the comic possibilities of laws not fully known, of survival subject to mutations and subconscious interruptions of order, cynical but tolerable premises of faith.

Svevo's self-advertised dilettantism in the world of such intellectual revolutions has often been assumed to be a defense against the necessity for responsible partisanship, especially in a crumbling Hapsburg world suffering from political and existential absurdity. He admits freely his resistance to spending too long with an idea and, in an essay on dilettantism—a subject perhaps inspired by Schopenhauer[107]—Svevo defends the dilettante who is made in the image of Mother Nature herself. Goethe and Machiavelli, with their predilection for many subjects, are cited. If such men needed more than one interest, is it not excusable that a businessman or banker satisfy the desire to play with various ideas which, irrationally, Mother Nature has put into his blood?[108] The playfulness of the dilettante's approach to subjects pays tribute to the mother of his whims. In a review of "Polemiche artistiche" of Salvatore Grita, Svevo coins an aphorism which, like Zeno's definition of life, is at the very heart of his disposition:

> Truth is a lady who gives the finger to whoever excitedly runs after her, while she surrenders herself, indeed, imposes herself, on the man who does not seek her.[109]

Svevo's trust in temperament over doctrine, his natural resistance to zealous intellectual systems might well be defensive, but he gives his fiction the advantage of being surprised by the truth. Perhaps in this adaptation of what others, and he himself, may deem his weakness, he most resembles Montaigne, who persuades us by his amateurism. The *Essais* themselves, he writes in "Of Giving the Lie," are

> for a nook in a library, and to amuse a neighbor, a relative, a friend, who may take pleasure in associating and conversing with me again in this image. Others have taken courage to speak of

---

107. Cf. the philosopher's essay "On Men of Learning," The Art of Literature, *Essays of Schopenhauer*, trans. T. Bailey Saunders (New York, 1942) , p. 39.
108. Svevo, "Il dilettantismo," OO, 3: 594.
109. Ibid., 3: 585.

themselves because they found the subject worthy and rich; I, on the contrary, because I have found mine so barren and so meager that no suspicion of ostentation can fall upon my plan. (2: 18, 503)

This is the pretense of nonchalance and modesty that infuriated Rousseau, but the importance of Montaigne's example lies in the casual transformation of his failings into strengths. Dilettantism is a necessary protection from salvation by mystery or reason. What begins in the essay on education as a listing of personal debilities of mind, ends as an affirmative example of tolerance. The dilettante may fail to develop his subject deeply, but he allows the widest vision and the healthy discomforts of relative perspectives.

The movement that turns personal defect to public asset is most clearly exhibited by Svevo in his essay "Soggiorno londinese," in which he turns his disappointment about Edoardo Weiss's verdict, that *Confessions of Zeno* has nothing really to do with psychoanalysis, to good account. Svevo recognizes that Einstein's theory of relativity is at the center of a new universe, and that it may be distorted by the language of literature. Suppose, he muses, a man were constructed whose heart beat only once every ten minutes. That man would see the sun pass from one horizon to another with the rapidity of a firecracker. This experiment with the rhythms of the blood and of perception was a favorite idea of Svevo, and corresponds to Montaigne's habit of looking at civilization from a primitive angle or the changing of sizes of man by widening or narrowing the universe. Now, the writer with this translation of Einstein's theory receives from him the same rebuff that Svevo received from Weiss: "The idea is very nice, but it has nothing to do with my theory of relativity."[110] But by this time the artist has pushed off and developed a structure of fiction that serves him well. The notion that the novelist is inspired, like the dilettante, by truths that he does not completely understand, that marriages are made that are not completely discovered, that conversations are completed that are not mutually grasped, is a way of rescuing, by the humor of natural mystery, human and literary relationships from the charmless clarity of full exposure. The artist and the philosopher produce children in a marriage neither understands and that only one desires. Antonio Testa perhaps makes Svevo seem too settled a reader when he writes of the

110. Ibid., 3: 687.

novelist: "He studied Freud while smiling,"[111] and consequently kept the most dramatic attributes of psychoanalysis, but Svevo would have enjoyed picturing himself like this. And why should not an artist smile when Schopenhauer writes back to Wagner, who had thanked him for his inspiration, that it was, after all, the music of Rossini that better fit his philosophy?[112] The mutations of Darwin and his thesis of survival, the lapses of Freud and his theory of the unconscious, the capitalistic insensitivity to economic justice and its reliance on the crazy fluctuations of supply and demand—these give Svevo the contemporary metaphors he needs to protect himself from those who would make of the laws of biology, physics, psychiatry, and economics predictive systems of control. In his return to what R. S. Baker calls "the classical impulse to emphasize not the roots from which things spring but the goals toward which they tend,"[113] Svevo, like Montaigne, enjoys new perspectives by which to view an unchanging human condition.

Any process of interpretation applied to the understanding of personality that loses the flexibility of metaphor was particularly suspicious to Svevo. His reluctance to credit therapy with curative objectivity derives from the fear that gradually the subject becomes a means to the truth, rather than an end. His criticism was not so harsh, but it complements that of Nigel Dennis, who pictures the "*artistic* satisfaction" of the therapist involved in reconstructing personality, a most dangerous editing and one that Freud recognized.[114] It is, like Rousseau's Original Virtue, only replacing one tyranny by another.[115] Zeno's memory inventions, following upon his visions, reveal to us the thin line between the pictures that a fallible and distorting memory legitimately lays out for inspection and those that are willed, inspired by a desire for consistency or rebellion. In either case motives can be discovered, but the analyst is subject to the temptation to will them, as the patient is to will his memories. Again, Svevo would rather abandon the search for cause and adjust to an attitude of acceptance, surrendering the quest for perfect health. It is not really paradoxical that Svevo's vision, classical and conservative

111. Antonio Testa, *Italo Svevo* (Ravenna, 1968) , pp. 102–03.
112. Svevo, "Il dilettantismo," OO, 3: 687.
113. "Italo Svevo and the Limits of Marriage," *Essays on Italo Svevo*, ed. Thomas F. Staley, University of Tulsa Monograph (Tulsa, Okla., 1969), p. 87.
114. Freud, "Constructions in Analyses," Standard ed. (1937) , 23: 257–69.
115. Nigel Dennis, *Preface and Two Plays* (New York, 1958) , p. 77.

in its intellectual reticence, could serve, with its vulnerability to so wide a range of contemporary thought, as a revolutionary impetus to the young Italian writers associated with *Solaria* and *Il Convegno*. So too, Freud created a revolution with a vision of life that one would hardly associate with progressive theorists. As Philip Rieff describes it:

> Freud's well-known pessimism as a social theorist must be seen in terms of his conception of time as repetition. No future is open, no past is closed. . . . The lot of rational humans is to face up to the comfortless world as it was, is, and will be.[116]

When Svevo attempts to theorize about socialism or peace, in the grand line of liberal political philosophy, he seems uncomfortable and awkward. Nothing in his incomplete essay on peace seems typical except the recognition that "no victory, no defeat can come about that would bring a stop to the game of life, and the fruit of each victory remains in play for the successive combatants."[117]

The defensive withdrawal from partisan commitment to intellectual theory, out of which Svevo makes a humane philosophy of life, is poignantly recognized as an affective flaw in the "Diario per la fidanzata." But for all the regret poured out in the pages of his letters about the involutions of his affective responses in contrast to those of Livia, Svevo salvages some satisfaction, by no means complacent, that his union matches those natural open marriages performed by Mother Nature that are constantly vulnerable to shifts of weather. Fated in his own self to double the observer with the liver, a doubling that can be exploited not as tragedy but as bitter comedy, the groom accepts early the consequences of his high consciousness and the impossibility of cure:

> Even when I enjoy life at your side, there remains in my soul something that does not enjoy with me and that cautions me: Take care, it is not as it seems to you and everything is but a comedy because the curtain will drop. What is more, indifference about life is the essence of my intellectual life. Whatever my words might posesss of wit and energy, comes out as irony and I fear that the day you succeed in making me believe in life (an impossible feat) I will become a smaller man. It's almost as if I wanted to pray you to let me be the way I am. I am afraid that if I became happy, I would

116. Rieff, *Freud*, p. 239.
117. Svevo, "Sulla teoria della pace," OO, 3: 651.

become stupid, and then vice versa, I am happy (how you must pity me) only when I feel moving inside my big head ideas that I think move in very few others. What proves how sincere my desire is not to wound you, however, and I would do this only for you, is my desire to give up smoking, an activity I dared to place in competition with you.[118]

The dangerous and alluring delusion of perfect marriage goes up in smoke, like the dreams that would forget the businessman. Svevo accepts as a motto for the "Diario" the lines of Joseph Freiherr von Eötvös:

> So innig zwei Menschen einander lieben mögen, sie können doch nicht vollständig ineinander aufgehen. Nur diejenigen werden sich stets nahe bleiben welche fortwährend das Bedürfniss fühlen, sich einander zu nähren.[119]

And Zeno, in a touching confession, admits of his feelings for Augusta: "I am compelled to believe that true love is compatible with . . . doubt" (CZ, 127). At least the novelist can be continually reminded by the suspension between the critical and feeling self, man and Mother Nature, husband and wife, the dreamer and waker of the vain quest for perfect union, equilibrium, health. Svevo's universe is one of comic marriages, like that arising out of Zeno's courtship, standing on its own feet and delightfully compromised by secular mysteries and misunderstandings,[120] compulsions and inhibitions.

This amateur of marriage, who complains from time to time in his letters of Livia's bourgeois prison, this self-styled dilettante of the world's thought regularly foreswore the melodramas of divorce incessantly performed in modern literature. Renato Poggioli seems to me absolutely right when, in speaking of the wide modern adoption of the literary theme of tension between the bourgeois spirit and the artist's mind in Flaubert, Nietzsche, Wilde, Shaw, Joyce, Proust, and

118. Svevo, "Diario per la fidanzata," OO, 3: 772–3.
119. Ibid., p. 767:

No matter how intensely two people may love one another, they can never completely become as one. Only those who feel the constant need to get nearer each other remain close.

120. Marcel Brion speaks in "Italo Svevo," *Nouvelles littéraires artistiques et scientifiques,* 24 March 1928, of the mysterious intimacy between Svevo and his characters; Silvio Benco, "Italo Svevo," Umana, 20 (May-September 1971): 67 (republished from *Pegaso,* January 1929) singles out Svevo's talent for not destroying the mystery of his characters.

Mann, he excludes Svevo as "the only one among modern writers unable to conceive of such a conflict."[121] He accepts, claims Poggioli, the bourgeois spirit as a frame or state of mind, a datum or fact, as our own version of what Montaigne called "the condition of man." He possesses that "merry wisdom" which Montaigne had in abundance and which is so "alien to the modern mind,"[122] a wisdom premised on doubts about man's reason and his will. The adjective Poggioli uses to describe this wisdom, *innocent,* a term not meant to indicate naiveté, but a quality more interested in describing than judging, catches the Svevian spirit reluctantly at home in the bourgeois world. It is because of this temper that attempts to make him a Marxist judge of bourgeois decadence are so unconvincing.[123]

Typical of the Svevian suspicion of historical verdicts is the review of Taine's criticism of Napoleon.[124] To pretend that the superiority of one's historical documents will render a superior judgment simply ignores the distorting filter of temperament. "To cite a document," says Svevo cynically, "means giving someone else's words to your own opinion."[125] What produces diversity of conclusions from the same facts is the differing natures and temperaments of the writers.[126] Taine's work ultimately irritates us because, though Taine knows his man thoroughly,

> . . . he does not love him as Michelet loved him and he does not tolerate him with the good will of a practical man that Thiers possessed.[127]

His truth, then, will irritate us too. Svevo's critical essays are not intellectually impressive, and we may feel disappointed at the mildness of his chastisements, but the steadiness of his priority of response

121. Renato Poggioli, "A Note on Italo Svevo," *Spirit of the Letter* (Cambridge, Mass., 1965), pp. 178–79.

122. Ibid., p. 179.

123. See the interesting remarks of Sandro Maxia, *Lettura di Italo Svevo* (Padua, 1965), p. 20, that Svevo's socialism distinguished itself from that of other intellectuals by its pessimism and that, in the final account, social class and its limits became symbols of an ontological human condition from which there is no way out (see also p. 175).

124. Svevo, "Per un critico," OO, 3: 607–23. (From "L'Indipendente," Trieste, 17 November 1890).

125. Ibid., p. 608.

126. Ibid., p. 610.

127. Ibid.

to the presence in the work is undeniable and is consonant with his vision of himself as merely a temperament, a dilettante in a world of ardent historical and philosophical judgments. It is easier to place Svevo, through Montaigne, in a history of temperament than in histories of the time. No one gets so distorted in literary chronicles, not because the age fails to be reflected in his books, but because his character is so immune to historical formulas. There is something awkward about the elevating of Svevo's habit of introspection by Gian-Paolo Biasin, with Lukács and Auerbach at his back, into the major symptom of the bourgeois disease of the fin de siècle,[128] for while it is certainly accurate to designate compulsive analysis as a trait shared by superfluous men, and accurate too to see Zeno as a representative of this tendency, the unique quality of its playfulness and the direction of this analysis toward tolerance are slighted by the historical reference. Any attempt to make Svevo a typical embodiment of historical symptoms seems destructive of his delicate balance and tone, yet his books obviously do belong to his age. The slippery nature of his performance is caught by Pietro Citati, who writes: "As soon as he looked at things, he surrounded them with clouds of smoke: he filled them with possibility, with contingency, with 'as if's,' with Ariosto-like fancies."[129] We recognize the characteristic screen behind which Svevo could release "his outrageous silliness, his delight in play and irony."[130] The subtlety of this evasion and its charm seem violated by Marxist assumptions that Svevo belongs to those whose escape into the pathological represents a crippled moral protest against capitalism and by the psychiatric view that such screens are defenses against deeper truths of the personality.[131]

The most balanced and intelligent review of the way in which Svevo absorbed intellectual and cultural strains is the long article of André Bouissy on the novelist's ideological debts.[132] Svevo was eager

128. Biasin, "Zeno's Last Bomb," *Modern Fiction Studies,* Svevo issue, p. 20.
129. Pietro Citati, "Il violino di Svevo," *Il tè del cappelaio matto* (Milan, 1972), p. 159.
130. Ibid., p. 162.
131. In distinguishing the individualism of Svevo in relation to his contemporaries, Geno Pampaloni, "Svevo," p. 500, calls his introspective habit "a refined and insinuating mode of aggression" in contrast to the lyric evasions of reality practiced by so many other Italian writers.
132. André Bouissy, "Les Fondements idéologiques de l'oeuvre d'Italo Svevo," *Revue des études italiennes,* p. 1, 12, no. 3 (July-September 1966) : 209–45; p. 2, 12, no. 4 (October-December 1966) ; 350–373; p. 3, 13, no. 1 (January-March 1967) : 23–50.

to share the diagnostic perspectives of Schopenhauer and varieties of Socialism, Freudianism, and Darwinism without relying on their solutions. In general, Bouissy charts well the qualifications that temperament forced upon ideology, though at times he leans too far toward that polemical position of social criticism that makes of his subject an example. Though Schopenhauer was an enormous influence on Svevo for the pre-Freudian revelation of the layered consciousness, the deceptions of the world as will and rationalization, as well as a sanction for introspection, the novelist's temperament led him to resist the philosopher on two major points: Svevo never had the least toleration for the egoism of the solitary genius nor for his ascetic quarantine from the world of causality.[133] With loose adoption of the structure of psychoanalytic therapy for his major novel, with its emphasis upon repetition of psychic patterns and identities goes the refusal to accept cure as a serious possibility. It is because Svevo turns away from logical conclusions when considering the personality of men that he is able to entertain so many strains that may have proved, in a more dedicated student of ideology, mutually exclusive. Arguments taken from Darwinian materialism and Socialism might be seen as views that qualify and expand the psychiatric emphasis on the individual,[134] but that they presented a picture of the civilized sickness of industrial society at a far remove from what is just and natural for man, is only, despite the ending of *Confessions of Zeno,* of secondary interest to Svevo. When Bouissy cites Svevo as "the only one of the great bourgeois writers writing in Italian to know how to distinguish between the famous 'laws of nature' and the law of capitalism, that which is dictated by the owners of the means of production (and destruction) at the hour of imperialist concentration,"[135] we remember appropriate references in the fiction and the short story "La tribu," but we are not comfortable with such a tendentious ascription. Surely Svevo's social momentum takes us beyond the premise of Verga's naturalism that things are just like that, a premise that consciously confuses the social and natural laws, but the contexts of Svevo's humor continually stop us short of the spirit of exposure or complaint. The narcissistic socialism of *As a Man Grows Older* that blossoms into dreams and fantasies of patroniza-

133. Ibid., 1: 214.
134. Ibid., 2: 350–51.
135. Ibid., 1: 233.

tion, the drunken socialism of "Generous Wine," the fables on social injustice have the charming elementalism and carelessness that are the privilege of the imaginative amateur of social thought.

Svevo's acceptance of Nietzsche's insistence on the necessity for the psychologizing of philosophy is a more natural attitude.[136] His early reading of Schopenhauer[137] had already prepared the way for such an assumption. Zeno's incessant questioning of his desire for parental approval of his "goodness" certainly reflects a consciousness of the loss of security, to say nothing of conviction, in the old inherited terms of morality, now the social vocabulary of guilt. If Augusta and Nietzsche's Englishmen did not yet consider morality a problem, Zeno did. Schopenhauer's exposure of will was certainly studied by the novelist, and his reading opened him to Freud's thesis that morality can make us sick.[138] Zeno's limps of guilt are comic illustrations of such an affliction. But there is a difference between the boldness of Nietzsche, whom Zeno reads, in insisting that the philosopher must overcome the age in himself once he has realized that "apart from all theology and its contentions . . . the world is not good and not bad,"[139] and the modesty of Svevo, who never raises his recognition to the pitch of rebellion. Supermen, ascetics, and transvaluators are, for Svevo, always suspect. His humor keeps him in the world, exploiting tensions between the ethical and psychological, health and sickness, innocence and guilt. Though Zeno sees around Augusta's morality, he wants to be good by Augusta's standards, and he shares with his creator Freud's ambivalence toward a repressive culture. "He is not," says Pampaloni, "a prophet of chaos because it isn't worth the trouble: chaos is already with us."[140] And it is here to stay. For Svevo and Zeno both, this is the only world we have. No demolisher of bourgeois values, no prophetic castigator of bourgeois decadence, Svevo's irony has never known a moment of complacency. It is this wavering motion that for Svevo, as for Montaigne, assures us not the best, but the most real of all worlds. The novelist shared the pessimism of Schopenhauer, but would not take advantage of it. While the philosopher thinks of optimism as a "really *wicked* way of

136. Nietzsche, "Human, All Too Human," *The Philosophy of Nietzsche*, 1: 598.
137. Livia Veneziani Svevo, *Vita di mio marito*, p. 30.
138. See Rieff, *Freud*, p. 350.
139. Nietzsche, Preface to "Case of Wagner," *Philosophy of Nietzsche*, p. 131, and "Human, All Too Human," Ibid., 1: 498.
140. Pampaloni, "Svevo," p. 500.

thinking, as a bitter mockery of the unspeakable suffering of humanity,"[141] for Svevo it is merely an interesting phenomenon that exhibits a consistency and energy alien to him. Mother Nature's careless winds blow us on a course that looks to her like "il varco/ folle d'Ulisse," the mad passage of Ulysses described by Dante[142] and applied by a colleague of Dottor Menghi, Svevo's hero of a science fiction piece, "Lo specifico del Dottor Menghi," to the doctor to describe his youth as "nothing less than a crazy race to old age."[143]

The view of life as accident and mutation corresponds to Darwin's descent with modification and contradicts a universe planned by divine guidance. "Lo specifico del Dottor Menghi" plays out one of Svevo's favorite fantasies[144] of controlling Mother Nature's experiments and guiding them to insure equilibrium in the human body, prolonging or intensifying life. It is really a comic version of Zeno's final vision, in which spectacled man, lucid of brain and dull of feeling, leads us to the destruction of the universe, and since it is comic fiction, the serum is destroyed in the end. But the serum, according to the vain and rational Dr. Clementi, did not produce the desired change in physiological conservation, and leaves instead only the ether in which it is dissolved. Dr. Clementi, a form of Dr. S., by his sober presence, allows the hero to experiment in the same way that Svevo's bourgeois household and the conditions of therapy allow the fantasies of Svevo and Zeno. In the story we have fictionalized forms of the commercial competence of Svevo's mother-in-law while Dr. Menghi dreams on the job, and Svevo humorously identifies with the dilettantism of the scientist's experiment. His reference to the unscientific language necessary to explain it is certainly a sly and amusing poke at his own "linguaggio." The Balzacian experiment attempts to slow down life's excessive and wasteful energies by preserving heat so that an economy of vital forces can be effected. "Latent energy is the only energy" (SDM, 537), exclaims Dr. Menghi, a phrase that could serve as an ironic motto for most of Svevo's heroes and a playful, literal exposure of his own feeling that he was deficient in the healthy exuberance toward life that Dr.

141. Schopenhauer, *The Philosophy of Schopenhauer*, p. 269.
142. Dante, *Paradiso* 27. 82.
143. Svevo, OO, 3: 532.
144. See, for example, its recurrence in his discussion of Einstein's theory in "Soggiorno londinese," OO, 3 and in "This Indolence of Mine," (FCZ). Succeeding references to the story, OO, 3: 531–54, will be noted in the text as SDM.

Clementi exhibits. The intensification of the details of objects when the seeing subject is drugged corresponds to the prolongation and expansion of the world's material in the timeless fantasies of the study dreams. The experiment may even be seen as a physiological rendition of Freud's theory of psychic economy of dreams, art, and wit.[145] Like Zeno in relation to Dr. S., Dr. Menghi imagines that he tops those psychiatrists who seek the cause of criminality, by revealing that the experiment, treated loosely in the way a novelist uses modern science, suggests the hypothesis that the criminal suffers from a restriction of vital forces, an attenuation of life on what later becomes the Basedow line. Generosity derives from excessive life forces. This hypothesis results in a rather meek and conventional motto, much inferior to Zeno's aphorism, of acceptance of physical, moral, and psychological boundaries: "Let us remain, therefore, mortal and good" (SDM, 553), a recommendation that at least scoops Dr. Clementi with his patronizing, if accurate revelation. Without the rich meanderings into ironic self-analysis that we find in the last works of Svevo, the tale seems bare and fabled. But Svevo liked to exhibit in chaste forms physiological symptoms and complexes from which he could draw moral, psychological, and scientific metaphors to scold man's presumption of self-control.

The projection of psychic frustrations and aggressions into psychosomatic symptoms and adulteries and the vulnerability of biological selection to mutation gave Svevo the direction he wanted to humble the pretensions of those who would compete with Mother Nature by inventing tools that distance us from her rather unconsoling nest. If Dr. Menghi's applied dilettantism is a cause for critical laughter and his hypotheses a stimulus to comic scorn, there is in his experimentation a great deal of self-mockery by Svevo, who habitually fantasized the altering of life's balances. Svevo refers to himself (as to his fictional heroes) as one of evolution's incomplete sketches,[146] thereby giving us the autobiographical sentiment behind the proliferation of unequal contests in his fiction between the strong, fully evolved man and the inept sketch whose deprived anatomy feeds on analysis. We also see, however, in Zeno, the long-

---

145. The experiment seems to castigate authority economically, because Svevo, most likely using his mother-in-law as a model for the mother, manages to kill her off while exposing Doctor Clementi's vanity.
146. Svevo, "L'uomo e la teoria Darwiniana," OO, 3: 638.

range survival of the incomplete specimen. The very dilettantism of the unbalanced organism is, paradoxically, the source of its evolutionary adaptability.[147] Zeno's psychological and physiological survival, however vitiated by guilt, while his father and Guido disappear, is evidence of this oddity. Svevo himself, a mere sketch, like Zeno, will survive:

> I think that the animal most capable of evolving is the one in whom one part is in continual struggle with another for supremacy, the animal, now or in the future generations, who has preserved the possibility of evolving from one part or another in response to what is demanded of it by society, whose needs no one can now foresee. In my absolute lack of any marked development in whatever direction, I am that man. I feel it so strongly that in my solitude I glory in it and I wait, knowing I am nothing but a sketch.

Such a comic perspective on the advantages of incompletion is a pseudo-Darwinian version of Montaigne's patchwork self, and in its emphasis upon latent rather than applied power, in accordance with Dr. Menghi's lesson it clearly separates Zeno from the spectacled man who points us toward the earth's destruction. That man is devoid of the humor that receives life instead of controlling it. Zeno's humor and spontaneity mark him as one who awaits and respects Mother Nature and her surprises. The movement by which the world comes at Zeno and Svevo in the novel and the letters and the diaries is rendered by the passive tense of latent man:

> I do not understand how in my silly life something so serious as old age could have happened to me.[148]

It is an endearing structure that uses helplessness as a mode of defense, not apology. Into old age Svevo sees himself as a scribbler, available to the world's distractions. He regrets, in a diary entry of 1906, like old Zeno, that he did not fix the past in writing,[149] though by failing to do so, he saved humanity from the affliction of one more autobiography. His failure is by no means an aesthetic tragedy, and if literature's organizing of past time now seems of help in accepting death, it can never conquer time in a cork-lined room:

147. Ibid.
148. Svevo, "Documenti umani," OO, 3: 835.
149. "Pagine di diario e sparse," OO, 3: 822.

Everything around me dies daily into oblivion because I appear
entranced, distracted by a world of people who shout in my ears.[150]

This disposition is not to be taken as a bitter expression of self-pity,
any more than Svevo's occasional complaints about the prison of
marriage. It represents the posture of a sketch, incomplete still, waiting for time's last quirky strokes.

150. Ibid.

Chapter 3

The Fiction's Climb

I. A Life

ONE OF THE MOST INTRIGUING QUESTIONS to readers of Svevo has been the problem of determining the causes and nature of his announced literary renunciation after the failure of *As a Man Grows Older* to attract any extensive appreciation. From the turn of the century until the First World War, Svevo occupied himself, according to his own testimony,[1] with his entrance into the family paint industry, the security of his family, and his violin, turning his back on his literary career and the hopes he had cherished. There could be no compromise: "one line of writing was enough to make him less efficient in his practical work, to which he had to devote himself daily."[2] His diary entry of December 1902, in which he melodramatically states that henceforth he is giving up the ridiculous and harmful thing called literature,[3] at the same time assures us of a continuity of self-examination in the form of letters and diaries, not meant for publication. Bruno Maier convincingly hypothesizes a constant activity of drafts of the later stories, plays, and fables during this time. Three specific events help us to chart the motivating influences behind the emergence of the third novel: the meeting with James Joyce, the reading of Freud, and the sequestered leisure imposed upon him by the war. Yet we remain surprised at the dramatic leap of confidence and the full flowering of humor that mark Svevo's participation in

1. Svevo, "Profilo autobiografico," OO, 3: 805.
2. Ibid.
3. Ibid., p. 818: "Io, a quest'ora e definitivamente ho eliminato dalla mia vita quella ridicola e dannosa cosa che si chiama letteratura."

Confessions of Zeno. The enormous surge of trust in his fictive consciousness at the center of the novel recalls the plan of Henry James
noted in the preface to *Portrait of a Lady,* to free Isabel's spirit from
material need and from competing satellite consciousnesses, her story
from the support of underplots, and to release George Eliot's frail
vessel of girlhood into a sea that would make her altogether "dis-
ponible."[4] The change to first person can be seen as both a cause and
a symptom of this trust, as can the psychoanalytically inspired
breakup of traditional narrative order.

A long Italian preference for *As a Man Grows Older,* just now
largely abandoned in favor of *Confessions of Zeno,* only seems to
verify that the emergence of *Confessions of Zeno* represented a rather
startling change. It is probably for this reason that critics have busied
themselves so assiduously in tracing the links between the novels, in
establishing each hero as a stage in the growth to a full Svevian
creation. We have Svevo's own effort to assert a history of identity
between his protagonists: "Alfonso is obviously a blood brother to
the protagonists of the other two novels."[5] The novelist's regrets
over ensnaring his first hero, Alfonso, too syllogistically in Schopenhauerian theory, and his presentation in "a language crammed with
solecisms and dialectical formations"[6] did not prevent him from
more or less accepting Joyce's assertion that every novelist writes but
one novel. There is no doubt that dominating characteristics, abulia,
anxiety, a talent for rationalization, and a defensive alienation afflict
all three of the heroes, making them legitimate citizens of the
modern novel. Antonio Testa's qualification of a distinctively staged
climb from tragic pessimism to elegiac lyricism to humor as an over-
simplification is a good one,[7] and a necessary caution to schematic
criticism. Certainly it does seem excessive to attribute the term *tragic*
to *A Life* and misleading to speak neatly of the comedy of *Confessions of Zeno* as a final solution for the anti-hero, the "inetto." But
one cannot deny that the atmospheres of the three books, whatever
they may share superficially, are remarkably different, and that Svevo
seems to feel most at home in the third.

4. Henry James, *The Art of the Novel,* ed. R. P. Blackmur (New York, 1934),
particularly, pp. 42–53.
   5. Svevo, "Profilo autobiografico," OO, 3: 802.
   6. Ibid.
   7. Testa, *Italo Svevo,* p. 30.

By contrast to Zeno, the hero of *A Life,* Alfonso, is vulnerable to James's complaint about Frédéric Moreau, that he is too small a vessel for the author's vision and therefore suffers the limitations of the author's felt life partially withheld or diverted from the character's consciousness. And, indeed, all readers of the novel have recognized its debt to Flaubert's *L'Education sentimentale.* Marxist critics have seconded Lukács's complaints about Flaubert that the disease of bourgeois decadence in Svevo's novels seems a general disease of life itself, while psychoanalytic critics have identified the two heroes as classic Oedipal cases unable to persist in relationships that are not fantasized. Unquestionably, Svevo's reading in the French realists and naturalists is everywhere evident in the atmosphere, characterization, and even title of *A Life.* Because the ascent from this novel to Zeno indicates a throwing off of this influence with a concomitant reliance upon a less literary and more original Svevian temperament, the fictional education of Svevo can be used as an indicator of the national climb of Italian fiction into modernity. That Svevo was, though not intentionally, an initiator of this national education is suggested by Montale's letter to the novelist in December of 1926, in which he confesses that his early preference for *Senilità* over *La coscienza di Zeno* had to do with the difficulty for an Italian in reading Zeno's novel in the right way. "Now," admits Montale, "I see Augusta as the most vivid portrait of all Italian narrative from Manzoni to the present."[8] This compliment puts Svevo in the great tradition of Italian narrative, a position so long refused him by the conservative Italian literary world.

Geno Pampaloni sees the development from *A Life* to *Confessions of Zeno* as a moral, psychological, and artistic expansion that benefits the hero as he passes from a narrow and solipsistic impotence to a flexible and tolerant view of the complex and subtle affective zones between a man and his destiny, and the destiny of other men.[9] The recapitulation of two major scenes, tossed from novel to novel, illustrates well the course of this expansion. *A Life* comes full circle, from the opening letter of the straitened young bank clerk, Alfonso, in the city, to his mother in the country, in which he expresses a regressive desire to return to the country, to the last part of the novel in which

---

8. Montale, *Lettere,* p. 62.
9. Pampaloni, "Italo Svevo," *Storia,* p. 516.

Alfonso, desiring release from the responsibility of emotional engagement with Annetta and from the economic and social humiliation of his position in her father's bank, receives, with the news of his
mother's sickness, an ex post facto sanction for his decision to escape.
Annetta's companion, Francesca, herself interested in a marriage
with Annetta's father, pleads with Alfonso not to leave, and this,
along with the threat of Annetta's desire, presses Alfonso to depart
before it is too late. Safely on his way to the country, in the train, he
thinks of the dreary life of the Lanuccis, the family he lives with, and
of those like them:

> Oh! what dreary squalid people! The railway line running along
> the flat dikes seemed to be bearing him to a point from which he
> could judge all those people rushing after goals that were stupid
> and unreachable. And he went on to ask himself: "Why don't they
> live more serenely?" (AL, 255)

The mother's dying is a slow, drawn-out process, but Alfonso, in a
position that allows desire to correspond with necessity, experiences
in the midst of this suffering a sweeping sense of innocence in a
world without choice. One has no trouble subscribing to the thesis of
Marida Tancredi that the mother's deathbed is the only reality for
Alfonso, that the desire for union with her, a return to embryonic
innocence, is a major cause for his inability to enter a historical
reality.[10] Rationalizations, couched in the conditional like the
Flaubertian fantasies of Frédéric Moreau and Mme Bovary, serve the
cause of self-justification released into timelessness, where "one day
was so like the other that he could not tell how long he had been in
the country" (AL, 287). This atmosphere is measured by the
rudeness of its interruption in the form of a letter from Francesca,
the biased negotiator between Annetta and Alfonso, who hopes to
take advantage of a union that would insure hers with Mr. Maller,
Annetta's father. The letter warns Alfonso that all will be lost if he
does not return. The world of time, engagement, and responsibility
is banished only when Alfonso writes back to Francesca, by which he
turns, for the second time, his retreat into Annetta's betrayal, thus
again achieving the innocence his dying mother grants him. Daydreams of humiliation, Annetta's hatred, and visions of being turned
out of the bank alternate with the consciousness of his mother's

10. Marida Tancredi, "*Una vita* di Svevo," *Angelus Novus* (1972), p. 76 n. 21.

suffering until, after his mother's death, he experiences his own collapse, his own "fake" death in a bed at the notary's house in the village.

In his fever, he erases chronology by dreaming, in a Proustian confusion of identity, of another convalescence, with his mother close by in the kitchen. It is a "sweet fever which had made him live among dear ghosts of the past" (AL, 307). With recovery, he feels himself to be a new person and prides himself on having put aside his boyhood. But Svevo inserts: "It was not the first time he thought he had left boyhood behind" (AL, 306). His resolution to marry Annetta if she still wants him is completely protected by his knowledge, from Francesca, that it is surely too late for that and by his unrealistic determination to tell Annetta that he will reform her. The alternative, a retreat into solitude, again puts him into the more innocent position of victim of another's decision. Thus, if the affair destroys possibilities of advancement in the bank, he reasons, his contemplative life gains by the denial of riches. With no more risks of love affairs and in the spirit of Madame Bovary's "saintly" convalescence, he imagines "he would live with desires that were simple, sincere, thus lasting" (AL, 308). The presence of this pseudo-Schopenhauerian alternative indicates, from here to the end of the novel, the inadequacy of Alfonso for the Schopenhauerian vision, as his will, in the guise of rationalized passivity and retreat, dogs him to the end. The decision for suicide, directly counter to Schopenhauer's recommendation, carries, as we might expect, the infection of the will. It would enable him "to become superior to the suspicions and hatreds of others" (AL, 397), just as originally his privileged position with Annetta had made him superior to his fellow clerks.

Before leaving his village for the city, Alfonso visits the graveyard and sees his father's grave: "How simple had been his feelings at his father's death," he claims, and at the end of the novel, retreating to suicide to evade a duel with Annetta's brother, he pictures the peace and green of the cemetery as his new home, the childhood home in which he was still innocent under the protection of idealized parents. On the train back to the city, a Flaubertian voyage that gets nowhere despite reversals of direction, Alfonso sees a shabby man thrown precipitously off the train for not having his fare. "Whatever would he do," he wonders, "in that village where he had happened by chance and knew no one?" (AL 313). The hinted identification with a stranger, a favorite device again of Flaubert, throws an Alfonso unable to pay his dues into a hostile adult world in which all responsibility is a threat to the innocent life of the child. The graveyard in which his mother and father lie, so simplified by death, is a return to a childhood in which one's place is prescribed, securely, behind the parents. Such a projection converts guilt into an aristocratic scorn of others. Death poses, in this novel, as a tragic ending, the hero's suicide, but even in his first novel Svevo resists ascribing it such dignity. Self-deception turns it to bathos. Svevo cuts into Alfonso's hopeful conditionals with dry and short reminders of this deception, but not with the harshness of Flaubert's unvoiced castigations. An artificial death, ringed with mild authorial irony, is Svevo's only attempt to give the illusion of narrative progress and conclusion to a pattern of psychological repetition. The deliberate limpness of the last pages suggests more the anticlimactic death in life of Frédéric Moreau than it does the pitifully stagy death of Madame Bovary with the final kick of fierce irony in Homais's public self-advertisement.

And, in fact, the life of a survivor dependent upon a fantasized identity of a dead, saintly sister and a dead love affair with a prostitute is the more natural fate of Svevo's second hero, Emilio Brentani. I would like for the time being to pass over this second scene of familial death in order to juxtapose to Alfonso's last meditations with the great second section of *Confessions of Zeno*. Already subject to the humiliation of displacement following the comic and flippant initial section on the cigarette habit, the father's death is further subservient to the priority of Zeno's own psychoanalysis. The dead gets his vengeance by stretching his hand over the entire novel. The central struggle between father and son is not slighted or transferred, as it is in *A Life*. The mother's death this time is passed over with apparent philosophic calm, whereas the father's death is psychologically recognized as "an unmitigated catastrophe" (AL, 28). The loss of what protects Zeno's blameless latency ("I had passed from cigarette to cigarette, and from subject to subject at the University with an indestructible faith in my possibilities") and a concomitant guilt of replacement ("If it comes to comparing us, I am bound to say that of the two I was the stronger character"), recalled at the beginning of the novel instead of at the end, tell us that for Zeno there will be no soothing cemetery, and that life must go on on this side of the grave in full consciousness. The marital infidelities of the father may be repeated by the son, but not the complacency of the father's adjustments. Not for long will Zeno's tears allow him to "throw a veil over [his] faults and allow him to accuse Fate without fear of contradiction" (AL, 41). In the first stages of his father's death, the Zeno who is recording his memories at the psychoanalyst's suggestion links the last chapter of his novel to this chapter by means of an image that came to him while he lay on the sofa listening to his father's breathing. The image is none other than Alfonso's train interiorized—the "image of an engine drawing a string of coaches up a hill"—accompanied by a fear that the puffing momentum will stop and tumble the train into the valley. This train no longer measures the route of sentimental educations from provinces to Paris. As an image of anxiety, it rises shamelessly above chronology and runs the endless journeys back and forth along the chain of being, of love, fear, and hate. The train of thought that has gone forward and backward on the track between the father's death and the psychoanalyst's office, though it would appear to make even less real progress than Alfonso's train, runs on the track between goiters and dropsy. All the engines of love and authority that run out of steam in the novel do not keep the train from its shuttling pace, and there is no danger that the passenger will be hurtled into the valley or tossed off for lack of a fare. In fact, Zeno becomes in time his own chief engineer drawing a whole family of wives and mistresses, brothers and sons, fears and affections behind him.

The train ride at the end of Zeno's novel is a literal embodiment of this unmelodramatic journey. Riding through war, separation, exile, to a bed in Trieste, Zeno reviews the hopes and fears that chase each other, before each sleep, through his mind, a mind "accustomed by psychoanalysis to retain the images that come to [it]" (CZ, 395). With the acceptance that there is no perfect cure, no absolute innocence, that they are at best provisional, we are as far removed as possible from the delusive peace of Alfonso's cemetery. Alfonso hurtles himself into the valley behind dead engines, while Zeno realizes that his father's dying slap, shrouded in ambivalence, will forever deny the clarity and purity of absolution. So, to Ada, to the psychoanalyst, no proof of innocence is possible, and this in part accounts for the heightened tone of exacerbated frustration in Zeno's flippant arrogance. The attempt at self-justification never ceases, but its motion is tamed by repetition and analogy, by the acceptance of the mortality of man and the immortality of his images.

In one of the most famous scenes of *A Life,* Annetta's cousin Macario, who assumes a traditional Svevian role of sophisticated superiority in the mock-Darwinian scale of evolution, takes Alfonso for a boat ride on a windy sea, and the contrast between Macario and his aristocratic hand, evidence of a fully evolved species, and Alfonso and his hands clutching in fear, proof of an abortive development, like Svevo's own, reveals early signs of the irony turned against the self that is the novelist's most attractive mode of adjustment. The scene has been prepared for by a long description of the closed and myopic life of the bank clerk and his colleagues, the equally hermetic and cramped atmosphere of Alfonso's lodging at the Lanuccis', the sense of alienation in the spacious chill of the Maller house, nights in the library. The release from confinement by dreams of glory housed among the books is only intensified by hikes into the hills of Trieste. The movement from the interior to the exterior world is antithetical merely in the most superficial way. Alfonso's vision is decidedly confined by his dreams and, in the manner of Flaubert, apparent contrasts of scene indicate only more poignantly the monotonous and monolithic atmosphere of the soul. The nature of the dreams has a great deal to do with this state of arrest. The library musings are punctured by Svevo's satire:

> He had found his path! He would lay the foundations of modern Italian philosophy by translating a good German work and at the same time writing an original work of his own. The translation remained purely an intention, but he did start on the original work: a title, *The Moral Idea in the Modern World,* and a preface in which he declared the aim of his work. This aim was theoretic and without any practical intention, which seemed to him quite new for Italian philosophy. (AL, 96)

For this, adds Svevo, he "lacked neither the courage nor the sincerity," terms that seem consciously disproportionate to the rhetorical and conventional nature of his ambition. "After an hour spent with the German idealists," Svevo had noted with a wink in an earlier scene, "everything in the street seemed to be calling a greeting" (AL, 73) . Yet the point to be stressed here is that the sentimental contrasts between books and nature, or a job and the love of reading, remain just that, for the vision of the hero is not up to the energy and humor necessary to take advantage from alternating perspectives. Here is an evolutionary sketch that never gets beyond the stage of latency.

The biological superiority of Macario is accompanied by a superiority of wit. Alfonso is too shy to refute Macario's glib condemnation of Balzac's rhetoric, "as original as it was false" (AL, 103), and generally allows him the lead since he himsef does not sufficiently respect and understand the difference between the taste born of class and genuine knowledge and sensibility. Alfonso is terrified in Macario's boat while Macario waves nonchalantly, and Ferdinando, his sailor, laughs at Alfonso's fears. The final patronization of Alfonso by Macario comes in the form of a fully developed metaphor that later becomes a Svevian fable. Sea gulls, reflects Macario as he prepares his putdown, are made merely for fishing and eating. They have very little brain, but large effective wings that allow them to drop like lead on a prey. All the library evenings of Alfonso cannot make him a successful hunter in life if he does not have wings that can whip him down upon a prey: "One dies in the precise state in which one is born, our hands mere organs for snatching or incapable of holding," says Macario from his position of the fully evolved specimen. To Alfonso's question: "Have I got wings?" Macario wittily answers: "Only for poetic flights," and again his artistocratic hand gestures his metaphor into being.

The application, which although it comes from an unreliable analyst nevertheless appears accurate, gives to Alfonso a moment of sad reflection, but also, in the last resort, a determinist excuse for his neurotic evasions of the affairs of the heart. This excuse is mocked by the meaninglessness of his final suicide, but even nature, not yet the great mother of Confessions of Zeno, is not allowed to exhibit her capricious independence from such a vision. In As a Man Grows Older, she becomes an agent of Emilio's lyric powers of delusion and, as such, is granted the capacity for metamorphosis that she does not have in A Life. But even there, though she sometimes blows up a storm, she is dominated by Emilio's needs. Only with Confessions of Zeno does nature come into full being as an independent character, because she accompanies a consciousness that stands on its own feet. Superior in her gay neutrality to a Zeno wracked by a never-ending recapitulation of moral resolutions to be good, she leads him, as we have seen, to a vision both humorous and lyrical that cannot be reached by those doomed to mere "poetic flights." Here Mother Nature is hardly made to play the conventional role of nurse to city life, nor is she content merely to offer her animals for fables of moral application. The scenes in which Guido and Zeno are fishing together are measures of the distance between the Svevo of *A Life* and the Svevo of *Confessions of Zeno*. Superior specimens are baited and the sea and sky have the colors of the unconscious without being confined by the vagaries of any one. Nature's originality is as genuine as Macario's is false.

Macario's determinism, accepted by Alfonso and nature alike, is part of the price the novel pays for carrying in the open the baggage of literary influence. Everywhere, the signs of Flaubert and Stendhal are apparent. The German writer Paul Heyse had criticized *A Life* for too heavy a dependence upon the realist and naturalist example, à la Zola, of too much detail and stress upon secondary character and scene, particularly in the bank, and a concomitant weakness of nature in the hero that makes him almost too uninteresting to justify the analysis. Heyse attributes this flaw to the adoption of a false principle of modern art derived from the naturalist theoreticians, and notes that Svevo's "earnest striving towards inner truth" deserves a larger scene and consciousness.[11] However prejudiced Heyse's own literary expectations, and however much we sympathize with Stanislaus Joyce's complaint about the futility of Heyse's demands for something not given, we respond to the German critic's sense of literary strain, on Svevo's part, when he deals with his hero and his surroundings as the anatomy of an age, and we also respond to a more natural and original tone in the psychological analysis, only tentatively shared with the hero.[12] Flaubert's critical poise in *Sentimental Education* permits a mutual infection of age and biography, which is so well modulated that the two parts seem to absorb each other. Svevo's cynicism, by contrast, is never strong enough; it is

11. Reprinted in the original as an appendix to Ferdinando Pasini's article on Italo Svevo in *Annali dell'Università degli Studi Economici e Commerciale di Trieste* 1, fasc. 1 (1929) : 180–182.

12. Stanislaus Joyce, *The Meeting of Svevo and Joyce*, ed. Sergio Perosa (Trieste, 1965). See also Antonio Testa, *Italo Svevo*, for a good analysis of the lack of integration between the psychological analysis and the dossiers.

more allied to depression than complaint, and his social criticism is not bold enough, nor his distance from his character sure enough, to give us that homogeneity of surface, substance, and parts that Proust admired in Flaubert's novel. Yet we are not surprised to see Crémieux call *A Life,* in the crucial Svevo edition of *Le Navire d'Argent:* "a Flaubertian novel, perhaps the only one in Italian literature."[13] Most readers of the novel would find puzzling, however, Crémieux's identification of Alfonso with Monsieur Bovary ("Italo Svevo has placed before us, in his first book, a Triestine Monsieur Bovary"), but his affinities to Frédéric Moreau are obvious.

There is certainly no way to shake the impression of literary models, particularly Flaubert and Stendhal, just as it is impossible to miss the strains of Schopenhauer which, by Svevo's own admission, are perhaps too rigidly applied rather than absorbed.[14] The Svevian world does not yet stand firmly on its own feet. Yet Pampaloni is surely right to note symptoms of modernity in the subtle irony of the central chapters,[15] which picture the literary courtship of Annetta and Alfonso—scenes that, deliberate as they are, presage the accidental courtship of Augusta while at the same time drawing from *The Red and the Black* and perhaps even from the Francesca-Paolo episode of Dante's *Inferno.*[16] Alfonso does not possess that attractive spontaneity that questions the nature and motive of each action after it is taken which we identify with the Stendhalian hero, and he has not the privilege of energetic naiveté. These are qualities we associate more with the improvising Zeno, whose aspirations, as Furbank notes perceptively, "towards good conduct are not in vain; it is simply that they bear fruit in unexpected ways."[17] This first "man without qualities"[18] in Italian literature certainly does assume, however, the Stendhalian habit of analyzing action before the fact, of stimulating passion by strategy. It is in the peculiar texture of this

13. Benjamin Crémieux, "Italo Svevo," *Le Navire d'argent,* 1 February 1926, p. 25.
14. Svevo, "Profilo autobiografico," OO, 3: 801.
15. Pampaloni, "Italo Svevo," p. 502.
16. On Stendhal's influence see Debenedetti, "Svevo e Schmitz," p. 69. As proof of Svevo's interest in Dante, in *Confessions of Zeno* the music book that brings together the heads of Carla and Zeno is called, like the romance in the Francesca-Paolo scene, "our Galeotto" (CZ, 170).
17. Furbank, *Italo Svevo,* pp. 187–88.
18. This term, taken from the hero of Musil's novel, is applied by Pampaloni, "Italo Svevo," p. 502.

analysis, its provisional suspension from the "naturalistic" atmosphere of Trieste, of the Maller bank, and of the Lanucci household that the most natural Svevian temperament resides.[19]

Certainly, as Debenedetti reminds us, Svevo is not a novelist who competes like Balzac with "l'état civil."[20] Even the apparent naturalistic mechanics, like the cold framing of the novel with Alfonso's letter to his mother and the dry report of his death, are structures that are more important for our judgment of the psychological than for the sociological anatomy. In the face of a large body of criticism complimenting Svevo's picture of the decadent, exploited, and superfluous "piccolo borghese" of a dying age, it is important to hear Marziano Guglielminetti's plea against burdening *A Life* with too much historical consciousness:

> *A Life* is a novel still too unripe and immature as a whole to support such a range of meaning, above all, it we want to consider it as a denunciation of contemporary bourgeois society. To define it as an "open work" implies seeing in it a vulnerability, but it also points at the same time to all the potential and renewed substance and weight of the old nineteenth-century novel.[21]

The way in which Macario copes with his age, superfluous though he be to its welfare, and the constant puncturing of Alfonso's conditionals with Svevian irony, make it difficult for us to believe in the priority of class distinction between the Maller household and Alfonso's social status, any more than in the mother's sickness, as the determining factor in Alfonso's emotional responses. So too, Annetta's brother Federigo and his lower-class counterpart, Gustavo Lanucci, seem less-convincing representatives of exploiting and exploited social casualties than sons made weak, in one case by a dominating father and in the other by a weak one. The presence of a psychiatric distortion consistently precedes our recognition of a social disadvantage. Tancredi makes an intelligent identification between the economic and psychological momentum when he reminds us that making a success in the business world depends upon the willingness to

19. See also Marco Forti's comment on chap. 6 of *A Life* in his *Svevo romanziere* (Milan, 1966), pp. 30–31 and the comments of N. Jonard, *Italo Svevo et la crise de la bourgeoisie européenne* (Paris, 1969), pp. 88ff. on the ambivalence of Svevo toward the provincial bourgeoisie of *Una vita*.

20. Debenedetti, "Svevo e Schmitz."

21. Marziano Guglielminetti, *Struttura e sintassi del romanzo italiano del primo novecento* (Milan, 1964), p. 129.

compete with the father, and exclusion from the Maller house sets up dreams of a return to the mother. Affective security and economic availability are interdependent.[22] Alfonso's shying away from manhood is a psychiatric retreat that gets a social sanction. But the social eviction casts an illusory light, seems suspiciously immaterial (not that distant from the unexplained arbitrary evictions of Kafka's heroes) in comparison to the psychiatric regression. Ironically, in this "pre-Freudian" novel, there is more justification for assuming the paralyzing priority of unresolved Oedipal conflicts than there is in the "post-Freudian" Svevian hero. This impression is, of course, determined by the degree of consciousness and control of the character over his sophistic protective rhetoric.[23] Alfonso's lack of humor, his drabness in comparison to Zeno, the limitations of his vision, and the absence of Augusta help to account for the lowering of the reader's resistance to the psychiatric interpretation. A scene properly singled out for its symptomatic suggestiveness is the early reprimand of Maller, a figure of authority standing in for an absent father, concerning Alfonso's letter to his mother in which he had indicated his dissatisfaction with his job.[24] When Maller shows him a letter from his mother to Francesca complaining about both Maller and Alfonso, Alfonso blushes:

> "I've changed my mind now," he stuttered. "I'm quite content! You know how it is . . . distance . . . home-sickness." (AL, 17)

" 'I understand, I understand,' replies a patriarchal Maller, 'but we're men, you know!' He repeated the phrase a number of times. . . ." The continuing emphasis by Svevo on Alfonso's arrested adolescence ("His was the dream of a vicious boy, in which she abandoned herself to him coldly, for pleasure, to revenge herself on a third person, or even out of ambition" [AL, 125]) complements this repetition, as does the almost eerie nature of Alfonso's introduction into the Maller household by Santo through private rooms, particularly Annetta's bedroom. When Maller asks Santo brusquely what he is doing in that part of the house, Santo himself stutters in embarrassment. The picture of the capitalist patron fades before that of the

22. Tancredi, "Una vita di Svevo," p. 61.
23. Cf. André Bouissy, in "Les Fondements idéologiques de l'oeuvre d'Italo Svevo," 3: 35.
24. See Paula Robison, "*Una vita* and the Family Romance," *Modern Fiction Studies,* Svevo issue, p. 36.

forbidding father. The importance of seeing the psychiatric distortion in Alfonso before the social exploitation is properly emphasized by André Bouissy:

> It is because he feels guilty that the character spends his life in hesitations, self analysis, rationalizations of his impulses and acts.[25]

By the time we come to the central scenes of Alfonso's courtship of Annetta, the simultaneous social and sexual climax of the novel, the literary nature of Alfonso's strategies and self-protections seems to have come some distance from the post-Napoleonic hero's sentimental educations by forbidden women of superior class and to draw closer to the world of Freudian case histories of emotional paralysis. In the manner of Flaubert, Svevo indicates an identity between the task of drafting chapters for the novel he is writing with Annetta, the muse of the provinces, and the work at the bank, but by giving the recognition to Alfonso himself, Svevo leads us to concentrate on the nature of the mind rather than upon the experience (AL, 154). That mind, which sees itself as superior in its feelings to those around it, brings together the fantasy of success in business and marriage. Such ambition can thrive only in fantasy, and when it is forced out into action, it protects its self-imposed failure by secondary fantasies of the superiority of retreat to engagement, renunciation of riches, and passion for peace. It is with this perspective that we view the contest between the apparently cold and self-willed Annetta and an actually cold and self-willed Alfonso disguised as a stuttering, subservient, and lyric suitor. The contest immediately calls to mind its literary model, the great debate between Mademoiselle de la Môle and Julien in *The Red and the Black*. We have already noted some similarities, but the differences are, by this comparison, made even more striking. The debate between two ambitions, each swaddled in costumes of the past, of Napoleon and Rousseau, of Marguérite of Navarre; the violence of the fluctuation of sentiment and behavior along the whole range of sadism and masochism; the freshness of energy that belies the constant presence of literary models and historical precedence, the originality of each encounter, however staged it may seem, are at a far remove from the provincial debate between Alfonso and Annetta. Alfonso's courtship is never allowed to become

---

25. Bouissy, "Les Fondements," 3: 36.

superior to its literary pretext, secondhand because of the *lack* of faith in the fantasies of literature, history, and passion. The Stendhalian fantasy, however isolating and egocentric, comes to life in melodramatic actuality, tossed between competitive wills on alternating currents. That melodrama has been forced to live in heroic timelessness and classlessness, pinched as it is in the present by repressive bourgeois intrigue. The constant capacity for wonder and surprise, which so effectively voids self-conscious strategy in the Stendhalian hero, is a symptom of superior character, a nature determined, it would seem, by chance. Though the rhythm of the analysis succeeding passion may seem similar in *A Life,* the analysis itself is lodged in a mind of such inferior energy and boldness, more intent upon protection than discovery, that what is the sign of distinction in the Stendhalian hero becomes in Alfonso flabby self-justification. After his conquest of Annetta he thinks in tired disillusion:

> He felt ill at ease with this weeping girl, and had he not feared to displease her would have left at once, maybe even promising never to return. He was surprised to feel so calm and so far from the desire which had led him to such risky action ten minutes before. (AL, 225)

Alfonso is not equal to Annetta in the play of passion, while the Stendhalian couple is checked by mutual strength. Because Svevo grants to this confession no value in the display and discovery of character and consciousness, because Alfonso does not have even the rights of exorcistic scorn, deprived as he is of a vision large enough to give to disillusion itself a dimension superior to the experience of the surrounding bourgeois policies, his reactions are stranded by his psychological retreat. Without Zeno's winning spontaneity, without the candor, freshness, and humor of response and action that make of Zeno a kind of modern Stendhalian hero, Alfonso cannot rise above his author's irony. Because of the narcissism of his self-justifications, his analysis of Annetta's motives is "harsh, even unjust" (AL, 182). He typically projects his own desire for vengeance onto Annetta in cathartic displacements:

> he was drawn by sensuality, not by anything else. Annetta was the more to blame since the excuses he had found for himself did not exist for her. From beginning to end she had acted out of sensuality and vanity. He had always had an urge to sweeten their love affair

by words and gestures; she had merely tolerated his love without showing she returned it. So, eventually, he had found his feelings getting similar to hers—ceasing, that is, when desire ceased. (AL, 234–35)

By contrast, Marcario's apparent harshness is, in fact, the amusing manifestation of a comfortable teasing of jealous affection. His social ease gives only a superficial advantage. (After all, Julien Sorel's social inferiority, much more severe than Alfonso's, becomes, for all the obstacles it encounters, a decidedly romantic preeminence.) With the realization that he does not love Annetta, Alfonso reasons, his problem is solved (AL, 236).

Recalling the judgment of his "wings," he assumes that Macario's verdict was mistaken. He had, after all, fallen upon his prey (AL, 231). But the self-deception is immediately exposed with Svevo's reminder of his habit of assuming superiority, a criticism that, typically, is half realized by Alfonso himself:

He had spent some happy hours. . . . It had been a strange happiness, continuously finding sops to his pride by seeking weaknesses in others from which he was immune himself, by watching others struggling for money and honors while he remained calm, satisfied by the sense of talent burgeoning in his brain, by a sweeter emotion in his heart than falls to the lot of most human beings. (AL, 231)

Recasting the Darwinian metaphor, he regrets now that "the struggling people whom he despised had drawn him into their midst and without putting up any resistance he had felt the same desires as they, adopted their weapons." Macario's determinism is gratefully accepted, after all. The Svevian attributes of pleasurable latency and dilettantism are played into life by Zeno, but at this stage they serve as Svevo's own tempered but self-castigating reminder that he who uses literature to protect possibility is even more pitiable than the Don Quixotes and Madame Bovaries who infect life with literature but at least live it out, thereby gaining a compensatory vividness that never could be Alfonso's. Renunciation comforts itself with other spurious dreams, that, for example, of self-sacrifice: "If he had two lives, he thought, he would dedicate one to the Lanuccis' happiness" (AL, 205). This brief fantasy will fully flower, at the end of the novel, into the ironic recognition that Alfonso, an evolutionary abortion that insisted on being completed by dreams of superiority, can leave only the most literal of all legacies, money.

The most cynical and naturalistic demystification of Alfonso's sophistic dream of sacrifice is, in fact, the grubby negotiation with the printer's foreman, Gralli, concerning his marriage to Lucia Lanucci. The Lanucci household, throughout the novel a terrible contrast with the Maller shrine, is gloomy and economically pinched, lightened only by the empty freedom of Lucia's ne'er-do-well brother, Gustavo. Along with the bank atmosphere swarming with a supporting cast of frustrated clerks, it frames the scene of courtship and the pastoral retreat, and the reader might well be tempted to see such atmospheres as instigations to Alfonso's dreams. In fact, because neither the bank work nor potential relationship with Lucia is ever really taken seriously by Alfonso, we feel that the novel's naturalism serves better as a justification after the fact for Alfonso than as a motivation. Tancredi is right to claim that the negotiations between Gralli and Alfonso show the real link between economics and affections in this novel, that only Lucia's cry for real happiness breaks through the financial calculations of the household, and that here, as in the Maller house, the capitalistic structure and the pattern of the family romance are joined.[26] Yet there is something secondhand, literary, and stale about the presentation of the Lanucci subplot that, for all its precedents, we do not feel in the courtship scenes. It seems strangely schooled for a Svevo who is more at home as a master of light irony observing the latest literary question of the day in provincial salons:

> At that period whenever literature was mentioned there was always a discussion about realism and romanticism; this was a cosy literary argument in which all could take part. Maller was a partisan of "realism" but, as he always wanted to seem more witty than learned, he confessed that he liked the realists all the more because they were not moralists. He also pretended to despise them because he considered their methods made it easy for them to achieve popularity. (AL, 142–43)

Alfonso's *psychological* negotiations dominate the Lanucci scenes because the household's linear and ineluctably chronological calcula-

26. See Tancredi, *"Una vita,"* p. 78.

tions cannot compete with the rich undated time in which rationalizations and self-justifications are hatched. Svevo feels more comfortable when, in the Jamesian tradition, he frees his last hero from
financial constraints to play with illicit desires against an atmosphere
of emotional and economic security. One way to measure the ascent
of Svevo's fiction from *A Life* to *Confessions of Zeno* is by noting the
gradual loosening of the Svevian atmosphere from the social transac-
tions of the nineteenth-century novel and the opening of a more
generous universe of moral and psychological exchange.

That this freer atmosphere of mixed time and temper, modulated
by the author's relationships of irony with his character, is already
begun in *A Life* is apparent if we study the ways in which Svevo
manipulates the verbal tenses of Alfonso's rationalizations. The interruption of the chronology of events by the indirect time of psychological repetition owes something to Flaubert's method, but the
presence of the author in this novel is altogether different. Svevo has
neither the confidence nor the temperament to let Alfonso's rhetoric
alone hang him. Authorial irony, which insinuates itself to nest in
Alfonso's mind beside the rationalizations that succeed event, is more
interested in widening the psychological scene than in condemning
psychological evasions. The interference has none of the harshness of
Flaubert's absence. Marziano Guglielminetti has sensitively analyzed
the modulation of tenses in the passage from the indicative of event,
to the conditional of the author, across the mediation of the imperfect.[27] The event is widened by analysis through this change and,
in turn, is subtly touched by the presence of the author lightly pushing off from his hero by means of a qualifying conditional, but never
really letting go of him. In its simplest form, this structure is evident
in the description of the first meeting with Annetta. Macario and
Annetta are teasing about her playing, and Alfonso's sense of alienation from their familiarity stimulates a desire for escape and successfully translates inferiority into fatigue:

> Alfonso forced a smile [sorrise con sforzo]. The continual effort to
> appear at ease tired [stancava] him. If he could have found a way,
> he would have left at once. (AL, 38)

Variations of this modulation hover around Alfonso's musings. After
the first kiss, the hero imagines the feelings of Annetta:

27. Guglielminetti, *Struttura e sintassi*, p. 119.

She liked such daring, and hesitations imposed by respect merely satisfied her vanity. When drawing her to him, he had muttered aloud: "If I'm killed for this, it would be a fine death!" [Se adesso mi uccidessero, sarebbe pure la bella morte!]

He had not needed to say the melodramatic phrase, as his action was already excused in Annetta's eyes—so Alfonso had grounds for believing. [Era una frase melodramatica che non ci sarebbe stato bisogne di pronunziare.] (AL, 182)

At yet another encounter, Alfonso rises to the offensive and reasons:

He did not know if he could nourish any great hopes, from these changes, of bringing their relationship back to the point it had reached before, and this time with Annetta's explicit consent. From one day to another he put off that step which he had to take sooner or later and which would definitely show the results obtained; but a week later, he was no longer thinking of taking it because he felt all right as he was. He had hoped to speak words of love, but to ask for them would have been silly and equivalent to a retreat. [Egli aveva sperato di dire delle parole d'amore, ma ora sarebbe stato poco abile a chiederle. Sarebbe equivaluto a retrocedere.] (AL, 220)

A fine example of the conditional as a means of exposure and a carrier of irony occurs after Alfonso decides, following his sexual "triumph," to seize an opportunity to retreat from Annetta since she herself, as a kind of test, suggests his temporary absence. Though Francesca tries to show him the folly of this act, Alfonso has what he wants, a sanction for escape:

He was free at last. No one could any longer try to change his mind; he would leave knowing that by that step he was renouncing Annetta. Francesca had convinced him; departure was equivalent to renunciation. He felt calm and happy. If what Francesca foresaw took place, he was free from all doubt and remorse. She had said that if Annetta abandoned him, he would go back to being a wretched quill-pusher at the Maller bank. No! He would be superior even to the position that Annetta wanted to give him, a superiority shown precisely by his renunciation. (AL, 245–46)

After Annetta has backed down from her suggestion and left the choice open to Alfonso, Alfonso composes a letter in which his cold rhetorical deliberations are exposed by the same series of verb changes, but Svevo never leaves the range of his hero's consciousness:

He would have to be more careful and astute in his reply, or it would eventually make her think him stupid, or indifferent in spite of his melodramatic phrases. Like this, it was pointless or mistaken. If Annetta still cared enough to study his letters, she was clever enough to realize soon that Alfonso was pretending and not even taking much trouble about his pretense. This should have worried him a lot because he had tried to make her think he was the betrayed, but such was his indifference that he could easily console himself. Annetta would not pore over that note of his for long. (AL, 253–54)

While waiting at his mother's bedside, he uses his dying mother's idyllic innocence to castigate Annetta and to pacify his doubts. At the end of his reproachful juxtaposition, the usual suspicious conditionals undermine the defense:

His revulsion to Annetta, he said to himself, was explicable, indeed natural. . . . Her chief motive when she spoke was a desire to please; when she wrote she was vain, vain and sensual when she loved. He compared her with the poor woman whose sleep he was watching. Even in that state, Signora Carolina betrayed how much and in what manner she had loved her husband, so humbly that she still kept as a living memory, and unconsciously imitated, his gestures and ways, even something of his physiognomy.

It would have been torture for him to live with Annetta. She would have made him rich and held to her right to enslave him; the vanity and sensuality which had flung her in his arms might lead to her doing the same with others. (AL, 271)

For all the finesse of this authorial entrance, at times Svevo's presence suffers from its self-imposed restraints and presses to come out of hiding. It seems suspended between the "old" omniscience and the "new" "style indirecte libre." The nature of his ironic sympathy and exposure is, we have seen, entirely different from that of Flaubert, marked as it is by timidity of identification and reluctance of separation. He gives to Alfonso enough perception to hold him by his side. When, for example, Alfonso betrays his assumed pose of resignation, he himself notes: "Soon he had to laugh at himself, seeing the obvious contrast between his intentions and feelings" (AL, 357) and, viewing Annetta for the last time, he remarks to himself: "Perhaps it was his own fault" (AL, 380). Still, Alfonso's perceptions, his compulsive analyses, are habits without the muscle to refuse rationalizations or to transform these into Zeno's comic and spontaneous leaps of adjustment. It will be the great originality of *Confessions of Zeno* to break through the conventional link between self-analysis and paralysis to a new identity of self-analysis and gay, sociable wisdom. At the point of Alfonso's suicide, Svevo is at the furthest distance from him. The choice seems to the hero a saintly solution, but in its terrible misreading of Schopenhauer's recommendation of renunciation, it takes its place next to "the dull, optimistic, Protestant-rationalistic, or peculiarly Jewish view of life [that] will make the demand for poetical justice, and find satisfaction in it."[28] Alfonso is not of the stature necessary for true tragedy; he is unable ever to be that hero who atones for Original Sin, the crime of existence itself.[29] The last movement of the book deliberately flirts with the existential justification, only to underline the inability of Alfonso to embrace it. Yet Svevo's most developed hero is comic and, even with a character stronger than Alfonso, we cannot imagine that the novelist would interest himself in a death immune to irony.

In the midst of an interesting, if somewhat overdrawn, rush of miserable lives in emotional and financial collapse, from old clerks to abandoned mistresses, climaxing in Lucia's frail and ruined desire for happiness, Svevo offers Alfonso the existential temptation, the excuse of universal misery. While Zeno can make of this perspective more than an apology, Alfonso betrays the narrow narcissism of his range. First he rises to a general pity: "He pitied both victor and vanquished" (AL, 351). Next, Alfonso accepts Macario's deterministic definition as a general law:

> Now he knew why he had renounced Annetta. He had nothing to blame himself for, because he had acted according to his own nature, which he had not recognized then. It was good to know at last the motivating forces in his own organism, which brought him new surprises every day. By knowing them, he could now avoid other deviations from the road his nature imposed on him; a pleasant, easy road without a goal. (AL, 353)

What a contrast to Zeno, who accepts the impossibility of knowing, or the partiality of one's knowledge of the self and others! His is the

28. Schopenhauer, "World as Will and Idea," *The Philosophy of Schopenhauer*, p. 198.
29. According to Schopenhauer, the hero who atones for original sin, and existence itself, is tragic.

positive aspect of Svevo's defense, while Alfonso's acceptance is the negative aspect, the rationalization that protects *against* surprise. In response to the pressure of what he imagines to be Maller's contempt, Alfonso's mind typically races back to the school gardens and his mother's embrace, his father's praises. The strain of a showdown with Maller, however, turns up a father unwilling to excuse a bad mark. Alfonso muses:

> How wrong his father was! Even at that young age, Alfonso already knew from experience that none of his efforts could lessen a hatred roused through no fault of his own. (AL, 380)

The cheating of genuine self-knowledge by settling on a premature resignation to the *father's* attitude, a philosophical gloss never quite believed in, is the final evasion, the final submission to "senility," psychological old age fed by delusion instead of wisdom. The great existential perspective is humiliated by an infantile desire to show himself superior to the suspicions and hatred of *others,* a mockery of self-liberation. That Alfonso's social and psychological rhythm is different from that of the others does not give him the Stendhalian distinction of being among the privileged few. What could deviate more from the suicide of Alfonso, its dry registering, than the melodrama of Julien's self-willed execution, also dryly rendered, which overcomes its absurdity by sheer energy and greatness of spirit. Neither the naturalist, realist, nor romantic excuse is left to Alfonso.

Svevo well knew his favorite philosopher's attitude toward suicide, that it "thwarts the attainment of the highest moral aim by the fact that, for a real release from this world of misery, it substitutes one that is merely apparent."[30] If this is a mistake, rather than a crime, it is still a far cry from ideal moral freedom. Suicide is, in fact, rather than a denial of the will to live, an assertion of this will:

> Far from being denial of the will, suicide is a phenomenon of strong assertion of will; for the essence of negation lies in this, that the joys of life are shunned, not its sorrows. The suicide wills life, and is only dissatisfied with the conditions under which it has presented itself to him. He therefore by no means surrenders the will to life, but only life, in that he destroys the individual manifestation.[31]

30. Schopenhauer, "On Suicide," Studies in Pessimism, *Essays of Schopenhauer,* p. 29.
31. Schopenhauer, "World as Will and Idea," p. 324.

Alfonso's self-deluding solution cannot then be Svevo's. If Svevo could not rise above the will on Schopenhauer's wings, neither could he settle for Alfonso's poetic wings.

II. As a Man Grows Older

Though we are not really given in *A Life* alternative lives that proffer a generous moral vision, the mere presence of Annetta's energy, Maller's authority, the fitful intrusion of the air and hills of Trieste, and the shy irony of Svevo prevent us from feeling the spiritual claustrophobia we feel in Flaubert's bourgeois novels. The execution is not fine enough, as it is in Flaubert, to compensate us for inhabiting such a small world, but there is promise of a wider atmosphere. In the second novel, the scattered phenomena of the busy external world, which took up so much space in *A Life,* are drastically cut, and the inner weather of psychological exploration, delusion, rationalization is expanded and poeticized to give us almost a classical purity and consistency of effect. Yet ironically, because there is less to distract us from the psychological life, we are aware of a more liberal atmosphere in which Svevo can feel more at home. On the second page of the novel, Svevo describes in one paragraph Emilio Brentano's petty job, his "impieguccio" and his small literary reputation, his "reputazioncella," economically reducing the practical life of his hero by diminutive endings to both a minimal satisfaction and a minimal success. The artificial tension between a world of grim economy with social inferiority and psychological patterns of evasion that disturbed the homogeneous atmosphere of *A Life* is minimized in this novel because the mind of the hero possesses the entire atmosphere. Even the titles of the two novels lead us from the case history to a state of mind. From the first page, Emilio's protective devices against emotional engagement emanate the timeless color of senility that envelops the motley world that others live in. On the first page, Svevo dryly cuts into the poetry of Emilio's reservations about his courtship of Angiolina, "figlia del popolo": "I have other duties in life, my career and my family" with the question "And his family?" Emilio's sister, Amalia, is the family, who "made no claim at all on him, either physically or morally." But sharing his house, she appears older than her years, small and pale. Emilio's literary career, long past, "brought him in nothing, but also took nothing out of him." His novel is senile in its own right, "ingiallito" from the passage of time. We realize now that the yellow cast of its pages has spread across the novel's introduction, filtering the variegated light of the world into a monotonous hue. When the desire Emilio has sidled up to is at least experienced, it too becomes an old novel, and the last page of Svevo's story shows us a subject who lives in a "new" past "like an old man on the memories of his youth," a simile that ironically suggests the chronology of the normal history of experience when in fact Emilio's great adventure was yellowed before it began. At least the "writer's idle imagination" fantasizes forth a metamorphosis that is colored now by the gold and white of the idealized face of Angiolina reflecting the reddening rays of the horizon. It supplants a vacuous reality and, hanging beneath religious transvaluation and above the vision of the street, it lifts us by its timelessness almost to a belief in its independence from Emilio's mind. If such an image prevents the full vision of reality that Zeno achieves, it also avoids the bankruptcy of Alfonso's suicide. Emilio keeps the image alive by painting on Angiolina's face the anticipation he projects from his state of latency, while in fact the daughter of the people has not lived for one moment in the future. Svevo's irony fiercely qualifies the lyricism of the metamorphic vision, and keeps it from integration into any social reality. He hovers over the yellowing pages of Emilio's literature and the golden face of his dream without yet releasing his mind into a universe of independent vitality and color that permits such fantasies, but not their tyranny over consciousness. We have to wait for Zeno's novel to find a world in which defenses and experience are not enemies, but already what one critic calls "the dark music"[32] of *As a Man Grows Older* is the sign of a much more confident novelist than the one who wrote *A Life.*

If Emilio's habitual coloring of life keeps us at a distance, it also liberates us from the naturalism of *A Life,* which seemed often to be for Svevo an obligation. It is set off as a conscious literary term in the second novel, subject to a parodic irrelevance in relation to the life of the street. At one point in the novel, when Emilio, after talking to Angiolina's mother at the door of the house, understands that once again Angiolina has lied to him, he fantasizes the scene that would

32. Mario Lunetta, *Invito alla lettura di Italo Svevo* (Milan, 1972) , p. 88.

follow the cornering of the prostitute "in flagrante" (AMGO, 114) .
He consoles himself with these words:

> Why be so miserable? Why revolt against the laws of nature?
> Angiolina was a lost woman even in her mother's womb. . . .
> It was useless to punish her: she did not even deserve it; she was
> only the victim of a universal law. The naturalist who somewhere
> lay hidden in him revived, but he could not at once give up his
> desire for vengeance. (AMGO, 90–91)

Naturalist has now become a term halfway between Emilio's consciousness and that of Svevo, but while Emilio assumes it to achieve
an attitude of resignation, one that relieves him of his habitual and
jealous analysis, Svevo himself has another intention. The release of
standard literary terms from fixed definition prepares for the release
of man, in an age of Schopenhauer, Nietzsche, and Freud, from the
certainty of old moral formulas. In leading Svevo's second novel up
to *Confessions of Zeno,* John Gatt-Rutter astutely comments about
its language:

> In *Senilità* Svevo stops this side of paradox, but leaves the strong
> suspicion that words have become merely provisional indicators, as
> the conventional assumptions on which they rest are being under-
> mined. Flags of convenience, they will be shot to tatters by Zeno, for
> whom paradox becomes a new aesthetic, if not a new aestheticism.
> Love, truth, goodness, health, conscience, life are then really dis-
> sected till we no longer know what they are.[33]

And it is fruitful, in this regard, to recall Sartre's praise, in his essay
on Mauriac, of Conrad's unsettling of terminology that is both
literary and moral:

> Conrad suggests to us that Lord Jim may be "romantic." He takes
> great care not to state this himself; he puts the word into the mouth
> of one of his characters, a fallible being, who utters it hesitantly. The
> word "romantic," clear as it is, thereby acquires depth and pathos
> and a certain indefinable mystery.[34]

The literary quality of the designation *naturalist* is for Emilio both
apt and grimly amusing, since Angiolina represents, for this dilet-

---

33. John Gatt-Rutter, *"Senilità* and the Unsaid," *Essays on Italo Svevo,* ed. Thomas
Staley, p. 28.
34. Sartre, "François Mauriac and Freedom," *Literary Essays,* p. 15.

tante, the hope of living the novel he could not write (AMGO, 170).
She is his novel as well as his life ("He hoped to live the novel he
found himself unable to write" [AMGO, 135]), and this is the reason that she can never be absorbed on her own terms into either of
them. Emilio can no longer be satisfied, however, with Macario's
image of deterministic evolution. The consolation is quickly rejected
as inadequate, not only by Svevo, but by the hero himself, who refuses to renounce the sweet dream that softens the long-delayed
posession of the flesh:

> Angiolina really gave him everything: the possession of her body
> and—since one gives birth to the other—the poet's dream as well.
> (AMGO, 153)

Such a synthesis will be quickly disturbed by a mind that anxiously
breaks marriages. Next to Angiolina's body, Emilio constructs visions
that transform the flesh:

> It was a dream which he continued to develop while with Angio-
> lina, and regardless of her being there. He dreamed that they were
> very unhappy because of the unfair conditions of society under
> which they lived. He was so persuaded of this that he even imagined
> himself capable of performing an act of heroism in order to ensure
> the triumph of socialism. All their misfortunes were due to the
> poverty of her family which drove her to do so. (AMGO, 153)

Again he rises to the use of naturalism as a moral patronization, and
again the consolation is humiliated:

> But she did not perceive this implication and only regarded his
> words as a caress, and thought that he was blaming himself.
> (AMGO, 153)

The triumph of Emilio's socialism is a dream of moral salvation for
Angiolina, a compensation for the "moral" lectures that failed to
change her (so vividly mocked by the scene in which Emilio writes
for Angiolina the coarse letter to Volpini) :

> In another order of society he would at once have acknowledged
> her publicly without obliging her first to sacrifice herself to the
> tailor. He entered into Angiolina's lies in order to make her kinder
> to him and induce her to join in his ideas so that they might dream
> together. She asked for some explanations and he gave them to her,
> only too glad to be able to utter his dream aloud. He told her of the

enormous struggle which was to bring liberty to all, to them as well. He talked to her about the abolition of capital and the short hours of agreeable work which alone one would be obliged to do. Woman was to be the equal of man and love a mutual gift. (AMGO, 153–54)

Earlier, as Emilio and Angiolina had been walking in the city, Emilio thinks of Trieste as "the city of labour" and remembers that "in the past he had indulged in socialistic ideas, of course without ever stirring a finger to realize them" (AMGO, 47). Like naturalism, socialism becomes paradoxically a fantasy that provisionally *releases* him from reality, a reality that, in the mouth of a relentlessly actual Angiolina, mocks the narcissism of his moral lessons, his dreams of justice:

> She asked for some further explanations which disturbed his dream, and finally concluded: "If everything was to be divided there wouldn't be much left for anybody. The working classes are jealous good-for-nothings and will never succeed, however much you do for them." (AMGO, 154)

At last, when he realizes that "the child of the people was on the side of the rich," he gives up his lesson. The mouth that utters this deflating opinion is the same that early in the novel complained of a toothache, the same that is amusingly transformed by Emilio momentarily emancipated from his habit of cynical analysis ("Passion had for a moment freed him from his painful habit of observation" [AMGO,146]):

> "This one," she said, opening her delicious mouth for him to see, and displaying her red gums and strong white teeth, which seemed like a casket of precious gems chosen and set there by that incomparable artificer—health. He did not laugh, but gravely kissed the mouth she held out to him. (AMGO, 17)

The juxtaposition of the socialist dream and the naturalist rationalization with the clichéd regressive fantasy of the lover as nurse, a mother tending a sick child, and the disappearance of these images with Angiolina's words of assent, shows up the cheat of all Emilio's fantasies, their consuming jealousy that will not leave the objective world alone.

The most desperate attempt to subdue the struggle between dream and reality, classless idealization and social debasement, affection (which Freud identifies as the feeling, among the bourgeois, toward the sister and mother) and sensuality (which Freud views as satisfied by a short-circuiting of Oedipal conflicts through dalliance with the lower classes), is the projection of virginal radiance, beamed from the eyes of her poet, to the image of Angiolina. Angiolina is perpetually coming out of sunlight, crowned with her golden hair, her eyes crackling fire, her cheeks pink with health. Her color of good weather makes her seem a creature of nature to the literary Emilio, who is busy transforming scattered light into a unifying semi-religious metaphor of effulgence. Emilio's eyes see an image of bold innocence in "her white dress . . . with its pinched waist and wide sleeves, almost like inflated balloons," that "clamoured to be looked at, and existed for that purpose. Her face rose out of all that whiteness, in no wise overpowered by it, but flaunting its roses unabashed" (AMGO, 41). At a later, vengeful stage, he still cannot get rid "of the tendency to reconstruct the *Ange* who was daily broken into fragments" (AMGO, 153). The gray cast of Amalia's saintly resignation and the harsh secular winds and rain off the sea, which put Angiolina, fearful of spoiling her dress, to flight, set off the elemental ingenuousness of her amorality, so natural in its refusal of idealization. Angiolina's reality is immune to gossip and, while she is present, to Emilio's imagination. She never forces nature to reflect her moods as does Emilio by the stalest of literary tricks, the pathetic fallacy. At peace,

> he had loved her in the moonlight, in the warm evening air, with all that boundless lovely landscape spread out before them alone and for their love. (AMGO, 25)

and in turbulence,

> Emilio felt the confusion of the elements was attuned to his grief, and it helped him to attain a greater calm. His habit of always thinking in images made him read a comparison between the scene before him and the spectacle of his own life. (AMGO, 202)

How comforting for Emilio "in the tumult of the waves, where each transmitted to the other the movement which had roused it from its own inertia, where each in turn strove to rise from its place only to fall again into a horizontal position, [to] read the impassivity of fate.

No one was to blame for all the vast destruction" (AMGO, 202).
Seeing busy sailors, he creates a melodrama of motivation to action
possible for him only in his fantasy:

> Emilio thought that it was the inactivity of his own fate which had
> been responsible for his misfortunes. If only once in his life he had
> had to untie a rope and knot it again at a given moment; if the fate
> of one fishing-boat, no matter how small, had been entrusted to
> him, to his care, to his courage, if he had been compelled to over-
> ride with his own voice the clamour of the wind and sea he would
> have been less weak and less unhappy. (AMGO, 203)

Never to have been pressured by fate is the familiar retreat into
latency.

His fantasy absorbs the moonlight as well. The moon that will, in
Confessions of Zeno, live such an independent life, carefree enough
to mock the faces that are sent up to it, the kisses of Zamboni's
poetry, serves merely to lyricize Angiolina:

> Her face had become grave, almost austere, and as he kissed it he
> felt himself to be more than ever a seducer. He was kissing the pure
> virginal moonlight. (AMGO, 23)

The homogeneous atmosphere of the novel, the sad erotic courtship
of experience through dreams, cannot develop more than a narrow
cast of characters screened through Emilio's egoism. Their lives can
be used in Emilio's fantasies because not one of this group exhibits
the ability to form an attachment that survives neurotic distortions,
such as that between Zeno and Augusta. Zeno himself willingly out-
lasts his fantasies of Ada. However tenacious his desires and dreams,
he releases the objects of his affections and hostilities into independence where they, again and again, get the best of him. Emilio is not
equal to this, although his dreams have a thicker dimension than
Alfonso's rationalizations, and we are, for all our impatience and
antagonism, brought closer to his texture than to that of Svevo's first
hero. Depressed by his own idealizations, he is, after all, susceptible
to the thought that "the whole fault was his. It was he who was an
abnormal, unhealthy creature, not Angiolina" (AMGO, 87). When
Emilio laments his fate "with an irony of self-analysis which removed
from it every trace of the ridiculous" (AMGO, 107–8), we are certainly being lured to a larger sympathy. Because Emilio's sense of
superiority, based on his dreams, and his defensive assaults and with-

drawals are of a more apprehensive nature than those of Alfonso, the delayed possession of Angiolina seems to exploit a greater and deeper range of feeling. In a fury of vengeance, he makes the unpardonable remark to Angiolina: "I am not worth much more than you are" (AMGO, 152), but his shame at his patronization prods him into dreams of socialist equality, a transformation more frenetic and more painfully ironic than those less complicated rationalizations of Alfonso. Emilio manifests an energy, however distorted its purpose, to reconstruct the fragments of experience into a visionary shrine, while Amalia sinks to suicide. By no means can we see Emilio's solution as one that at last closes the rift between experience and fantasy. The progress of his moral education, from the first Svevian intrusion of irony: "Are not good health and corruption always assumed by the rhetorician to be incompatible?" (AMGO, 8) to the final summation: "How astonishing reality was!" might remind us of Zeno's trajectory, but Emilio's mind is never sprung free enough from his needs to see these questions, like the moon, like the personality of others, in all their contradictory independence, never enough, certainly, to tolerate a universe in a permanent state of paradox.[35]

Emilio's final fantasy, fragile as it is, represents a last effort at a synthesis that will keep reality from breaking into fragments:

> Yes, Angiolina thinks and sometimes cries, thinks as though the secret of the universe had been explained to her or the secret of her own existence, and it is sad as though in all the whole wide world she could not find one single solitary *deo gratias*. (AMGO, 224)

The originality of this poetry, which Joyce much admired in the Italian,[36] its absolute appropriateness, lies in the refusal of Emilio to allow Angiolina the satisfaction of her short-sighted naturalness, in the egoism that insists on pushing her, by the gentle hands of poetry, into a state characteristic of *him*, not *her*, of unconsoled and anxious meditation, delicately personalized by the artificial dignity of her church Latin learned from lovers. He shapes her out of his own

35. For an excellent charting of Emilio's "progress" see Eduardo Saccone, *"Senilità di Italo Svevo: dalla impotenza del privato alla ansiosa speranza," Modern Language Notes,* 82, no. 1 (January 1967) : 79–102.

36. The last passage, which Joyce had memorized, perhaps failing to realize its full irony in context, is one of the most musical of Svevo's prose:

Si! Angiolina pensa e piange! Pensa come se le fosse stato spiegato il segreto dell'-universo e della propria esistenza; piange come se nel vasto mondo non avesse piú trovato neppure un *Deo gratias* qualunque.

absurd dreams of socialist distribution, his own anxieties of expectation:

> The image embodied the dream he had once dreamed at Angiolina's side, which that child of the people could not understand.
> (AMGO, 223)

With the help of a transfusion from the ghost of Amalia, the lover's troublesome body disappears, that body that kept bringing down the dream. It is indeed a "metamorfosi strana," but perhaps the strangest aspect of the vision is that we cannot dismiss it, so impressive is its poetry, in the way that we can dismiss Alfonso's visions of rising above the hate and suspicions of others. The fantasy of the incorrigible dreamer,[37] evasive and distorted as it is, projects enough persuasion to give us, momentarily, the illusion that Angiolina's vitality deserves such expansion. If the vision has the practical advantage of helping Emilio to forget the life Angiolina might now be leading without him, a life of daily vanities, it also paradoxically honors Angiolina's resistance to such dreams and the tenacious reality of her existence.

A great deal of the force and originality of *As a Man Grows Older* depends upon the fact that such poetry can be only a pretense of liberation from an anxious world of fragments and a dilettante's version of spiritual transformation. Consequently it remains the negative side of his dilettantism that Svevo exposes here. Emilio's projections lack the charm, abandon, and vulnerability of Zeno's. The ridiculous pomposity and ineptness of Emilio's plans for the moral education of Angiolina, the rhetorical nature of his "maturity" ("He was fond of talking about his experience. What he was pleased to call so was something he had absorbed from books: a considerable mistrust of his fellow-men and a great contempt for them" [AMGO, 12]) do not qualify him for life. Though Angiolina does not need his help, Svevo delights in boosting her by displaying the Molièresque absurdity of the dreamer's advice to look out for her own interests:

> As he spoke, he felt himself to be a superior being, an immoralist, who sees things as they are and is content that they should be so.
> (AMGO, 20)

37. "Incorregibilmente sognatore" is the name applied to Emilio by Saccone, "*Senilità*," p. 52.

The rhetorical nature of this vision that prides itself on being beyond good and evil is exposed by the artless medley of affectation that Angiolina has grafted to her speech, learned from lovers, Latin church tags, coarse Venetian canzonette, a bad Tuscan accent ("ella toscaneggiava").

Emilio is not ever close to achieving Schopenhauerian calm. Writing gives him too much pain; Emilio wants "to spare himself all possible pain, and he did not feel strong enough to study his own incapacity and to overcome it" (AMGO, 134). At the opera, listening to Wagner's music, Emilio wonders if "he had perhaps found a cure in art?" (AMGO, 131). The ever-absorptive narcissim is beautifully depicted in one paragraph that holds together his insensitivity to his sister and his habit of enslaving experience:

> Art had only given him an interval of peace, and it would not be able to give it to him again, for now certain fragments of the music which had remained in his mind were already adapting themselves too perfectly to his own sensations, his self-pity, for example, and the sympathy which he felt for Angiolina or Amalia. (AMGO, 131)

The individualistic aesthetic ideal of spontaneity sponsored by Emilio's best friend, the painter Balli: "a certain ruggedness, a simplicity, or, as he preferred to say, perspicacity of idea from which he thought his artistic 'ego' must emerge purified of all that was not original either in form or idea" (AMGO, 13) seems on the surface to be a moral alternative that corrects the selfish dilettantism of Emilio's dreams and habits; but Svevo's reminders, following fast upon this ideal, of Balli's incapacity to love, of his vanity, of his lack of real success, and of the desire to play the part of a superior being help us to realize that such a philosophy in his mouth is only a more seductive, because more shameless, kind of narcissism than that of Emilio's.

At the famous "cena di vitelli"[38] scene particularly, Emilio feels unlike the others (Balli, Angiolina, and Balli's mistress Margherita), but Balli himself had claimed his difference to be one of degree, not kind, and calls him an egoist less fortunate than himself (AMGO, 13). The real difference between Emilio and Balli is, as Eduardo Saccone has asserted, not one of character so much as one of con-

---

38. This is Balli's phrase, "the dinner of veal dishes," to describe the central scene of Emilio's humiliation in Balli's own version of a sentimental education.

sciousness.[39] The malice, possessiveness, guilt, and generosity of Balli distinguish themselves by the simplicity of their structure ("Balli, now that he had recovered the conviction of his own innocence" [AMGO, 63]), the shortness of their duration, and the absence of hangovers. Balli and Angiolina represent not a moral alternative, but a biological superiority ("Balli, who was a man in the true sense of the word . . ." [AMGO, 14]) that enables them to feel more at home in the world, oblivious to the historical progress of bourgeois decadence and superior to Emilio's protective morality. One critic, Giacinto Spagnoletti, has suggested that Angiolina is able to convince us of her reality largely through her need and ability to make herself loved,[40] and surely this holds true for Balli as well. The novel plays upon the harsh irony of inversion that forces emotionally passive characters, Emilio and Amalia, into active roles of emotional pursuers. Emilio's customary position of child to the father in Balli, mistress to his master (". . . in Brentani's company, [Balli] had almost the sense of being with one of the many women who were entirely dominated by him" [AMGO, 14]) is wrenched out of joint by desire and jealousy, and nothing is more awkward and artificial than Emilio's fitful attempts at imitating aggressiveness that end in a possession vitiated by the disappointment of a realized dream, the collapse of the great fantasized synthesis. Amalia seconds this clumsy reversal when she pathetically imitates Angiolina as, mesmerized, she strolls in her hopelessly old-fashioned dress. Svevo's cunning and amusing inversion of order is accomplished by rendering Emilio's great escapist dream of the socialist unity of the sexes antithetical to Balli's applied capitalist exploitation of slave by master in such a way that the myth of the natural is condemned by even pseudo-dreams of justice and equality, and the myth of political solutions to emotional problems is exposed by the pseudo-pragmatism of Balli's animalism. The peculiar jarring of psychological complexity in Emilio's tensions and the concomitant patterns of fantasy played against the biological simplicity of Balli's behavior yield a comic dimension that will be fully exploited in *Confessions of Zeno* and *Further Confessions of Zeno*. The "cena di vitelli" scene, in which Balli at a prearranged dinner with his mistress, Emilio, and Angiolina, uses the pretense of sentimental education (a nice reproach to Emilio's "moral"

39. Saccone, *"Senilità,"* p. 33.
40. Giacinto Spagnoletti, *Svevo* (Milan, 1972), pp. 51–52.

pedagogy) to fully enjoy his "natural" talents of mastery, develops this contrast. The two names given Angiolina, the ridiculously idealizing "Ange" of Emilio and the contemptuous, but to Angiolina herself more comfortable, "Giolona" of Balli, set the almost farcical melodrama of the scene. Balli's domination of everyone is enjoyed because it is played with a confident humor (his kiss to Margherita is given with "habitual brusquerie and mock severity" [AMGO, 56]), highly sociable in its concentration on the body's vanity. Even Balli's art is pressed into the service of bodily lure: " 'Dear Angiolina,' " he says abruptly. " 'She looks at me like that in the hope that I may admire her nose too' " (AMGO, 54). Angiolina's vanity, in turn, cele-brates the insensitivity of her physical health, and the pervasive physiology of the atmosphere thoroughly isolates Emilio, accustomed to feeding on dreams. Balli's quip, a mock reproach to Angiolina for taking away Emilio: " 'We used to get on so well together. I, the most intelligent person in the town and he the fifth, for there are four places immediately below me, and he comes directly after that' " (AMGO, 56), amusingly turns Angiolina to "thinking that the fifth intelligent person in the town was not worth very much" (AMGO, 56), whereby she concentrates her admiration on the first. Mean-while, Balli "good-humouredly burie[s] Emilio beneath the weight of his own superiority" (AMGO, 57).

The subsequent guilt of Balli for assuming the role of rival instead of friend is typically short and simple, and recognized with attractive candor:

> A little sound argument would probably be more efficacious than example in curing Emilio, and even if it did not altogether work, it would at least enable him to appear again in the guise of a friend and to give up the role of rival which he had only assumed from weakness and for the sake of a moment's distraction. (AMGO, 60)

Balli thoroughly publicizes his "bizarre autobiography" (AMGO, 69), calming its hubris by the notion of natural luck. Again and again we have the sensation that Balli and Angiolina are beings born lucky, yet nothing in their external biographies cooperates with this sensation except their physical and social attractiveness. Just as their lives are loud, so the lives of Emilio and his sister are hushed and drab, marked by a repression that internalizes their biographies. Like Alfonso, Emilio exhibits in his emotional patterns a strong impulsion to flight and infantilism that marvelously counterpoints Balli's manliness. The family, in the novel, is represented by a brother and a sister on the one hand and the sordid household of Angiolina on the other. Angiolina seems perfectly adjusted to her atmosphere, passed on from the Lanuccis and cheapened, of an interior marked by the pathetic traces of luxury from her "career." The household that sells itself is countered by the household that saves itself, that hoards passion and desire. The two households are miles apart, but the social distinctions are not so significant as one might think. Rather, they represent two different orders of consciousness that seem, in their contrast, to bypass moral evaluation. Inherited morality appears homeless in a world that pits the biological against the psychological.

It is, in fact, the helplessness of the moral order in the natural world that invites pity for Emilio's exile into fantasy. Paula Robison's view is persuasive, that if Emilio has to contend with the images of women as maternal angel and degraded plaything, both inaccessible to marriage, and with ambivalent feelings toward Balli's paternal authority, there is some justification for his feelings of innocence, some truth in his gentle passivity, some self-knowledge in his rationalizations.[41] Emilio's vision procures escape, but his puritanism reveals that he demands more; his idealism is humiliated by experience, but the ghosts of his fantasies give us a lyric dimension which, by being in touch with the unconscious, widens the atmosphere and deepens the universe in which others act. The final irony is, in fact, that if Angiolina represents a standard of reality by which to measure the sick fantasies of Emilio's *senilità*,[42] his poetry, an illegitimate grafting of Amalia's sensitivity and sadness onto Angiolina's radiant health, grants her a fictive immortality that raises her power to a level beyond good and evil. Impelled defensively by his neurosis rather than actively from his imagination, the image guarantees us the perspective of Svevian irony that refuses any lasting independence to such sterile transcendence. Wagner's music checks the distinctiveness of Amalia's fate instead of expanding it. Not for her even the romantic energy of Madame Bovary, which moves a life

---

41. Paula Robison, "*Senilità:* The Secret of Svevo's Weeping Madonna," *Italian Quarterly* 14, no. 55 (Winter 1971) : 74.
42. Russell Pfohl, "Imagery as Disease in *Senilità*," *Modern Language Notes* 76 (February 1961) : 143–150.

to a higher pitch of intensity if not fulfillment through projection
into art. Emilio's fantasy is allowed only to immortalize the reality of
another who still lives. The terrible possessiveness of Emilio's mind
appropriates all fates in a moral vacuum. No feeling and no character
are ever quite free of Emilio's transmutations. We are relieved for a
moment by Balli's limited pity of Amalia, for it is just what it claims
to be, while Emilio's feelings slide into inauthenticity:

> It is true that his remorse ended by changing into profound self-
> pity, which made him find relief in a fit of weeping. So for that
> night at least remorse lulled him to sleep. (AMGO, 116)

We measure the distance from this self-absorption to the range of
Zeno's sympathies when, after musing "strange . . . it almost seems
as if one half of humanity exists to live and the other to be lived,"
Emilio adds: "Perhaps Angiolina only exists in order that I may live"
(AMGO, 221). Zeno will be able to indulge his passions as if they
were, as Pampaloni puts it, "another gift offered to him by life,"[43]
and his remorse will soften rather than rebuke his marriage. The
hero's acceptance of the independence of characters from his dreams
is one of the great changes that mark the passage from *As a Man
Grows Older* to *Confessions of Zeno*. (For this reason, Augusta's
health can socialize with Zeno's sickness.) It is the honoring of this
independence that keeps Zeno in the game. Ultimately, no rationalization, no fantasy, will be able to organize life or protect him from
it. He is forced, again and again, to affront the conventional morality
of marriages. Yet, for all the distance in time and consciousness between the two novels, the way has been prepared for Svevo's master-
piece. Guglielminetti alerts us to the fact that alternating modes and
verbal times, so complex in *A Life*, are reduced in the second novel
to a minimum, and that the imperfect realizes the most constant tone
of the narrator's voice.[44] Expressive condensation is effected through
an increase in adverbs of manner, pejorative noun endings, superla-
tive adjectives. Though the decreasing dependence upon a reality
described outside the bounds of a central consciousness dead ends in
the second novel in Emilio's synthetic lyricism, it furthers the liberation from the givens of naturalism and prepares for the equalizing of
class (Carla seems a quite natural adjunct of the bourgeois world),

43. Pampaloni, "Svevo," pp. 523–24.
44. Guglielminetti, *Struttura*, pp. 131–33.

the socializing of consciousness, and the release of the poetry of
metamorphosis from personal desire into the hands of Mother
Nature.

III. "Confessions of Zeno" and After

The maturing of Svevo's fiction is greatly aided by a new muse
courted during twenty years of relative dormancy, psychoanalysis.
The structure of haphazard, unchronological perception within the
conventionally ordered bourgeois marriage sets up a rich tension that
eliminates dependence upon a stark opposition of the hyperconscious
hero and the biologically adaptable.[45] The hero is given a weapon
formerly wielded by the author, humor, which enables him to co-
operate, often with kicking feet, with the forces that control fantasy
and infantile desire without being possessed by them. Through this
cooperation, Zeno's uniqueness is made normal and his improvisations acceptable, especially by comparison to the even more original
and unpredictable ones of Mother Nature. To see all human life as a
sickness may have been an excuse in Alfonso. In Zeno it is a truth
beyond personal need and a mode of sympathy rather than a sanction
for isolation. The whole universe conspires to keep Zeno going with
a peculiarly unsentimental receptiveness. It laughs at his jokes.

With a new availability between the universe and the hero, the
hero and others, and author and characters, the narcissistic parasitism
of Emilio's world disappears. If those of higher consciousness are
more susceptible to modern existential anxieties and compulsions,
they do not have to bear all the responsibility for that sickness. Beyond Emilio, it is man himself who is a parasite on earth. All the
characters in this new world are, like Angiolina and Balli, open to
luck. Yet they live in an atmosphere suffused with bourgeois order
and apparent health, hardly dependent for its life on the debased
naturalness of Angiolina. It is a world of business concerns, not one
charged by the casual and carefree career of Balli. The Malfenti
household, patriarchally structured, is not the forbidding Maller

---

45. As Gian-Paolo Biasin puts it in "Zeno's Last Bomb," *Modern Language Notes,*
Svevo issue, p. 19:

Between *Senilità and La coscienza di Zeno* psychoanalysis . . . provided him with
the link which he had long sought between positivism and subjectivism, between
objectivity and relativity.

house, nor does Carla's life, with its façade of respectable singing lessons to disguise the selling of favors, have anything to do with the grim Lanucci life, or that of Angiolina's family. It is absorbed into the dominating bourgeois aura of physical comfort. So basic is this order that it accommodates, by its central metaphor, the stock market, all conceivable vagaries of fate without prejudice. As one reader remarks, even the war, an absurd bankruptcy, is soothed by the humors of commercial volatility.[46] While, in their struggle with antagonistic worlds, Alfonso and Emilio employ imaginations desperate to preserve their sense of superiority, Zeno, in a world that only mildly reproaches his eccentricities, works to become acceptable to it. The high innocence so desired by the first two heroes, to escape from an adult world of engagements, is to them a matter of life or death. For Zeno Cosini, the yearning for innocence is no longer isolated from the moral world of marriages. It is humorously demoted to the conventional wish of the bourgeois child to be good. Zeno's obsession to find the health that will make him a full member of the bourgeois world, however impoverishing from a historical perspective, is plotted with such charm that we come to think of that world as the only living space available.

Because of the pervasive presence of the bourgeois order, some social critics ascribe historically diagnostic purposes and intentions to *Confessions of Zeno,* implying that one of its primary purposes is "the literary transcription of a precise moment in the history of the European mind; the moment in which the crisis of post-romantic individualism opens up into a larger crisis, into a deeper denunciation of the structures of 19th century civilization."[47] The substance of such a claim, if we think in terms of what we might derive from Svevo's creation, seems defensible. But the scope of the claim and its assumption of a dominating sociological bias in Svevo misrepresents the Svevian texture. I would certainly second Spagnoletti's contention about the distracting nature of such claims, even if he may go too far in his assumption of Zeno's historical insensitivity.[48] He sees Zeno as a psychiatric opportunist rather than a conscious historical actor, one who draws no moral or political consequences from his times, but instead, in a rather timeless Darwinian emphasis upon the

46. Spagnoletti, *Svevo,* p. 133.
47. A. Leone de Castris, *Italo Svevo* (Pisa, 1959), p. 203.
48. Spagnoletti, *Svevo,* p. 123.

struggle of the weak for survival, concentrates on how to manage his neurosis profitably. Zeno's self-absorption, apparently too near-sighted to see the relationship between personal and historical neurosis, actually is relieved by a humor that clearly links internal and external determinations on Basedow's absurdly nonprogressive line. It is not a dispassionate or insensitive humor, but one that arrives at the Freudian attitude of active resignation to the suffering imposed by civilization and its cultural super-ego, since the self's censors collaborate in this oppression.[49]

It is not the purpose of such a perspective to denounce the modern bourgeois society in which Zeno performs his comedy of self-pity.[50] While recognizing that social criticism may be implicit in the busy humor of anecdote, I cannot willingly subscribe to the more sweeping assumption of Leone de Castris, writing on the section called "Story of My Marriage":

> The denunciation of a society, levelled at the inside of a rich bourgeois family, without deep ties and without genuine moral structure, is present in the comic preparations of the event, in its narrative representation.[51]

More convincing is the comment of old Zeno upon a younger one, a judgment cast in the typically cynical humor that sees life as a bourgeois "comédie larmoyante," manifesting more disturbance over changes of role than over cultural decline:

> And now I see my life, commencing with childhood, passing on into turbid adolescence, which one fine day settled down into young manhood (something in the nature of a disillusionment), then hurtling on into marriage (a state of resignation interrupted by occasional rebellions) and then entering upon old age, the main characteristic of which was to push me into the shadows and rob me of the role of leading actor. For everyone, including myself, my *raison d'être* from now on was to provide a background to others— to my wife, my daughter, my son and my grandson. (FCZ, 29)

49. See Freud, "Civilization and Its Discontents," Standard ed., vol. 21 and Lionel Trilling's perceptive discussion in *Sincerity and Authenticity*, pp. 151–59.
50. See Spagnoletti, *Svevo*, p. 127.
51. de Castris, *Italo Svevo*, p. 239. See also the statement on p. 34 that forces the Svevian comedy:

All the analytic descent into Zeno's childhood, from his anarchic boyhood to his father's failure to understand him, is a smiling but bitter diatribe against traditional morality and education.

We might examine as well Zeno's own suspicion of a transference from personal to social criticism. In a scene that finds him on his way to Augusta from Carla's apartment, thinking of the complications of having a wife and a mistress, he admits:

> As I hurried home I was even bold enough to begin attacking our social system, as if that were responsible for my shortcomings. I thought it ought to be so arranged as to allow one to have intercourse occasionally with other women without having to fear the consequences. (CZ, 194)

By dint of such an analysis of remorse, Zeno manages as usual to feel innocent by the time he gets home. Zeno does not expect us to take seriously his displacement from personal to societal guilt, since he himself cannot be taken in by it, but with his tentative explorations he leaves us free to entertain such a double perspective. There is evidence in Svevo's letters and in Zeno's comments about Augusta of irritability in relation to the bourgeois complacency of marriage, and there is no question about the ambivalence of Svevo, which rises from an unwillingness to close the gap between social subscription and existential discomfort. But Zeno's own doubts and pleasure over setting himself up after his marriage as the bourgeois patriarch he once resisted is a psychiatric sentiment, not a historical judgment:

> I was collaborating in the building up of a patriarchal family, and I myself was on the way to becoming the patriarch I had previously hated, and who now stood for me for an emblem of health. It is one thing to be a patriarch, and quite another to be called on to revere someone else who has assumed that position. (CZ, 142–43)

This preference for a mixed Freudian and Darwinian vision of the stages of man demotes the historical view and deflects demands for political responsibility.

The bourgeois scene, unruffled by the harsh ironies of the rise of modern fascism, is decidedly disturbed by an existential view of man no longer at home in the universe. When Zeno comes into the Malfenti house in pursuit of health and happiness, he feels as if he were "coming safely into port," but later in the novel, we recall, after he has coined for Guido the famous aphorism about life's originality, Zeno meditates in this way about life's unpredictability:

> And one did not need to get outside it in order to realize how fantastically it was put together. One need only remind oneself of

all that we men expect from life to see how very strange it is, and to arrive at the conclusion that man has found his way into it by mistake and does not really belong there. (CZ, 299)

Yet the bourgeois comedy survives and even exploits obsessive interruptions by the metaphors of division, the absurd mental dissections of Zeno's anatomy. Zeno speaks to his first doctor about his sick tendency to divide women into the parts of their body and the sane desire to embrace the whole woman (CZ, 14). The recognition, like the resolutions on smoking, sends him to the sanatorium in search of a cure, away from the security of the marriage hearth, but with Augusta's smiling approval. Zeno's friend Tullio runs over the lines of Zeno's script of his comedy of self-pity, and while Tullio delights in giving Zeno the pity he desires, he talks about the most delicate wonders of human anatomy. Zeno's attention is self-consciously turned to the legs that propel the "infernal machine" (CZ, 94), so casually taken for granted by his father. Such concentration on the parts rather than on the whole, a symptom of the disease of hyperconsciousness, leads to a psychosomatic limp that, in various disguises, hobbles Zeno throughout the novel. A climactic separation of parts occurs in the image that Zeno conjures up when he is actually betraying Augusta:

> The higher part of one's body bends down to observe and judge the lower, and finds it monstrous. The sense of horror it experiences at the sight is what we call remorse. In classical tragedy the victim did not return to life, and yet all remorse vanished; which meant that the deformity was cured and that it was idle to lament any longer. (CZ, 194)

But Zeno's world is not classical; it is incurable. In the section on psychoanalysis, Zeno reminds us that such tragic consolation and purity are out of place in the comedy of bourgeois repetition. On hearing of his Oedipus complex, Zeno, with mock rapture, exclaims:

> It was a disease that exalted me to a place among the great ones of the earth; a disease so dignified that it could trace back its pedigree even to the mythological age! (CZ, 367)

The final vision of the fracturing of the earth from its parasites, a result of the meddling of the infernal machine with an innocent nature, explodes the whole comedy, leaving behind no choral chant, no legend, only its revival in the heart of Zeno.

With this prophetic burst, capping domestic death and disease, the security of the Malfenti household is ravaged, and we see Zeno, temporarily unhoused by the war, plunge into the vagaries of a speculation only slightly resembling the comfortable order and play of Giovanni's business. Still, it would be a great mistake to construe the bombardment of the bourgeois ramparts as the end of an epoch, like the financial attrition and bad marriages in *Buddenbrooks,* as representing the decline of the bourgeoise at a precise moment in history. Neither Svevo nor Zeno, clinging to his comedy, ever emigrates from the bourgeois situation to chart its ruin. Distanced from the war in "horrified inaction" (CZ, 396), Zeno will go on dreaming beside his wife of "limbs, gestures, of a voice more perfect still" (CZ, 372). No final grammar can make political language of the play between the controlled repetitions of Augusta's duties and the uncontrolled compulsive repetitions of identity and situation in the psychiatric order. The bourgeois earth of this novel will never be free of this mixed time. Zeno is delighted to use its pragmatic capitalistic metaphors to describe the value of Carla and Augusta, priced in terms of market fluctuation (CZ, 208). The acceptance of the modern bourgeois stage as the basic ground upon which we stand paradoxically makes possible a timeless comedy that can acknowledge the Marxist complaints about the obsessive application to life of the cash nexus, but cannot stop laughing long enough to worry about them. The marketplace is too good a metaphor for human life itself to be made into a target of political or social conscience.

The superior man of parts is quite willing to crawl into a well-made bourgeois bed. In that bed, sick with the guilt of adultery, Zeno is comforted by Augusta as he murmurs by mistake, thinking of his mistress: "Poor Cosini" (CZ, 148). Augusta's ignorance of cause by no means humiliates her, for her indulgence is generous enough to account for death and desire, for "all the things that drive men to desperation" (CZ, 141), without worrying about them herself. When Zeno reflects upon the nature of Augusta's "perfect health," he finds that its quietness is based upon the acceptance of the present as a tangible reality, a reality that, instead of employing jealousy and adultery as protests against the impossibility of perfect union, builds a shelter, a sanctuary of marriage (CZ, 141). The indicative world of Augusta's bourgeois well-being gladly accommodates the subjunctive vagaries of Zeno's guilts and anxieties. The modal mediocrity of her

time tenses checks, as firmly as the naturalistic indicative of
Angiolina's, the fancies of Zeno's consciousness, but because Zeno
accepts the need for this simple time and lives under its roof, we are
freed from the necessity of contrasting social classes. If the conditional of imagination is still in play around Ada, it is no longer the
mode of evasion but of exploration. The novel's space is opened by
the punctuation of spontaneous exclamation, improvisations in the
present indicative, to unpremeditated dialogue—all entertained in
bourgeois salons. And Svevo, liberated, can now sit in the audience,
confident that Zeno's voice alone can carry his spirit as well as its own
criticism. He embodies at last the positive attributes of what Svevo
saw as his own weaknesses and constructively applies his author's
favorite defenses and qualifications. Svevo realized that Zeno was the
more resilient reflector of his values because he was not under his
thumb:

> When I was left alone I sought to convince myself that I myself was
> Zeno. I walked like him, like him I smoked, and I pursued in my
> past all his adventures that could resemble mine, only because the
> reevocation of one's own adventure becomes quite easily a com-
> pletely new construction when it is successfully transposed to a dif-
> ferent atmosphere. The flavor and value of the remembrance, even
> its sadness, are not lost by this process.[52]

Svevo gives to Zeno a multidimensional present tense that draws
upon the past and imagines the future without the temptation of
escaping its bounds. He remains in the thick of it, always vulnerable
to "surprise, fright, and confusion" (FCZ, 17–18). The old Zeno
featured in the last stories feels relieved that with old age's trunca-
tion of the future, his breadth of hope, hence anxiety, has been
narrowed. But even he continues to live the common fate of man in a
mixed time. Man's "grammar also contains pure tenses," but "they
seem designed for the lower animals, who live joyously, when not
frightened, in a crystal-clear present" (FCZ, 17). Zeno is master of
all Svevo's tenses, while characters like his father and Augusta, not so
lucky as Mario Samigli's sparrows, still are closer to them on the
evolutionary scale rising toward complicated temporal patterns.
Doubtless the concentration upon this competition of tenses owes as
much to a contemporary European atmosphere of narrative experi-

52. To Eugenio Montale, 17 February 1926, OO, 1: 779.

mentation as to a familiarity with psychoanalysis, despite Svevo's assertion to Montale of his ignorance of modern literature.[53] But it is well to remember Debenedetti's insistence on the conservative nature of Svevo's structure and technique, a point seconded by Renato Barilli, who emphasizes the originality of Svevo's ethical, epistemological, and cultural vulnerability while refusing to his technical organization a progressive nature.[54] We remember Svevo's own suspicion of technical innovation:

> The great virtuosity of Joyce (I never liked it, and for good reason) was a great danger.[55]

In fact, the syntactical metaphor applied to life was one of Svevo's favorite devices for giving bourgeois respectability and order to the undependable rhythms and divisions of the poems of the unconscious. Zeno's reflections are assuredly not streams of consciousness, and are always controlled by the succession of analysis to anecdote. It is important to recognize Svevo's unwillingness to break the bonds of bourgeois scene and grammar. Even the inversions of chronological order, the equalization of events of disparate proportion, the imitation of psychoanalytic association, and the reversal of its direction can be seen as a conventional "progression" from symptom (in love and work) to understanding to acceptance, or, as a secular calendar of traditional religious rites—birth, marriage, death—as a contemporary Protestant ethic of business speculation or the Catholic confession. Svevo's vision, his humor, the richness of his atmosphere *depend* upon the recognition and acceptance of conventional restraints. For this reason, one is reluctant to place Svevo's narrative irregularities with the experiments of Joyce, Kafka, and Pirandello as Mario Lunetta does in this equation:

> The interior partitioning of the individual is the psychological equivalent of the imperialistic phase in the socio-economic sphere.[56]

Svevo and Kafka obviously suffer most from the pressures on their textures to assume a historical consciousness, for their approach to

53. Ibid.: "I was really ignorant of such literature when I wrote because after the neglect of *Senilità,* I refused myself even this reading."

54. Renato Barilli, *La linea Svevo-Pirandello* (Milan, 1972), p. 105. Giacomo Debenedetti deals with this evaluation in his sections on Svevo in *Il romanzo del novecento* (Milan, 1971) and we shall look at it more fully in part 2.

55. Svevo, "Scritti su Joyce," OO, 3: 729.

56. *Invito alla lettura,* p. 140.

the world is one of defensive, delicate humor. An illuminating and useful correspondence may emerge, as it has done so often in relation to the literature of the Habsburg empire. But, as always, imposing such implications upon Svevo's humor tends to coarsen his unique overtures to reality.

The large problems obsessively explored in the modern novel and associated with the modern world, the man without quality in a Godless universe, the relation between sickness and art, health and morality, the eruptions of the unconscious and the threatening attraction of the irrational, the absurdity of war, the evil of business as usual in a world of collapsing trust and values—all are reflected in the pages of *Confessions of Zeno,* tempting critics to comparisons with *Der Zauberberg, Der Mann ohne Eigenschaften, La Recherche du temps perdu.* Yet it is questionable whether the determination of such a place for Svevo's novel is authentic. For Mother Nature, as for the Greek gods watching battles, history appears as alternations rather than crises. We can certainly see the logic of referring to the development of Svevo's fiction as one that leads us from the fin de siècle crisis of naturalism and positivism, of the petty bourgeois, in *A Life,* through the intellectual and psychological crises of *As a Man Grows Older,* to the larger and more complex crisis of the powerful, mercantile, Triestine bourgeoisie in *Confessions of Zeno.*[57] But the experience of the novels revolts against such a design. Zeno's novel lives through historical pressures but does not organize and point them, for while it may register the hardness and absurdity of the mercantile world, the growing distance between man and nature, the restraints of marriage and the obstacles of social competition, the primary narrative momentum derives from the comic and desperate scrabbling of an unconventional consciousness for approval within a conventional morality. The ability to see around social institutions with an eye as whimsical as Mother Nature's (in "The Old Old Man," Zeno, hearing in a lovely pastoral scene the hammer on the anvil long after he sees it, reflects: "I am a child, but Mother Nature is very childish too, creating such contrasts between light and sound" [FCZ, 18]) gives Zeno neither the capacity nor the instinct to transcend society. At times one is persuaded that Zeno cherishes his desires and his improvisations because they *trap* him in the "given"

57. Forti, *Svevo,* p. 100.

bourgeois world, feeding his sense of density. If Svevo, in historical perspective, came to have a revolutionary position in Italian literature, if his books appear to reflect rather neatly the stages of the decline and decadence of the European bourgeoisie, its political paralysis and social superfluity, it is because, as old Zeno says of his own re-creating memory that selectively eliminates surprise, fright, and confusion (FCZ, 17–18), the individual case has been "translated into the past" (FCZ, 18).

In such a consideration, it does not seem an exaggeration to see in the play between internal and external orders in *Confessions of Zeno* a leap into polyphonic modernity. Not to be underrated in our sense of narrative liberation is the fact that at last we have a likable hero (though likability in the twentieth-century novel is bound to be a neurotic symptom) who, by his wit and self-irony, relieves us of the task of judgment unleavened by the comedy of grace. I cannot agree with readers who have complained that the job of evaluating Zeno's psychic authenticity is made even more difficult by this change. From the beginning of the novel, when Zeno mocks his own parody of medieval number magic by ordering the calendar around the cigarette habit and resolutions to stop it, until the end, when Zeno mocks his own lies of spite against diagnostic rigidity ("The sweet proof that I never had the disease is that I have not been cured of it" [CZ, 367]), he *contains* the mixed time of the Svevian vision:

> In order to make it seem a little less foolish I tried to give a philosophic content to the malady of "the last cigarette." You strike a noble attitude, and say: "Never again!" But what becomes of the attitude if you keep your word? You can only preserve it if you keep on renewing your resolution. And then Time, for me, is not that unimaginable thing that never stops. For me, but only for me, it comes again. (CZ, 11)

The times of conscience and consciousness, both implicit in the title *La coscienza di Zeno,* exist side by side from the first page to the last. As Poggioli remarks: "In a certain sense, one might say that the aim of Svevo's works is to express conscience in terms of consciousness, and consciousness in terms of conscience."[58] By the rhythm of remorse and resolution, guilt and confession, Zeno reforms each calendar by means of the other. The obsessive "senilità" is charted in

---

58. *The Spirit of the Letter,* p. 175.

two times. The dread of old age and death, which Zeno farcically trivializes ("At that time I was attacked by a slight illness from which I was never to recover. It was a mere trifle; the fear of growing old, and above all the fear of death" [CZ, 145]) is by the newly married Zeno attributed to jealousy of Augusta's health. To an older Zeno it will be associated with the diminishing of desire, which, by its dreams, startles bourgeois time. A fine consciousness in Zeno of the alternation of these times, those of the bourgeois and the dreamer, biological man and psychological man, subjects experience to a high degree of volatility, for if—unlike the fly, who assumes that lost health can be found again since he lives for only one season and has no time to learn by repetition (CZ, 296) —diseased man both learns from experience and is unable to profit by it, the deed loses its cast of necessity and becomes instead anecdote. Zeno learns from experience that there is no perfect health or innocence, but he is compelled in his comedy to seek them. Whatever debasement experience suffers by this circular race, it gains in value by serving as a premise for the acceptance of the round of life. We are as far as possible from a syllogistic universe. "Resolutions," says Zeno, "existed for their own sake, and had no practical results whatever" (CZ, 225). His adultery arouses in him new tenderness for his wife (CZ, 224). Copler dies in proper order, but his resurrection, an improvisation of Zeno, becomes a family joke. Cured of its finality, death serves Zeno as an agent of social harmony. The unpredictability of the relationship between unconscious and conscious time, cause and effect, which often leads to a disastrous paralysis and evasion, as in Alfonso and Emilio, in Zeno produces a rich, new, comic imperative—that of receiving life as original. In no way, as I have indicated earlier, does this mean that all is permitted. The difference between Zeno, Alfonso, and Emilio is that Alfonso and Emilio never really *lived* in bourgeois time. For them, dreams and the conditional mode are a means of survival. For Zeno, they are surprising, disturbing, and funny. Zeno is the first of Svevo's heroes who knows how to keep his hands off time. He twists and turns under its pressures, which he invites, but he always allows it to have the last word. This is why he scribbles his notebooks and dabbles in psychoanalysis. Zeno continually falls short of chronological mastery and, in this way, cooperates with the process of therapeutic association even when he thinks he is resisting it.

One might well assume that the compulsive nature of repetition of obsessive patterns like the inevitable Svevian reversal of strong and weak figures—the fathers cut down by sickness, death, and failure—would make a shambles of moral education. As Zeno is thinking of Carla in the presence of Augusta, Augusta supposes that he is ill because of Ada's marriage (CZ, 195). When he discovers this, he feels freed from guilt by dissociation. During the night, as he longs to hold Carla in his arms, he plots his confession to her of his love for Augusta (CZ, 188), which would be "part of her education" (CZ, 189), one that has come a long way from Angiolina's. His resolutions in the area of love resemble those which slyly motivate his smoking, and "Last Betrayal" replaces "Last Cigarette" (CZ, 186). The revolt against the father, doctors, and the wife become one. The desire for confession and for acquittal is aroused in the face of any figure of bourgeois authority.[59] Drawing on a comment of Freud in *Totem and Taboo* concerning the working of conscience, Gian-Paolo Biasin contends with good reason that Zeno's consciousness is moral when it "perceives a condemnation and projects it outward onto the others who become would-be and omnipresent judges—the objective correlatives of his sense of guilt."[60] Pushing off from the reproach of his father-in-law, based upon his suspicion that Zeno was trying to injure Guido in the eyes of Guido's own father, an angry Zeno feels sanctioned, like a child, to visit Carla "without thinking of Augusta," Giovanni's daughter (CZ, 178). After all, conscience had tricked him in the first place to take what was good for him. Zeno runs the gamut of all the A's, alphabetically convinced that he was "about to choose a wife from a far country" (CZ, 62), and indeed, in the seance, itself invoking fake spirits from a distant land ("I have no objection to anyone making attempts to spy on the world beyond the grave" [CZ, 106]), Zeno puts his arm around Augusta's waist, virtually sealing his choice but thinking it the body of Ada.

All this comedy of repetition, of psychic lapses,[61] seems to bind conventional time to that of psychological determination and to mock moral order. But in fact, the identifications, like Zeno's ap-

59. For an interesting discussion of how this desire masks a fear of death see Eduardo Saccone, *Commento a 'Zeno'* (Bologna, 1975), pp. 103–20.
60. Gian-Paolo Biasin, "Zeno's Last Bomb," p. 22.
61. See Anthony Wilden, "Death, Desire and Repetition in Svevo's Zeno," *Modern Language Notes* 84, no. 1 (January 1969): 98–119.

parently self-consuming analysis, often carelessly tagged as a product of fin de siècle decadence, take an entirely different direction. Zeno's desire to kill Guido the rival, hilariously motivated by the violin competition, ultimately becomes a desire to father him, even as that desire itself involves a kind of unconscious cooperation in his death. Compulsive patterns become, through the help of Mother Nature, unexpected modes of moral discovery. Zeno's criticism of Guido's violin playing turns out in the end to be more than jealousy, a rather convincing prediction of what is wrong with Guido's character. When Zeno the son feels concern about his dying father, a slap in the face reminds him of his desire for the father to die. If Zeno uses Augusta as a mother confessor, he also reveres her and loves her as a wife:

> Who could have foreseen it, that day I went limping from Ada to Alberta to arrive at last at Augusta? I discovered that far from being a blind beast driven by another's will, I was a very clever man. (CZ, 140)

If he thought of Ada only as a lover, Zeno befriends her in the end, a gesture that furnishes a reply in advance to her accusations. Mother Nature mixes identities and imaginings but, like the novelist, she plots social survival. Augusta herself says to Zeno: "One can never be bored if one is with you. Every day you become a different man" (CZ, 244). That is because, as a true child of Mother Nature, he can control neither his compulsions nor their social effects. Then too, as a careless student of Darwin, Mother Nature herself confounds the logic of bourgeois syllogisms while supporting their purpose. She ordains that "the mate you choose renews for better or for worse, her own race in your children," but she cannot, any more than psycho-analysis, lead us straight to the goal ("because when we get married it is not of children that we are thinking"). She "persuades us that our wife will bring about our own renewal—a curious illusion which the facts in no way support" (CZ, 55–56). She betrays our expectations; she frees man from moral and psychological claustrophobia but does not subvert bourgeois history. The entertainment of such external manipulation is the proof of Zeno's relinquishment of the willful control—a surrender that Dr. S. desires for him—a cause for both hope and cynicism.

It would appear that with a decadent age, Mother Nature at the helm and psychological determinism boring from within, the Svevian hero of consciousness could easily find cause, like Flaubert's Frédéric Moreau, for a circular sentimental education. The passing from one woman to another, in one's presence regretting the other's absence, by which a social climb is leveled, is turned to a different purpose by Zeno. There is no license in *Confessions of Zeno* for blaming the age, and no displacement of sentiment is allowed to give lasting relief. Life's originality, a highly unchronological phenomenon, establishes a new history and ignores the social determinism of the nineteenth-century novel, so long the most convincing picture of reality. We are amused by the intrusion at the beginning of the section "The Story of My Marriage," of the Napoleonic model that is such a staple of the nineteenth-century European novel:

> In the minds of middle-class young men life is associated with a career, and in early youth that career is usually Napoleon's. They do not of course necessarily dream of becoming Emperor, because it is possible to be like Napoleon while remaining far, far below him. Similarly, the most intense life is summarized in the most rudimentary of sounds, that of a sea-wave, which from the moment it is born until it expires is in a state of continual change. I too, like Napoleon and like the wave, could at any rate look forward to a recurring state of birth and dissolution.

The paragraph displays a mischievous dissolution of expected climax. In an earlier short story, "Il Malocchio," the provincial hero Vincenzo had also dreamed of Napoleon, but his frustrating indolence and mediocrity lead him to the realization of a fantasy, the evil eye that can injure enemies. The distance between Julien Sorel's dreams of Napoleon and his education in hypocrisy and the bathetic dreams of vengeance that are embodied in the magic organ of Vincenzo, tells us something about the anachronistic nature of the Napoleonic dream in the modern age. In *Confessions of Zeno* the dream seems even more arbitrarily a legacy from literature. Napoleon cannot stay on an objective and independent footing for even one paragraph. He is quickly absorbed into the rhythm of Zeno's unsystematic consciousness, and the new life, so early willed in the French provinces, takes a devious route through a new father (Giovanni) and a comedy of financial speculation to an "accidental" marriage. Napoleon and his history are humorously joined to the wave in a pseudo-universal rhythm of birth and dissolution. Even the seance, which in the drawing rooms of other modern novels and poems becomes a favorite sign of the emptiness and artificiality of bourgeois values, in *Confessions of Zeno* is undone as social criticism by serving as the ground for important rituals of bourgeois sanity, marriage, and business success.

The career, or any other goal sanctioned by bourgeois authority, even health, cannot be pursued without these crazy deviations into other worlds, not, certainly, by a son of Mother Nature. The old rehearsing for professions is abandoned for the privilege of latency, and law and chemistry are merely distractions. This amateurism could well have been attributed to the plight of the sensitive bourgeois son in Trieste, a city allowed as a Hapsburg outpost only a business college and accustomed to educating its sons in Germany and Florence. Svevo himself, we recall, had to find literature in a commercial school in Germany. Yet Augusta attributes Zeno's lack of success to personal qualities: "Your kindness of heart and simplicity seem to disqualify you for business" (CZ, 152). A bored Zeno tries religion under the pretense of getting closer to Augusta and her health. But health, as he had earlier noted, does not analyze itself (CZ, 146). Nothing could be farther from Augusta's religion than Zeno's conscious and scholarly approach:

> Augusta's religion did not take time to acquire or put into practice. You bowed your knee and returned to ordinary life again immediately! Religion for me was a very different thing. If I had only believed, nothing else in the world would have mattered to me. (CZ, 152)

Zeno is disinherited in all tradition's wills, disqualified from the present's business and from the future's reformers of government and society. But the "normal" man is not an enemy as he is to the underground man. Zeno cannot claim to be a heroically representative victim of distorted "normal" philosophies of life. The "sham activity" (CZ, 153) that bores Zeno might be extended to an indictment of all modern bourgeois activity, but Zeno is not allowed even the half-justification of the underground man, an appeal from personal sickness to the sickness of modern ideologies and expectations. Zeno's restless availability is turned in this novel to moral and spiritual advantage but not by an earnest and transcendent conversion.

Even his babbling, a legacy from the underground man, is refused the irritable martyrdom of Dostoevski's hero. Without a final grammar, the tongue is condemned to twist its way through the circumlocutions that hyperconsciousness designs. When Ada describes to the family, at the time of Zeno's courtship, her recent impressions of England, with "no idea of making [us] laugh or exciting our astonishment," Zeno envies her understated directness:

> I liked her simple way of talking all the more because I myself could not open my mouth without misrepresenting things or people, for otherwise I should have seen no use in talking at all. Talking seemed to me an event in itself which must not be hampered by any other events. (CZ, 68)

We recognize the dangerous dissociation of word from body so often cited as a major symptom of modern decadence, a disease most melodramatically embodied by the underground man. Yet, Svevo has already given to Zeno's habit of babble, as to his hyperconscious habit of analysis, an unexpected sociability that makes the reader aware more of the contrasts with such an inevitable juxtaposition than of comparisons. The literary language of the underground man, a symptom of cultural fragmentation, is gratefully used to save him from love; his one-sided debate with the "normal" man indicts the education of both the forties and the sixties, but it also can be employed to save him from brotherhood. Zeno's language has a life of its own, but its spontaneity of mode and matter establishes affection while it serves as defense. It is often a substitute for action, but it is never divorced from his social responsibilities. When Guido speaks Tuscan fluently (whereas Zeno is confined to his "inelegant dialect" [CZ, 98], a linguistic inferiority complex familiar to Svevo), the distinction of Guido in the Malfenti atmosphere is humorously accentuated. It is food for Zeno's envy but not for the censure that sanctions withdrawal. Later, we remember, Zeno will use the Tuscan tongue as a target for his defense against psychoanalysis. The doctor should not take the confessions too seriously for "he has no idea what writing in Italian means to us who talk dialect but cannot express ourselves in writing. A written confession is always mendacious. We lie with every word we speak in the Tuscan tongue" (CZ, 368). When he adds: "Naturally it would take on quite a different aspect if I told it in our own dialect," we hear the intimate echoes of Svevo's

own self-irony. The plea is conventional and unconvincing. The attitude toward that truth, one of conscious hyperbolic humor, is
original and persuasive. A long line of essayists from Montaigne to
Heine have accepted the inevitability of the lie in written confessions. Rousseau's hope that his could tell the truth in the language of
the heart could never be entertained by a self-ironist like Zeno. The
Tuscan tongue as an obstacle to truth is a ridiculous ascription of
cause. The humor becomes even more evident when Zeno defends
himself against his omission about Guido's property holdings by saying: "It is only another proof that no confession made by me in
Italian could ever be complete or sincere" (CZ, 377). The absurd
reasoning that follows this claim, replete with barbaric dialectical
names for various kinds of wood, is such a deliberate psychic romp,
though by no means a liberated one, that it is surprising how many
readers have insisted on the literal nature of Zeno's "rationalization."

The real concern is not, of course, the dialect, but the question of
how much distortion any literary self-consciousness inflicts upon a
spontaneous and impulsive sincerity. Sincerity itself is a social art in
the Svevian world, and the language of the heart must find its way to
ears that are willing to hear the spirit in the distracting noise of
letters. Not the least of Augusta's functions in the novel is her role as
Zeno's indulgent editor. The necessary announcement of the death
of Copler, Carla's original patron, carries with it implications of
Zeno's guilt in relation to his adultery and stimulates the need for
confession. In an exemplary scene already touched upon, Zeno comes
late to the wedding banquet for Guido and Ada—itself a situation
guaranteed to bring into play unresolved tensions in Zeno—and uses
literature and its impure grammar to achieve a more satisfying vision
of reality than the mere factual truth. Zeno is to serve as a model of
the good husband to the new couple, but he has in his mind the face
of Copler, his "pimp," whose expression in death seemed to dis-
approve of Zeno, the "malade imaginaire," or perhaps of Carla, who
would not learn her singing lessons well (CZ, 202). He also sees the
face of Carla pitying Augusta. To speak of Copler's death would
bring into the Malfenti house the taste of adultery, in Zeno's mouth
at least, and the social situation gives him a perfect excuse to say
instead that he is still alive. Why dampen the spirits of the occasion?
The naughty boy, sneaking food to avoid the reproaches of a father-
in-law constrained by prescribed abstemiousness, is at last "caught"

and becomes even naughtier. With a new guilt on his head, Zeno's desire for confession and absolution, furthered by the wine, is filtered through the remembrance of Copler's death. Here is news that might make his behavior understandable. When Guido reproaches him for "no longer caring whether you depress us or not" (CZ, 204), Zeno begins laughing and claims once again that Copler is alive. Temporarily indignant, the family gives him finally "the affection that I knew I did not deserve" (CZ, 205), accolades for marital fidelity. Now Zeno is to make a toast, and the psychological pyrotechnics that have killed and raised Copler from the dead, the guilt that has lowered his pride, and the wine loosen Zeno's tongue so that it seems to have that independent existence so often noted by Zeno before ("By dint of exercise my tongue was beginning to arrive at a certain degree of sincerity" [CZ, 128]). It tells, for the second time in the day, the story of his marriage and honeymoon, misrepresented for Carla once by omission of his love for Augusta and now by omission of his passion for Ada. The spirit of hyperbole pushes the tongue to claims of having made love to Augusta in all the museums of Italy:

> I was so up to my neck in lies that I even threw in that mendacious detail, though it served no purpose whatever. And yet they say, "In vino veritas." (CZ, 206)

Of course, it does serve the purpose of bringing together the passion and affection so often separated. When Augusta sets him straight by her own quip, Zeno, in mock protest, pretends: "She did not see that she thereby threw doubt on the whole story, and not only one detail of it!" (CZ, 206). With Augusta's final interruption, the laughing becomes contagious and Zeno has achieved his goal: "I laughed too, seeing how I had been instrumental in bringing about that state of noisy mirth which is *de rigeur* on such occasions" (CZ, 207). The lies and improvisations, so absurdly dressed that they elicit the laughter of absolution, are once again mediators between private guilt and public acceptance. In a marvelously apt image, in view of Copler's death, Augusta soothes Zeno's post-party guilts by saying that before he arrived the wedding banquet had seemed like a funeral (CZ, 211). The literary babble of the underground man attempts to convince him of his superiority to the normal man. The improvisations of Zeno, darting in all directions, depending on the irresponsible impulsions of guilt and desire toward affection, ultimately serve, whatever the origin, to relieve the lives of others as well as his own, a fine example of the psychic economy of wit.

The qualification of conventional modern formulas, such as "health is action, talking sickness," is yet another of Svevo's subversions of expectation. Zeno realizes that the difference between Guido and him is that "all the knowledge I had acquired was used by me for talking, and by him for action" (CZ, 250), but Guido's capacity to act leads to disaster, Zeno's tongue to consolation. So too, Augusta's active health is allowed to be bested when Zeno's lies have the power to change funerals into weddings. Of course, Zeno's babbling is a symptom of modern decadence; of course, it is a compensation for the lack of desired and necessary action. "Talkativeness was an absolute necessity to me," says Zeno (CZ, 134) as he is trying to persuade himself into an acceptance of Augusta as his wife. In a resolution reminiscent of Emilio's, Zeno convinces himself that he should undertake Augusta's moral education. The insanity of such an enterprise only reveals the necessity to talk *himself* into "gentleness, affection and, above all, fidelity" (CA, 134). When Zeno recognizes that the content of his sermons was unimportant in comparison to the act, we would readily agree. And when he claims that they had a good effect on his marriage, we would, surprisingly, agree too, for they helped to make Zeno marriageable. Augusta is the most generous of Zeno's readers, and she is touched, here and elsewhere, by Zeno's effort, ignoring or laughing away the absurdity of its content. That he shows his respect for the conventional expectations of marriage, however rhetorical his purpose, does prove that words are not necessarily the enemies of intention, even if they are often ignorant of them and mocked by action. Talking becomes the circuitous route to truth. For Zeno, rhetoric can become an agent of discovery. It is important to see the diseases of modern man in the bones of Zeno, but it is more important to see how persistently they are diverted from their anticipated ends. The compulsive uselessness of Zeno's resolutions to be better reveals his distance from the perfectly adjusted bourgeois health of Augusta, but it also leaves the moral world open to uncalculated infusions of goodness. One of the most delightful developments in the novel is that Zeno comes to be for the bourgeois Malfentis the model spouse. Mother Nature reroutes infidelities back to the marriage bed.

Because the novel depends more upon reaction than action, attitude than philosophy, spontaneous anecdote and analysis than plot,
some readers have felt that it suffers from an unearned "gravezza,"
teases us with its momentum of deep inquiry that really doesn't get
anywhere,[62] for no one is expected to believe, least of all Zeno himself, in his cure. Can we believe in the acceptance of his disease? Is
this enough for us? Giacomo Debenedetti is right to suggest that
Zeno never really learns from experience to experience to expect the
overturning of predictable order. He astutely notes:

> Indeed, the authentication of chaos at the end of each adventure is
> the only thing truly dependable in Zeno's story.[63]

There has been even more complaint about the narrative stasis of the
last works of Svevo than about this novel, and there is no doubt that
the hostility of the Svevian temperament to ethical and historical
climax is hard on our narrative expectations. Yet obviously, in this
novel, Zeno's vision, which we come to trust, reaches a kind of climax,
however vulnerable it may be to the continuing fluctuations of life.
While the bourgeois world suffers disease, death, and financial
failure, and loses its beauty, Zeno's world of mixed time seems to
grow less hysterically anecdotal, more lyrical and secure. The favorite
Svevian pattern of the weak and strong changing places on the scale
of evolution is apparent in the larger design of the novel itself, for in
the end it is Zeno who, reluctant to begin marriage as a bourgeois
patriarch, now wins, through humor, at the serious bourgeois games
of marriage and business. By contrast, Guido's failure is ascribed, in
"The Old Old Man," to "a fatal lack of humor" (FCZ, 34) .

The flippancy of Zeno's argument that he has been cured by business seems to us confusing, for Svevo has whimsically severed it from
his own authority. The collapse of the strong sends Zeno into action
to fill a vacuum in the struggle for survival and sanity. His speculation on Guido's behalf gave acceptable motivation to his action, even
if we had our reservations. The final speculation seems perilously
arbitrary and selfish, but Zeno is acting out the premise he discovers,
that life is original. To rise to a calculated principle of consistency
would be to overturn the reality principle of the book, which is both
cynical and generous. While Svevo sits out the war, Zeno acts out a

62. Eugenio Montale, "Presentazione di Italo Svevo," *Lettere,* p. 110.
63. Debenedetti, "Svevo and Schmitz," p. 74.

new version of his adulterous fantasies and joins the game of survival in a way that takes account of one of Svevo's deepest beliefs; that war, unlike the animal struggle for survival, destroys all sides, all that is fought for, and for generations to come.[64] Business is Zeno's toy gun that helps him make a killing without touching a body. The evil of war, writes Svevo, is not diminished by patriotism nor by heroism.[65] In a touching and typically contorted lament that reflects the spirit of Zeno neutralizing bad feelings, the novelist in a diary entry talks about how he has, over the years, lost many of his feelings of hostility. He laments:

> When the World War broke out, I was grieved over every defeat because I certainly had no need of a war to free me from hate.[66]

Somehow, though his profiteering must undergo moral criticism from the patriots, in *Further Confessions of Zeno,* the impulse of Zeno to play like an animal for survival instead of calculating like a man for destruction allows us to share his elation and get pleasure out of his rebuke to the analyst, without being taken in by it, but without the desire to judge.

IV. The Last Period: "The 60-year-old smiling public man"

The five pieces that make up the unfinished continuation of Zeno that Svevo was working on at the time of his death are laced with the same metaphors and the same spirit as Zeno. The change from anecdote to portrait, the loosening of the space between characters and between Zeno and the universe, and the relaxed, desultory pace of the narrative reflect a natural running down of Zeno's energy and desire in old age. Now that Zeno is the father of grown children, he

64. Svevo, "Sulla teoria della pace," OO, 3: 661.
65. Ibid.
66. Svevo, "Pagine di diario e sparse," OO, 3: 828. One might compare to this attitude the more lyrical and softer resignation of the young, but influential critic, Renato Serra, killed in the war, whose well-known "Esame di coscienza di un letterato," published in the *Voce,* 30 April 1915, became an emblematic meditation for the next generations, for it questioned the relation between art and war, like the French existentialist literature of the Second World War:
> La guerra non cambi niente. Non migliora, non redime, non cancella, per sè sola. Non fa miracoli. Non paga i debiti, non lava i peccatti.

Scritti di Renato Serra, ed. G. de Robertis e A. Grilli (Florence, 1968) , p. 398.

himself moves to a more static situation. His own father's hand, which gave rise to a drama of growing consciousness in *Confessions of Zeno,* has not disappeared, but it has lost some of its power as it is spread over a space in which Zeno takes his father's place. An older Zeno, more contemplative, more immune to surprise, converts his image of the higher part of the body observing and judging the lower (CZ, 194) to that of "half of humankind devoting itself to studying what the other half has written" (FCZ, 27). He is no longer a moving target, but one set up at tables to witness the disputes of others, dieting like the old Giovanni. His body has moved from center stage. Old age has robbed him of the role of leading actor (FCZ, 29); his body's twitches have become old companions past both cure and analysis. And the body's machine, which had been oiled part by part in Zeno, now becomes life itself:

> Later, during childhood, when we begin to examine the colossal machine which has been consigned us—life, railway tracks that end where they begin—we still find no relation between it and us, and we study life with objectivity and joy, interrupted by lightning flashes of terror. Adolescence is terrible, because it is then one gets the first inkling that the machine is designed to bite *us* and among all its cogs and teeth one hardly sees where to put one's feet. (FCZ, 77)

In old age the machine has become so familiar that its fierceness itself is merely an amusing habit. Now Zeno "entertains" a different fear:

> it frightens [me] when I think people might after all be better than I have always thought them, or life a more serious affair than it has always seemed to me. (FCZ, 78)

Zeno's irony is momentarily pierced, but it would be a mistake to take his perception itself too literally, for his irony has never been able to cancel his sympathies and make indifferent his hostilities. Once again, we must see that Zeno does not take this exception as a rule.

Zeno's meditation, stimulated by the company of his young grandson Umbertino, who is happily distracted by the machine, betrays the same rich and absurdly uncooperative relationship between the world we control and the world we do not that we met in *Confessions of Zeno.* Peace of mind is defined by the old Zeno as a "mixture of resignation and unquenchable curiosity" (FCZ, 77), a model of that bristly alliance which makes it almost impossible to detect where self-defense ends and the world as it is begins. The mind that lives among such large and wise metaphors must now walk beside another, that of his grandson, for that anxious, self-generated momentum of the young Zeno, no longer able to shake the old Zeno off his perch, is now divided between the head of Zeno, which thinks, and the bodies of others, who act. By far the most obsessive of the old metaphors that haunt the pages of the last Zeno is Svevo's comic and condensed adaptation of Darwinian heredity that treats psychological traits as if they were anatomical. The old Zeno is perpetually spying out signs of his legacy in the minds and bodies of others, peopling his wake with his neurotic leftovers. What could be more typical of Zeno the unbeliever than to be granted the undignified immortality of his habits? By means of Zeno's construction of the laws of inheritance, he comes back to center stage, even if other bodies must act for him, where his delightful social self-absorption can continue playing with the familiar irreconcilable forces of the universe. When his own body makes a last attempt to assume the position of protagonist, as it buys a last mistress, the affair ends in a wonderful scene of comic humiliation reminiscent of that between the Baron Hulot and Crevel in Balzac's *Cousin Bette*, in which two old men discover they are rivals in adultery and leave together; Zeno ekes out his last shred of biological dignity by noting the puffing of the fat Misceli as they tramp home, comparing symptoms. In a final effort to trick Mother Nature into thinking he is not finished, Zeno later climbs the steps for a visible demonstration of deliberated passion, and when he is put on the waiting list of those still to give a down payment, he groans a reproach, not confident enough to be a protest:

> Once again I said:
> "Ouf!" but not so loudly as to be heard by her. I said it to all the world, to society, to our institutions, and to Mother Nature—to everything that had permitted me to find myself on that staircase in that situation. (FCZ, 161)

We are amused to rediscover that persistent lack of persuasion, for Zeno as for us, of his half-hearted attempts to blame the world. Such general attributions of cause and effect are still, as in Zeno, punctured by the personal anecdote that stimulates it. When Zeno is forced to pay his mistress's "brother" for the last month (FCZ, 158), the most particular and personal humiliation gives way to this generalization:

> It is precisely the man of wide and long experience like myself who does not know how to behave: knowing as he does that a single word of his, a single deed, may lead to the most unforeseen consequences. One has only to read history to learn that causes and effects can stand in the most peculiar relations with each other. (FCZ, 159)

The absurd extension to such a contention is, as always, its own criticism. But the subject's humor prevents him from being flattened into a caricature of walking rationalizations.

His body must bow out and accept the tease of Carlo, Guido's son, that in old age fidelity is a biological necessity. Now, without a future, he is confined to the present, composed though it still be of various tenses. The time is shaped also by retirement from business (FCZ, 141) and the obsessive presence of medicine ("Unquestionably, a great part of my present is provided by medicine" [FCZ, 142]), where there used to be mock confessions and resolutions. The audience, however, no longer comes to see a leisured hypochondriac perform. So Zeno borrows from the lives of the young. The vagaries of Zeno's earlier sentimental education, a microcosmic reflection of the hoaxes of Mother Nature, now become the mysterious legacies and mutations between fathers and children. When Zeno, relieved at having a moment of peace with his daughter Antonietta, who has, after long and relentless mourning for her husband, forgotten to mourn him one evening, Zeno thanks her for a lovely time, whereupon Antonietta resumes her weeping, ashamed to have caught herself behaving as if Valentino were not dead. In a typical progression of sentiments, Zeno goes from annoyance to remorse, but now remorse is a trait as genetically solid and identifiable as the nose. It is detached for inheritance:

> And I recognized the possibility that a descendant of mine might be prone to total vows of self-dedication. I could see myself as Antonietta, more perverse and even less lovable. It was a minor nightmare. And was I also to blame for Alfio's painting? Now that, with the gramophone, I had so much improved my music I remembered that when I played the violin it had all been wrong notes and botched rhythms, not too much unlike Alfio's painting. I rolled about in bed, sick with remorse. (FCZ, 95)

By this means Zeno is guaranteed a present.

Many sections of the narrative are in fact set up as an introduction to a cast of characters. The perpetually mourning and over-virtuous Antonia is whimsically divided into psychiatric cells:

> her organism itself, I suspect, inherited cells with a tendency to exaggeration. I like to think that she inherited virtue from her mother, and exaggeration from me. . . . Although my own virtue has not been great, my desire for it has been excessive. It occurs to me I have just made an important discovery in the law of heredity, the accuracy of which may be verified by research. Antonia provides concrete evidence; from her mother she inherited a certain quality, and from her father the particular degree to which it manifested itself. (FCZ, 57) .

Though the energy of the younger Zeno's spontaneous first discoveries—that life is original, for example—has been somewhat diminished, Zeno still protests against those who claim he sees and hears less: "What I do see and hear always leads me to interesting discoveries" (FCZ, 73) . He still sneaks up upon disproportionate comparisons between sentiment and logic, the approach of the novel and that of science. Once Zeno has playfully paid his debt as a modern man to the laboratory of science, he can bring the Darwinian metaphor more comfortably into the realm of Mother Nature. Again poor Napoleon gets short historical shrift:

> Well, the evolution of flesh is a great mystery. Whenever I hear that history repeats itself, I can readily believe it; it does, but there is no telling where it will. There lies the surprise. A second Napoleon could be born in my house today without its startling me in the least. And everyone would claim that history had repeated itself, whereas actually there has been nothing to prepare its way. (FCZ, 61)

Like the strange and devious laws of marriage, analyzed by psychiatrists and sociologists, but ordained by an unpredictable Mother Nature, the laws of genetics are given over by Zeno to a universe that delights in the contradiction of purpose by desire. Augusta's untried intuitions read heredity from the heart and show up the comic artifice of Zeno's hyperbolic attempts to give intellectual respectability to sentiments. Once again Zeno allows Augusta's influence to subvert his organization, thereby keeping his theories sensitive to the novel's play:

> Smiling softly and affectionately, she confessed. I reminded her of Alfio. Both physically and morally. Women are never good at putting things precisely. She could not offer any proof to support her feelings. But she saw him, heard him and above all loved him, in the same terms as she did me. And not only that, but Antonietta also was like me—which she couldn't prove, either. "But there's something similar about the two of you, something I don't like, and don't like for the same reasons. But in you it gives me a feeling of pity, of not liking it for *your* sake, do you understand? Whereas in her it makes me a little cross." (FCZ, 102–3)

The mysteries of the human personality, so enjoyable and disturbing to Zeno's observation, now become, as so often in *Confessions of Zeno,* the gateway to the larger universe above resolutions to virtue and above the laboratories of biology, psychology, and politics. Zeno's anxious impulsion to order is eased by the scene in front of him:

> The sun had set a few minutes ago and it was bliss to rest one's eyes on the vast expanse of water, with its soft shimmer of tranquil tints which seemed of no kin to the dazzling colours they had replaced. I gave in to all this reposefulness, trying to forget the gentle woman beside me who had read my character better than myself (and, I hope, better than she herself realised) . (FCZ, 103)

Zeno's neat theory of the divided legacy in Antonia's personality is bested by a less studied vision, stimulated by Augusta's intuition:

> For a moment I had a vision of human characteristics being handed down from one to another, completely altered in content but still so patently alike in their form that even Augusta, in a flash of intuition based on no reasoning, was able to recognise them. (FCZ, 103)

We notice again the patronization of Augusta's health by hyperconsciousness, but Zeno's final abandoning of theory derives from the nature of Augusta's perception:

> But then I inwardly rebelled: what good was the law of heredity if anything could give rise to anything? Better not to know anything about it if one had to accept that Carlo could be descended from

that ass Guido and those little pests Antonietta and Alfio from me.
(FCZ, 103)

This is the comic correction of the absurdly literal acceptance of the laws of naturalism that is punished in one of Svevo's lesser stories, "La buonissima madre." The underground man's diatribes against the Enlightment's laws of nature and modern sociology's attempt to read man scientifically are a heavier, more acerbic, and much more ordered indictment of the spirit that plays human nature like a piano key, but Zeno's spontaneous and partial protest, as usual made intimate by direct reference to specific personalities, appears to belong to the same family. As I have remarked, the underground man cannot afford to recognize individual faces for fear that they might diminish the pure abstraction of his attack. Zeno, on the other hand, always exposes himself to this risk and, in fact, wants to be overrun by the anarchy of human nature.

But what are we to think of his cynicism about Alfio's Marxism, his deliberate and amusing peopling of Alfio's abstract paintings with the characters of social protest? Where is one constant in all Zeno's complaints about Alfio, in all his gibes? It is his impatience—impatience over the careless adoption of abstract and ideological organizations of life, which are, for all their differences of direction (principally theories of social justice and the cults of personality) like the abstractions both despised and illustrated by the underground man, identical in their unreality. It is not so much party itself that irritates Zeno. A passionate commitment to a system or to anything else that demands the sacrifice of personal indulgence would doubtless intimidate him and stir the dilettante's envy. To accept the advantages and disadvantages of intellectual dilettantism is one thing (and that is Zeno's fate and privilege), but to try to ennoble personality with the trappings of organized belief is to Zeno a pompous evasion. Of Alfio he writes:

Just after the war he was angry with us in the name of Communism. He was, in fact, not Communist in the least, but he really felt we were wicked for taking up so much room in the world. . . . But in all the world he didn't know a single worker. He walked the streets alone—concerned, just then, about social justice, and later, still just as alone, with art and personality. (FCZ, 37)

Such a claim rejects those qualifying and distinguishing adjectives so dear to the analyst of character:

> This business of being a personality seemed to me carrying things too far: it was presumptuous of him. One could aim at having a lovable personality or an attractive one. But personality in itself—! Sometimes "real" personalities ended up with life sentences. (FCZ, 37)

When Olivi fils asserts a superiority of action over Zeno: "No one in your family was being shot at. *I* was in the trenches" (FCZ, 116), the patriot becomes an unlovable personality. Zeno gets his vengeance by placing him in that category of Bolshevik capitalist:

> But despite his Bolshevism, when it came to business he was exactly as his father had been—shrewd, alert, and hard. The staff had been spoiled by me, who was not a Bolshevik. He straightened everything out. He saw to it that they kept to a rigid schedule, and whenever he could he cut their pay. (FCZ, 116)

There is in Zeno admiration and envy for the man who works in one time alone, but that man's subsequent humorlessness almost condemns him to be a caricature of the active man. The impossibly uneven contest between a flexible Zeno and the efficient and hard Olivi fils puts into perspective Zeno's wartime business success. Olivi's moral righteousness, which casts suspicion on such tainted profit, is just the weapon needed against the man who lives by affective instinct rather than principles. The apparent lack of historical seriousness on Zeno's part makes him susceptible to the claims of both Alfio and Olivi fils that the war has made him an anachronism. Yet they are bound by their historical pride to a generation that, in its heroism, cannot see the faceless horror of all war, registered so cunningly by Zeno's business. Zeno can imagine in his larger moments an earth free of the parasites of personality. But he can live only by an intense absorption in the relationship between his personality and that of others. Historical determinism gives way time and again to the mysteries of the heart, comically played out on a Svevian field of survival of the fittest.

The portrait of Cima, treated in an earlier sketch, returns us to the deceptive nature of this contest, in which the half-completed specimen, Zeno, ultimately comes out ahead. What has given Zeno the advantage now, as with Guido, is the very quality that proved such a disadvantage earlier, susceptibility to the wills of others and to "some imperious will preparing the way for the future" (FCZ, 109). The universe itself now becomes a continuation of man's body, and the reflections between the biological mircrocosm and the planetary macrocosm that soothed Zeno's anxieties without offering false releases from moral responsibilities have by now become habitual. The distraction of the will is not an ideal Schopenhauerian state of knowledge, but it is, at this point in life, without the advantages and vanities of appearance, a state superior to the caricatured, masculine, monolithic will of the Cimas. Thus, if there is no metaphysical solution, there is at least metaphorical extension. Viewing in a semi-biological, semi-mystical way, the way of metaphor, the predestined nature of disease in our organs (strikingly illustrated by Valentino's precocious senility and death), Zeno ponders the irregular disposition of evolutionary health by humorously domesticating the godless sky:

> I am too ignorant to know whether in the heavens, as down here on earth, there exists the possibility of death and reproduction. All I know is that some stars, and even some planets, have less complete movements than others. It must be that a planet which does not rotate on itself is either lame, blind or hunchbacked. (FCZ, 145)

And now it is the heaven's turn to lend itself to the body:

> But among our organs there is one that is the centre, a kind of sun in a solar system. Up until a few years ago this organ was thought to be the heart. At the moment everybody knows that our entire life turns on the sexual organs. (FCZ, 145)

This is a fine example of the way in which Zeno's humor, again and again, breaks up the deterministic nature of scientific observation, giving to secular modern man an atmosphere in which the playful imagination can stretch itself. The Freudian emphasis on sexual motivation, and Darwinian genetics give rise to fancies that let the man with visas of self-irony out of his bourgeois biological and psychological borders for saving strolls. It is this power that now, in old age especially, makes Zeno feel superior to the Guidos and Cimas. The biologically incomplete sketch is early a butt of humor, and later a creator of it. Death itself is drawn into the game of life, since Mother Nature herself, who orders it for life's sake, has a magnificent flair for the survival of the species:

> One must accept the fact, Mother Nature is a maniac. That is to say, she has the reproduction mania. She maintains life within an organism so long as there is hope of its reproducing itself. Then she kills it off, and she does so in the most diverse ways because of her other mania, that for remaining mysterious. (FCZ, 146)

By this vision, by his own honoring of the mystery of personality, Zeno learns to speak the same language as the universe. What an advantage for cosmic diplomacy! Zeno can enjoy "hoodwinking" Mother Nature by taking a mistress. Of course, such a counterpoison, as always, is tricky: "Another person is a complex medicine, containing a substantial proportion of poison" (FCZ, 146), and Felicita could be fatal: "It was impossible to take her in doses" (FCZ, 157). But Zeno is kept moving on the publicized line between poisons and counterpoisons. The satisfaction of the needs of the moment, a present without dimension, is the time in which the servants Renata and Fortunato live. When Zeno imagines that Renata too ponders the laws of heredity in selecting a father for her children, the wry Carlo refuses this expansive meditation as too large for those who are busy acting in the center stage of life (FCZ, 109). Zeno typically adjusts his view to this correction:

> Perhaps Carlo was right; but then again, perhaps I was too. What are the needs of the moment? Aren't they perhaps dictated by some imperious will preparing the way for the future?

In one stroke Zeno has his revenge on the youth of Renata by circling her with a vision out of her control. When Dr. Raulli gives Zeno the comic image of an "old man's body that stays on its feet because it does not know in which direction to collapse" (FCZ, 156), Zeno sets to work on it, turning it into a theory of biological economy and, at last, a comforting justification for Providence's interception in his last affair by means of its ambassador Misceli. The organs have by this time grown into a mighty metaphor, and Beethoven's Ninth Symphony, in which Zeno seeks peace, now is invaded by collaborating and quarreling parts of his anatomy. The customary impression of harmony "between the most divergent forces" (FCZ, 156) is broken by the rebellion of voice, "the least rational of all sounds in nature," against the instrument. The voice, like Zeno's other organs, slips from equilibrium. The world of Zeno and his

novelist is not one of permanent harmonies. The organs regularly
rebel to assert their freedom of anxiety.

But this rebellious voice, the voice of sincerity, cannot be easily
tolerated around the table. It desires confession, but quickly fades
into provincial harmonies of cooperation. The tension between the
need for confession and the necessity for improvisation, so rich a
contest in *Confessions of Zeno,* now seems eased in old age. Augusta
thinks Zeno's disease is cured because resolutions no longer inhibit or
torture the chronic smoker:

> That is what *they* thought! Still it was true I had to teach my
> disease not to reveal itself except in soliloquies, immediately for-
> gotten, and in resolutions neither written down nor spoken, nor
> indicated in any way on the calendar or the face of my watch—all of
> which left me in a rather pleasant state of freedom. There's no
> doubt, living so long cures all diseases! (FCZ, 52–53)

Private confession in scribbling is to be a tonic, hygienic, like Felicita. But like her, like Zeno's unfortunate confession of infidelity to
Carlo, it too has its poisons. Zeno alludes to his former attempt at
confession, which prepared him for psychoanalysis, a treatment that,
he notes, failed, though the pages remain. They have the advantage
over life being lived, of protection from confusion: "Time is crystal-
lized in them and can always be located if one knows how to open at
the right page" (FDZ, 16). No more than the harmony of Beethoven's Ninth as a synecdoche of a desired universe can this journal
solve competition between the time of life being lived and that of
life already lived. The increased seriousness of life that the journal's
organization and simplification effect will be broken again and again
by the search for hygienes to cure the wisdom gained from experience. "This indolence of Mine" ends on a note that mocks the power
of art to harmonize and transport. The unread novelist and the
pseudo-industrialist, that centaur Svevo, will never allow, either in
his life or in his business, any activity to close the gap inhabited by
irony. What began as a crippling fate, the lack of real success in
either field, became in time accepted as health. With the double
success that came to him in the end, Svevo joyfully complains in his
letters that he is once again plunged into the anxieties of ambition
and suffering a return to infantilism. Even this cannot be believed in

as a final conversion of fate, but as a new and lucky stroke of Mother Nature, like the money returned at the end of "The Hoax" on a nonexistent contract on a book.

The old Zeno, looking at a young girl on the tram, still plays at deceiving Mother Nature as he thinks: "It's clearly not time for me to die yet; for if this girl wanted me to, I would still be ready to procreate" (FCZ, 163). Her companion whispers "Old lecher" to him, and Zeno, warding off the death that Mother Nature, who might have heard, sends to those who do not reproduce, replies: "Old fool!" (FCZ, 164). With such a sally is art's hygienic power mocked.

———•—•———

In the two late novellas, "The Nice Old Man and the Pretty Girl" and "The Hoax," Svevo sacrifices the advantage of a full and sympathetic center of consciousness to concentrate upon the comedy of man's persistent belief in the possibilities of controlling desire within a closed order of art, of purifying it of time. While Svevo never allowed either art or business to carry the field, or to reach such a state of independent power that it could transform the accidental nature of reality by its pseudo-order, in the foreshortened atmosphere of the novellas the writer's art suffers a particularly restricting debasement. The novella "The Nice Old Man and the Pretty Girl," in which Svevo at a distance compares his central character to the old man of classical comedy (NOM, 76), satirizes the assumption that theory, stripping life of its distracting details, yields a higher truth than experience. As the "nice" old man, who, like Zeno, had tried to hoodwink Mother Nature by a last affair, moves closer to death, he purifies himself from thoughts of the pretty girl's flesh by rising to protective and exonerating theory:

> Theory was born in the old man's mind—pure Theory, from which both the girl and himself were eliminated. (NOM, 116)

His new and studied sincerity transforms him into "something quite different from all the others" (NOM, 116). No longer writing for the mere daughter of the people, he writes for the world at large, his treatise on the relation between the old and the young. The old man, almost smothered by Svevo's irony, cleanses experience and stops it from breaking down in time by morally ordering it into a plea for "life":

> It is essential to ensure that the old man should not desire the pretty girl on the footboard of the tram, without also listening to the appeal for help addressed to him by her. Otherwise life, now passionate and corrupt, would become pure, but cold as ice. (NOM, 118)

In a fit of high moral sentimentality, the loved object becomes a daughter. Against this rhetoric of self-righteous sublimation, Svevo flings the harsh words of the jealous nurse: "So you are still thinking of that woman?" (NOM, 119) and by one sharp injection deflates the abstract by the particular:

> Clearly any theory must die strangled if you begin by calling the girl who was its true mother "that woman." (NOM, 119)

The doctor, as well, humiliates the cure by borrowing the Svevian conviction that both youth and age are diseases, though the old one is closer to death. But the best critic of theories of life is the development of the theory itself, which spends itself in volumes of destruction before reconstruction and fights a losing battle against the complications of experience. Coming into the story with flat-footed confidence, Svevo gives us a short and delightful fable:

> Theorists appear preaching the destruction of a particular animal, cats, for instance. They write and write and do not at first notice that round their theory, as a necessary corollary, rats spring up wholesale. It is a long time before the theorist stumbles against this difficulty and asks in despair: "What am I going to do with these rats?" (NOM, 123)

Doubts and contradictions begin to tax the old man. On the sheets laid aside, rather than destroyed, they fester into this boil: "With whom must morality begin?" (NOM, 126). Senility has, by this time, become a state rather than an age. The theory, as a substitute for love, a ticket to health, kills him. The answer to the question: "What should the old expect from the young?" is "Nothing," and Svevo maliciously plants the pen in the dead man's mouth. The narcissism of the old man's virtuous art could not have been more effectively symbolized.

The treatise that makes of morality a compensation for the absence of experience, a harsh comic form of compensation forcefully cut off from all social activity, debases art into medicine, a process familiar to Mario Samigli's brother in "The Hoax." Art becomes a hygienic exorcism without the saving self-irony of Zeno's confessions that lie in the Tuscan tongue. Svevo's persistent anti-literary professions, his reluctance to read poetry, his insistence on keeping literary activity no more than equivalent to industrial or domestic activity by reducing its powers of transformation to daydreams and scribblings, have, as I have suggested, important resonances for Italian cultural history. But it is, first of all, the way in which Svevo could simultaneously come to terms with his disappointment and continue to write. In a charming letter to his young daughter Letizia,[67] he speaks of his antipathy to poets and presents a fable of two carpenters. One silently made beautiful wardrobes, but the other, more ambitious, started to describe wardrobes, for which he got money and attention. The literary carpenter began to ornament his descriptions with metaphors that took him farther and farther away from the natural colors and textures of the wood. He personified them, claiming actually to know live wardrobes. When a rich man expresses his desire to own such a wardrobe, the literary carpenter says: "Go and see my next-door neighbour; he *makes* wardrobes, I only describe them." The real carpenter replies to the rich man's request: "I don't know how to make living things . . . and if I did, I wouldn't be making wardrobes." This fable about the oldest of aesthetic tensions, between makers and describers, is the manner in which Svevo, a literary carpenter, kept his own literary pretensions from assuming the self-importance he might have fantasized for them in private. The direction of the fable, like that of Zeno's wit, goes through self-irony from self-justification to social acceptance. Quite the opposite is true of the moral treatise of the old man and the fables of Mario Samigli.

The more thorough the old man's isolation from the life of the street, from the war thundering in the hillsides ("Why haven't they yet found a way of killing each other without making so much noise about it?" [NOM, 91]) , which had given financial profits to him, as to Zeno, the more sentimental becomes his remorse: "And I am trying to seduce a girl of the people, who are suffering and bleeding there,"

67. Dated 10 April 1908, OO, 1: 473–74.

whereas Zeno's comedy of self-pity, always played to others, clings to a tough realism. Like a hypochondriac's symptoms, the old man's solipsistic sense of virtue and sin meets no resistance except in dreams that quickly become literature. A scene in the street of a child helping a drunken man and in turn abused for it, fills the old man with pity. Taken in by his new social generosity, which of course does nothing for the boy, he comes to associate this picture with others that show the girl as a victim of his seduction, justifying the high purpose of philanthropic patronage that cures one of perilously sensual relationships. The girl, like Angiolina, forever a girl of the people, has something simple, ingenuous, and fresh about her (NOM, 107), but the old man's abstract ascent to virtue, which makes him imagine himself as an objective observer of life, freed from the compromises of circumstance, blinds him to this nature. Thus, we have the favorite Svevian scene of the ridiculous lack of coordination between the needs of the girl of the people for sale and the patron's arrogant plans for education to bring her up to his class (perhaps some self-irony, on Svevo's part, directed against his own attempts to get Livia to read the books he recommended). What good is virtue if it does not patronize?

The dryness of the story's execution, the economy of emotion, the undisguised intrusions of Svevo, the namelessness of the characters all give the novella the aspect of a fable. The depersonalizing of the dreams that "occur at night and are completed by day" creates an atmosphere less parasitic on Svevo's sympathies. It is almost as if Svevo, in his last stories, with their homogeneous climate of impersonality, releases himself on holiday from the heavy authorial obligations of sharing his hero's heart by making public his own consciousness. In this story, and even more in "A Hoax," Svevo gives to his anxieties a burlesque form,[68] now past the need for self-discovery and exploration. Rather, we have the composure of summation, the flat economy of self-irony as free as a public joke.

In his impish reversal of evolutionary hierarchy, Svevo likes to imagine that while man is busy fashioning fables that envy the pas-

---

68. The story was inspired by what Svevo saw as his own childish anxiety over the delayed French translation of *La coscienza di Zeno*.

toral simplicity of animal existence based upon scent, animals are doing much the same thing:

> Who knows whether our life doesn't seem to the sparrows simple enough to be expressed in a fable? (H, 68)

Svevo tries out these whimsical inversions in an incomplete sketch, "Argo and His Master," in which he wryly contends: "Men are much simpler animals than dogs, because they smell more than dogs, and do so more readily" (A, 182). The master, in typical Svevian fashion, is again educating an inferior who winds up instructing him. The master learns Argo's language and translates it for us from the dog's monologues. Argo is given the role of the natural characters, like Angiolina, or even Augusta, who innocently expose the pretensions of overconscious man. (We have to believe that Argo dies of neurasthenia from having talked to his master.) Philosophic sincerity, which every hero of Svevo has courted, is achieved by Argo, for though he knows many natural categories of smell and sensation, he can theorize only three divisions. That is the limit of his arithmetic (A, 168). The refusal to ignore details simply because they cannot be generalized is the source of the master's admiration for Argo's sincerity. The search for the final grammar never ends. For those who know both that time does not exist and that "the containers that hold it do, and that they are virtually watertight" (FCZ, 10), the grammar of the fable is a temporal oasis. The scene of Svevo's drawn-out sketch of the clash of grammars is a miniature Magic Mountain to which the doctor has banished Argo's master, but what proved so rich a vantage for Mann from which to survey man's mixed tenses is not an atmosphere really suited to the modest scenes of Svevo's irony. He is more comfortable with the domestic fables of Mario Samigli (Svevo's first pen name), the protagonist of "The Hoax," fables that have more psychological than philosophical resonance.

From the beginning, Svevo clearly indicates that Mario's fables are not better, but reduced forms of literary life, channels for social disappointment when social hope has faded. His one novel took its inspiration from his young "admiration for people who were his superiors in rank and fortune, and whom he could only observe through a telescope" (H, 12). But now: "when it came to fashioning more of those shadowy beings, and making them live by sheer force of language, he felt a genuine repugnance" (H, 12). The discovery of a novel in his own humble life is not given to this sixty-year-old dreamer and so, excluded from what he imagines to be real life, he gives up real people to devote himself to animal fables:

> Tiny, rigid mummies—you could not even call them corpses, so quite without odour were they—the crevices of time began to swarm with them. (H, 12)

But for Mario, the fables, like Emilio's synthetic dreams, achieve a pure time, a "step towards perfection," a securely sealed container. Svevo himself, of course, was an inveterate fable maker, especially during his "silent" years, and he recognized the genre as the supreme and defensive form of the dilettante who could not stay too long with any idea. Yet Svevo chastises this desire for escapist purity by surrounding his fables with the texture of a fiction responsible to a larger life. Thus, Zeno's fables are swept into mixed time and must make their way in an atmosphere that questions their motivation. Mario's fable-making is an example of Svevo's tendency to expose the negative side of one of his own habits while giving us a larger world by which to transform them into gifts. Zeno's improvisations are forced to do social duty, and the access between public and private world is thereby assured. In "The Hoax" Svevo desocializes the fable's wit. Mario's fables represent literary atrophy because, in the Svevian equation, they protect from life that forces you to go where you might want to: "You can get anywhere you like with a fable, if you know where you want to go" (H, 37) . While Svevo uses the war to write *Confessions of Zeno,* Mario imagines that the war has made him a genuine threat, a literary conscience, and writes fables "of doubtful application," just pointed enough to pose as criticism of Austria, yet conventional enough to be ignored. Like the nice old man whose inauthentic voice of social protest is lost before it gets to the street, Mario's fables reach no ears. In an amusing parody of the standard advice to apprentices of literary careers, Svevo makes Mario think he writes about what he knows by having him go about "accompanied by fables, as a coat is furnished with pockets" (H, 14) . Exotic creatures yield their place to familiar sparrows, which could actually be seen starving in wartime Trieste. Like the old man's treatise, the fables compensate for loss of life. They are to Mario "nature's gladdest expression," incapable of prolonged anticipations of fear (H, 15) .

Though Mario may write of nature's gladdest expression, his is not
the gaiety of the drunken singer, devoid of malice and ambition:

> How came he to read such malice, such ingratitude, into the most
> joyous expression of Nature?

Svevo asks this in mock naïveté, fully aware of the process of projection. If the language of Mario's birds is spiteful, ungrateful, mali-
cious, what must human language be (H, 16)? Released by the
limitation of Mario's consciousness and situation to a climax of
willed fable rather than spontaneous improvisation, and by a public
atmosphere that prepares us for the independent life of the hoax,
Svevo enters the story undisguised and unshackled by the conditions
that bound him in the first two novels with younger versions of the
evasive hero and by the love that attached him to Zeno. Mario's self-
doubts, exorcised by fables, are not, as in Zeno, interesting in themselves, but are crucial for his gullibility:

> Perhaps Mario thought his own failure would be less hard to bear if
> he could come to regard this too as the result of circumstances out-
> side his own control. We laugh at the fable of the heedless bird
> which has completely forgotten the ruin that so lately threatened it,
> merely because it happens to have escaped itself. But when we recall
> the impassive face of Nature while she makes her experiments, our
> laughter is turned to gall. (H, 16)

Mother Nature is intimate with Zeno, for he himself is made in her
image, but when Svevo introduces her into Mario's atmosphere, he
keeps her so spaced that she can coauthor the hoax and its aftermath.
Mario's comedy depends on his practiced antisocial channeling of
desires and angers into private poems of vengeance. Only by courting
Mother Nature or the Malfenti sisters might he have tamed the hoax
by anticipatory self-irony. For such a hero, literature can be only a
consolation, not discovery:

> He often wrote fables on the disillusion which follows every human
> activity. It was as if he sought to console himself for the poverty of
> his own life by saying: "I am all right. I cannot fail, because I at-
> tempt nothing." (H, 16)

Halfway between the dreams that reveal but cannot be controlled
and wit that is necessarily social, the fable safely exorcises frustration

in solitude. Even the war, which so bothered the old man, becomes innocuous as the stage of deprivation for the life of the sparrows.

The Trieste that instigates the hoax is, on the contrary, a commercial, multiracial and public atmosphere that hosts versions of Svevo's own literary disappointments, allowing them to be simultaneously mocked and comically avenged. If Mario and his invalid brother, Giulio, his rival in frightened retreat from public life, suffer less hardship than others in wartime Trieste, it is because Mario has an admirer in a Slav countryman who brings the brothers fruit, eggs, and poultry. Svevo cannot resist noting: "And this unique success of his shows that an Italian writer is more likely to be admired abroad than at home" (II, 20), a recognition based upon absurd statistics and giving him comic relief, like the story "The Mother," from his own neglect by Italian critics. The constant reminders of a city indifferent to literary dreams have led some readers to place the story in the line of bitter polemics on the petty-bourgeois hostility to art:

> The sparrow fables offer a bitter indictment of the struggle for success in a bourgeois world which shows neither pity nor respect for the artist.[69]

While the fluke of real financial success from a mere fantasy of literary acceptance can be read as an ironic commentary on a commercial age insensitive to its artists, to such a major modern literary motif, this protest is, as we might expect, considerably tempered by the counterthrust of Mario's evasive dreams. The movement of psychological and artistic cowardice once again prevents the reader from putting too much stress on the contemporary cultural situation which, after all, comes to seem a given to be handled by various defenses, not the least of which is humor. The Svevo who was amused at Joyce's startled recognition of wickedness in his unsuccessful financial ventures comments with tongue in cheek:

> your surprise at being cheated proves that you are a pure literary man. To be cheated proves not yet enough. But to be cheated and to reveal a great surprise over that and not to consider it as a matter of course is really literary.[70]

69. Robison, "Una burla riuscita': Irony as Hoax in Svevo," *Modern Fiction Studies,* Svevo issue, p. 74.
70. Letter of 15 June 1910 in English, OO, 1: 539.

His childlike sense of joy at his late successes and his concern over the
French translation of *Confessions of Zeno* and the reissuing and revising of *As a Man Grows Older* betray a temperament incapable of
lashing out in bitterness and invective. Mario says in "The Hoax":
"I'm not so young as I was . . . and I should like to see my novel
translated before I die" (H, 41), and Svevo's letters of 1926 indicate
concern that he might not live to see it all. In these letters Svevo
complains more about his impatience and his incipient paranoia
than about publishers in a bourgeois age. By casting suspicion upon
the nature of Mario's dreams and fables, by having the promised
success disturb the literary habits of the brothers to such an extent
that a rift is inevitable in a relationship based upon the set cooperation of fantasies and illness, Svevo re-creates his own trauma. In a
remark typical of Svevo's own comments in his letters during the last
years, Mario's creator reminds us: "And although he now believed
himself certain of success, poor Mario discovered, by sad experience,
that it is a mistake to occupy oneself with literature after sixty, because it may be very damaging to the health" (H, 48). As for the
relation between art and disease, so obsessive a theme in Mann's
novels and those of his contemporaries, Svevo deflates by this kind of
comment the sinister and thrilling possibilities of the identification.
When Mario's brother needs literature to sleep, Mario, in a fit of
pique against the brother's complaints about the reading of Mario's
editorial corrections of his own novel, pretends to the cliché of artistic purity:

> One's individual life is not so important as to warrant turning all
> the noblest things on earth into drugs for it. (H, 52)

And Svevo adds: "The insult to letters had been met by a counter-
attack on disease."

Mario's victimization by a crass age is undercut not only by Svevo's
emphasis upon the psychological causes for Mario's gullibility, almost a justification for his punishment (except that his dreams hurt
no one), but by the fact that Gaia, his torturer, has that gaiety and
energy of improvisation, though without conscience and persever-
ance, which is missing in Mario's make-up. Thus, victim and victim-
izer must share the artist's soul, leaving neither enough for a whole
one. The fable and the practical joke are competing brothers at
heart:

Perhaps this love of practical joking was a relic of his suppressed artistic tendencies. For the practical joker is really an artist, a kind of caricaturist whose task is all the harder in that he has to invent and lie in such a way as to induce his victim to make a caricature of himself. (H, 27)

The antagonism between the private and public frustrations is superficially motivated by the war, but Svevo is careful as always to keep the war from being the genuine cause of *any* personal failure or success. Instead, as he does so often, he displays a casual flippancy in his treatment of public events that, by comic disproportion, tells us that apocalypses of catastrophe are no match for the psychic defenses and delusions, jealousies and desires of the human heart. In a gibe against the patriotic rhetoric so prominent in irredentist Trieste and so foreign to Svevo's nature, Svevo makes heroic speech the incentive for the hoax. A drunken Gaia works himself up into a rage against the pretensions of Mario, who would like to write of "Trieste's liberation with a pen of gold on an illuminated parchment." Inspiration is born of the desire for vengeance:

And so Gaia discovered that a practical joke, like all other forms of art, can be improvised. (H, 31)

The invention of the great character, the representative of the Viennese publisher, Westermann, comes into being and is finally embodied by a collaborator. The possibility of a German translation of Mario's old novel, amusingly called *Youth,* is metaphorically linked to the house of prostitution where the representative would likely be and where "the puritan Mario would probably not consent to follow" (H, 33). The battle between innocence and experience has now assumed farcical lines. Mario pays "the penalty of chastity" (H, 43) as Gaia, trying to cover up the collaborator's laughter, pretends that a brothel "pass" had been mistaken for the check. The fables at least had the purity of a private lyric exorcism immune to the bitch goddess of success. With the idea of success, the fables die (H, 56), and in their place comes the revising of the old novel, a "golden cage." The enslavement, this prostitution by gullibility, is finally purged, after the hoax is discovered, by a fable about a humble songbird in a cage. The monk's lot of ministering to the sick brother and the private fables are blessed by the only success *not* desired, financial. Only in such arbitrary ways does Mother Nature tell us about the strange relations between the world of the dreamer and that of the industrialist, not by angry polemics and indictments. After the discovery of the ruse, in despair at losing his "reason for living" (H, 61) , so superior to living itself, Mario manages to revive the chaste healing fables:

> They arrived in all innocence as if the Westermann affair was no business of theirs, and they found the ready welcome they deserved. For they were fresh and unsullied by that horrible joke. No one had been able to spy on them. (H, 61)

They now can be used as lullabies to put Giulio to sleep, for they are not literature debased into drugs: "Literature was a thing to buy and sell" (H, 64) . The practical joke is not, we must remember, powerless in the world of influence, but in the world of dreams. Mario himself will board himself up with fables. Not so Svevo and Zeno, who might scribble them in delighted fits of economy from time to time. The dream of latency supersedes the "business" of literature as the primary target of irony. A less virginal man would have been able to see through the helpless laughter of Gaia and his collaborator, for experience is challenged and endured by an education in social wit.

In a letter of 1927 Svevo accepts the judgment of friends that "The Hoax" is "poco avanguardista," and he himself calls it "figliouolo di padre vecchio," the child of an old father.[71] The well-defined twist of the plot and its careful and logical preparation certainly give the story the lines of the classic joke. The private fable seems to compete with the hoax as a closed form. But the daring, and to some readers excessive, intrusion of fables of private psychic relief and the subsequent halt in narrative momentum provided by the hoax itself open the story up to a stuttering vulnerability that is anything but a closed and conventional form. The story seems to end with a secure victory of the fable's organization over the chaotic interruption of experience, but there is also, in the fable atmosphere, for all its neatness, a kind of subversive resistance to climax and resolution, so important a habit of Zeno's humor.[72] The Svevian fable always stops short of moralizing with referents that can be adjusted according to the private, rather than the public need, and is by no means a traditional

---

71. Undated letter to Leo Ferrero, OO, 1: 848.
72. Cf. Renato Barilli's comments on the fables in *La linea,* p. 99.

form, except for its natural affinity for using the evolutionary scale to favor characters who struggle, the weak against the strong. Since Mario will not open himself up again to public experience, the fables, balanced on an axis of guilt and self-justification, court the ambivalence of dreams. They are subject to the dream's arbitrary direction, and to its economic but deceptive clarity, and this prevents the literary mummies from sealing Mario up in undisturbed peace. Mario's sassy sparrows make up in independence what Mario shuts out of his consciousness. They come to have such a life of their own, restricted and channeled though it be, that they put up a successful resistance to any pretense to universal application, to complacency and sentimentality. The sparrows claim the privilege of judging others, and, when Mario scolds one, Svevo adds at the end of the story:

> But if every animal in the world were obliged to mind its own busi-
> ness and refrain from endowing others with its own qualities and
> even its own organs, there would be no more fables. And Mario
> would surely have been far from wishing this. (H, 70)

The universe of beasts suffers, in "The Hoax," from anthropomor-phic controls, but it also seizes, like the beasts of nightmare, the privilege of revealing unconscious desires and rationalizations. The reader realizes that the private use of fable is a contradiction in terms, and that if Mario's appropriation makes for continuous fantasy and relief, the fables themselves, in their journey into universal-ity, cannot be confined to any immediate moment of justification or consolation. It is Mario who insists upon his infinite powers of manipulation and control, but when we are told of the last fable: "there is no end to this fable" (H, 69), we sense a double direction in Svevo's comment. Mario can reuse the fable and bend it to his need, but it in turn assumes the cockiness that comes with the under-standing that it will never be finished. Mario does not want the fables to end, but the fables take heart that they are never finally fixed and universalized. The small sparrows are not steadied by the traditional roles of representatives of the humility of Christian resig-nation, nor the social humility of the despised and forgotten, though these references are a motivation for their selection. They are petty scrabblers whose unsentimental push for survival and whose constant displacement of blame or praise, patronized by Mario's imagination, are the old natural foils to unnatural dreams, and we have met them before in Svevo's fiction. "We *are* the present" (H, 37), they tell Mario, a reproof that we can imagine Angiolina giving to Emilio, and with these words, however dependent the birds are on Mario's fantasies, they live in a world where "you can get anywhere . . . if you know where you want to go" (H, 37). Mario's fantasies can conduct them, giving him humble company, but they are never resigned. They assume the energy of Mario's anger and frustrated dreams, but by pecking around in a dreamless world they have the privilege of showing up his game. The fact that the fables go on indefinitely opens up a space that the hoax pretends to close, and provides a version of the leveling out that marks the last stories of Svevo.

The refusal to close upon a finished form is especially marked in the organization of the unfinished "Short Sentimental Journey," but is evident too in the beautiful "Generous Wine"[73] which, like "The Hoax," seems to have a closed form. The dream of a drunken hero appears to give a clear warning to him that his ungenerous and antisocial thoughts and behavior will be punished by remorse and by an unbearable picture of his own betraying self. But the neatness of the dream's character is disturbed by the scattered and ambivalent character of its cause. Unlike Zeno, who changes a funereal atmosphere to a wedding air in *Confessions of Zeno,* the hero of "Generous Wine" manages to upset the celebration of his niece's wedding with explosions of anger and spite. Setting up his family as police of an abstemiousness prescribed by his doctor, he takes vengeance by indulgence. He toasts the bride with this cynical reminder:

"May you be contented for a year or two, then you will endure the other long years more easily, thanks to your gratitude for having experienced enjoyment. One regrets past joy, and this is a pain, but a pain which numbs the fundamental one, the real pain in life." (GW, 129)

73. In a letter to Benjamin Crémieux, 15 March 1927, 1: 839, Svevo calls "Generous Wine" a relatively old story, dating at least back to 1914, though he had recently revised it.

It is tempting to image here the existential Svevo punishing the bourgeois Svevo, a condemnation present, but always kept in line, in the letters. In one, for example, to Benjamin Crémieux in 1927, Svevo describes his life as one that did not appear so beautiful, but was decked with so many happy affections that he would accept it all over again.[74] The generous wine stirs the hero to his old socialistic altruism, which he harshly launches against a bragging nephew, but only after experiencing anger against his guardians, his wife and daughter, for replacing dreams with medicines. A frightened and depressed guest at the wedding feast cannot get the best of his antagonist in his argument, for when Giovanni replies: " 'Yes, in practice all socialists end up by calling in the executioner' " (GW, 132), he reminds the hero of his own doubts. Svevo consistently centers the cause of anger in self-doubt and fear and allows it to be vented comically in paranoic anger. Punishments are visited upon the father by his family with such remarks as " 'How well he looks' " (GW, 132), and we recognize the presence of the old enemy, death. He shouts at his daughter, arbitrarily gives permission to his son to go out. And now the name of an old friend is mentioned, Anna, whom the hero had courted before marrying his wife. Feeling like a betrayer because of the brusque way he had dumped her in favor of his wife, he attributes her absence from the supper to resentment rather than to the sickness she claimed. The fact that she is happily married has no power against the desire for self-punishment. His own resentment flowers next to the peacefully sleeping wife, while he suffers a burning agony from overindulgence. His dreams throw up the face of Anna, young and beautiful, but bringing reproof and demanding remorse. The victory over that image, which comes with his winning her over, is paid for by a horrible dream of human sacrifice by suffocation in a glass chest. The audience is peopled with the figures from the feast, and the verdict of the hero's victimization, which the bride utters, seems inevitable.

Condemned once again by Anna, his wife, and the doctor, the hero desperately asks that his daughter be substituted. In the world of waking, his wife interprets his shouts for Emma as a sign of his love for her. Overwhelmed by the dream, the hero asks: " 'How can we get our children to forgive us for having brought them into the world?' "

74. OO, 1: 855.

(GW, 145). He is wisely and modestly answered by his Augusta:
" 'Our children are happy to be alive.' " That the dream, in its monolithic hyperbolic shape, is a reductive form of reality, like the melodramatic question posed to his wife, is understood by the hero, who
says in a spirit of adjustment:

> The dream-world was not my world, nor was I the man who wagged
> his tail and who was ready to sacrifice his own daughter to save him-
> self. (GW, 145)

Yet it obviously reflects a fuller process by which fear is transformed
into resentment and paid for by guilt.[75] The horrible cave will be
there when he becomes disobedient to the authorities to whom he
has entrusted both his life and his virtue. The dream's absurd distortion pretends to close the case once and for all but, like the fables, it
will go on forever, assuming different guises. Even though these projections are products of specific psychic tensions, they come to
achieve a kind of autonomy that disengages them from the personality that formed them. They, and the guilt and frustration that produce them in such concentrated and economic fashion, overwhelm
their creators in a way that Zeno's dreams, fables, and improvisations
never do.

———·•·———

It has often been noted that the more traditional narrative modes
of Svevo's shorter pieces, in relation to *Confessions of Zeno,* entail a
loss of intimacy between the author and the hero.[76] This is misleading, for there is a compensating intimacy between the favorite meditations of Svevo and the reflections of the last stories uninhibited by
distracting fictional mediation. The conventional journey structure
of "Short Sentimental Journey," a picaresque of the vacationing
mind, does not lead the hero, a likable and sensitive, but by no
means extraordinary man, farther from Svevo's atmosphere than
Zeno. It is only because his reflections, modest though they be, bring
us so comfortably close to Svevo's mind that Signor Aghios does not
destroy the new intimacy with displays of personal idiosyncrasy or
calls for attention. The evolution of Svevo's fiction into a less dra-

75. It is interesting to note that Svevo misunderstood Freud's statements on dreams
as wish-fulfillments (elaborated in his 1920 supplement to his theory of dreams) and
assumes in "The Hoax" that self-torture and wish-fulfillment are mutually exclusive.
76. See, for example, Sandro Maxia, *Lettura di Italo Svevo* (Padua, 1965), p. 32.

matic, more casual, and static form cannot be called regressive, for it takes a kind of aesthetic confidence and security to sacrifice the seductive world of chronologically plotted anecdote and captivating personality to an unprotected reflection, dependent only upon its own quality and pace for its charm and persuasion.[77] Some have ascribed the relaxation of narrative tension in the last Svevo, the "rassernamento dello stile,"[78] to the fulfillment of his latent ambition. Success brought to Svevo a diminution of the conscious struggle with technical difficulties and moral disquietude. Svevo himself, though irritated with the delays in translations and publications, admitted to Valéry Larbaud in 1926: "I am much more serene now because I have now had all I yearned for."[79] The disappearance of contrapuntal modes of syntax seems to at least one critic a symptom of a new confidence that expresses itself in the linear and fragmented rhythms of the diary.[80] The self-consciousness about his language, revived with his revision of *As a Man Grows Older,* is humored by the vision of Italian critics delighted to find badly written novels,[81] and helped by a growing conviction on the part of the young critics that Svevo's language was necessary to express the Svevian consciousness.[82] The recognition that there was a developing public acceptance, even in Italy, perhaps allowed him to assert more forcefully a vision less and less guarded by a rationalizing personality coming to terms with social acceptance. In addition, this natural development was complemented by a general atmosphere of narrative looseness and poetic structure, sensitive to the language of the mind. It was at this time too that Svevo, already very familiar with Joyce, was reading Kafka, in whose stories compulsions and dreams live autonomous lives.

But the most convincing explanation for the change is simply the fact that life is being viewed from the sixty-year-old mind, which lives without a future and in a present that draws freely from analogies with the past, rendering all experience simultaneous. Signor

77. Despite the fact that Svevo saw in the theater a mode of transmitting life more precisely and directly than in fiction, this tendency to stretch out in reflective space proved antithetical to the need for action that the stage at that time demanded. See Furbank, *Italo Svevo,* p. 213.

78. Leone de Castris, *Decadentismo e realismo* (Bari, 1958) , p. 57.

79. April 1926, OO, 1: 793.

80. de Castris, *Decadentismo,* p. 69.

81. Letter to Valéry Larbaud, 30 April 1926, OO, 1: 793.

82. Letter to Marie Anne Comnène, 8 February 1927, ibid., p. 832.

Aghios knows "from his personal experience of sixty years, that when one is born made in a particular way one stays like it" (SSJ, 243), and Svevo himself attempts to cheer Valerio Jahier with the recognition that the intimate self never changes, nor is it cured.[83] In the mind of old Zeno, characters assume the timelessness of states of being:

> Seventy years seem a lot when you look at them from the bottom up. Looking at them from top to bottom, they seem like nothing. . . . My father goes with me always.[84]

Once more, in "Short Sentimental Journey," Svevo chooses a hero who looks at life from the top down, imagining the impossibility of a vacation from bourgeois forms that prosaically mock the dreamed-of unity of desire and duty. Following upon the fine delineation of Signor Aghios's anxious irritability at the last goodbyes of his wife, the delusive embrace of an anaesthetic freedom, the movement from familial concern with the future of a son toward the carefree expansive flow of psychological time that is the luxury of the older man, the dreaming toward death in a railway compartment "crossing a countryside of which it was not a part" (SSJ, 272), all this appears to move the story into the symbolic climate of a long line of literary sentimental journeys. But the title, like "Generous Wine," with its comic reminder of limitation, snaps on the dream the typical Svevian domestic leash that guarantees to lead our animals back home. And, indeed, Svevo uses this very image to describe Aghios's failure to travel without the protection of cheating the world with words "being unused to so much liberty, like dogs kept on a chain, who tear up the gardens the moment they are set loose" (SSJ, 232). The poignant recognition in *Diario per la fidanzata* of a desire for perfect intimacy and the necessity to settle for less, is fully developed and examined in the leisurely atmosphere of Signor Aghios's journey. The lyric journey to freedom, intimacy, sincerity, and kindness in a world of strangers carries its own peculiar comedy, and Signor Aghios often seems like a naughty boy running away from home in the hope of finding parents better than the ones he has and loves. His Venice will not be that of Von Aschenbach.

---

83. 27 December 1927, ibid., p. 860.
84. Svevo, "Pagine di diario e sparse," OO, 3: 841.

We are a long way too from the adolescent train ride of Alfonso that leads to a sterile suicide. The solution of suicide, as the gondolier Bortolo is fond of saying, belongs to the young: " 'Ever since the world began, you young chaps have shot yourself once a day' " (SSJ, 271). In the mind of a sixty-year-old man, death has become a condition of life. Yet there is decidedly a suggestion that the older man is looking for a second childhood away from the intimidating, and sophisticated young who force him offstage. The designation of "poet" to Signor Aghios by his fellow passenger, the stolid insurance investigator Borlini, is a vacation tag worn around the neck in infantile delight as a badge of provisional parental release: "Would he have felt more vigorous in the great world, away from his household?" he wonders, and the great world grows smaller and smaller. Signor Aghios seizes upon the young generation's criticism, embodied in his son, and the old wife's devotion to her child as civilized pretexts for walking off stage to indulge his dreams: "He banished from his mind these phantoms of his wife and son" (SSJ, 224). But the shadow of the bourgeois household is cast upon the entire voyage, which is constantly colored by its origin of escape rather than spiritual boldness. The controlling conscience and chronology of bourgeois morality appear only to have taken a holiday. Aghios's own conscience is eased by the recognition, ruefully and mischievously noted in Svevo's letters to Livia, that "the farther I travel from her the more I love her" (SSJ, 216). With this sanction, Signor Aghios finds himself "in accord with both human and divine law, for he loved his wife sincerely" (SSJ, 216). Civilization's super-ego is quieted by his debates "with that vague being who must be somewhere, perhaps in the ether (which is supposed to be everywhere) and who superintends moral law" (SSJ, 223) concerning the commandment not to covet his neighbors' wives. The first dream of release is launched, which allows "compartment theory" (SSJ, 272) to smooth the tension between social conscience and desire. A civilized child, he sees himself as a classic Freudian victim of society and its discontents:

He judged himself to be a man who desired many things which were forbidden him and which—since they were forbidden—he forbade himself, though he allowed his desire for them to continue. (SSJ, 249)

Later in the journey he is captivated by a phrase used by the young thief Bacis, who refers to his passion for the girl Anna, whom he then betrays, as "the sincerity of flesh" (SSJ, 280). The oxymoron opens that gap between conscience and desire, the space of mixed time, which is that of evolved man:

> The sincerity of the flesh was the sincerity of animals, but even among animals it only lasted for a flash and did not represent a commitment. Bacis, however, had tarnished this sincerity of his, because in the very moment of sincerity he had thought of play-acting. Even his sincerity had only helped him to betray. (SSJ, 280)

Aghios reproaches his companion with this reminder:

> "You call me a philosopher and, in the same breath, invent such a terrifying concept as that: the sincerity of flesh being contradicted by the falseness of another part of the body—flesh as well, but *evolved* flesh." (SSJ, 280)

The story of Anna's seduction, most likely fictional, is already the story of the whole dead planet earth (SSJ, 273), never free from the parasites of division and destruction envisaged by Zeno. Crossing the Venetian lagoon in a gondola, Signor Aghios reflects:

> A few days before, he had read in a newspaper that it is now believed that when Earth became habitable, it was infected by some accident with life from another planet. From then on, everything followed naturally: the little animals, once here, began making love and betraying, and they invaded everything, the land and the sea, evolving, and continuing to love and betray, from stage to stage of evolution. (SSJ, 273)

The bourgeois Hebraic moralism that forbids coveting the neighbor's wife has relaxed its hold as it passes through biology to psychology. Earlier in the story, upon overhearing the psychiatric cliché from a sophisticated youth resembling his "superior" son, that the first wounds of infancy are the most persistent and important blows to psychic health, Signor Aghios reacts in anger to a complacent theory that gives priority to the young. His leisurely sense of temporal simultaneity has been violated and he is reminded of his son's future:

> On the threshold of sixty didn't he suffer from every injury ever done him by others and from every self-doubting of his own? Flesh,

composed largely of liquid, was never very resistant, and ignorance
went hand in hand with it to our last breath, persuading us to at-
tach importance to all the things that have none really, making
them a burden and an encumbrance to us, and a source of distress
and disease. (SSJ, 228)

That flesh that wants merely to love is betrayed by psychological,
social, and biological distortions of intimacy. In a wonderfully comic
touch, Signor Aghios watches the young man step down from the
train and disappear into the station building: "the gateway to a ham-
let where the great science of psychoanalysis was arriving" (SSJ,
229). Until the end, Svevo refuses to the dreams of perfect intimacy,
sincerity, and kindness both romantic fulfillment and tragic collapse.

Early in the story, in a vivid scene, Signor Aghios looks at his own
face in the glass of a framed photograph as he sits opposite his first
acquaintance, the insurance investigator. Depressed by the strange-
ness of the face, he nevertheless thrills to the recognition of "the one
intimate relationship existing in the whole of nature" (SSJ, 226).
The intimacy and honesty of the identity is counterpointed by the
necessity for social lies between the two men:

One only has to address a single word to a fellow-being and one
risks telling a falsehood. Truth exists only among people who do
not know each other. (SSJ, 226)

The little falsehood that social kindness dictated now is rewarded by
a return of kindness, which leads Aghios back temporarily from the
pure contemplation of self to "the human consortium" (SSJ, 227)
and the acceptance of the social lie. But the dream of love persists in
its antisocial tendencies:

He couldn't exactly say he loved some*one,* but he loved, intensely,
life itself—men, animals and plants—all anonymous things, which
was what made them so lovable. (SSJ, 230)

Such comforting distance, unfortunately, is periodically destroyed by
the existence of a beautiful woman. Indeed, had it not been that
among mankind there were also beautiful women, he would have
been able to await death with the serenity of a saint (the name
Aghios means saint in Greek). Signor Aghios is released from a discussion on prices with the stranger by a pastoral remembrance of a
day of natural happiness, "the most perfect of human intimacies"

(SSJ, 234). The details of the relationship between Aghios and his companion, a painter, riding in horse and buggy across the Friulian countryside, are dissolved in sunny contentment. But the painter (modeled, like Balli, on Svevo's real friend Veruda) had died and "recollection . . . is not truly a form of action" since both the "rememberer and the remembered are immobilized" (SSJ, 234). They cannot stay in a world that pushes on. This dream of intimacy is harshly countered by the "intimacy of sorts" with the insurance investigator, Borlini.

And it is jolted too by two disappointed children. One, a little girl, desiring to see herself, the countryside, and the train all in one image in the train's window is surrounded by mocking laughter by an insensitive world of businessmen and parents. Aghios is touched at the child's first intimation of the cruel sundering of the original unity that prevents life from seeing itself and acting at the same time:

> Only he felt and knew what sorrow there was in not being able to see oneself while travelling. . . . To see the landscape, the train and oneself at the same time—that really would have been travelling! (SSJ, 241)

The patronization of such expectation by an insensitive world of adults is continued by Borlini's stories of his younger son's dreamy nature that would seem to incapacitate him for life. "Poor Paolucci was most unlucky," thinks Aghios, "having been born into the wrong family" (SSJ, 243). With the "sentimentalism of the leisurely traveller" (SSJ, 258), identification with the pain of these early victims, "boundless affection for all the weak and defenseless" (SSJ, 248) dreamers in a world of social and industrial insurance investigators, Aghios once again resorts to the visions that "beautify or blur" (SSJ, 246) the world:

> Far off in the distance, at the foot of a mountain, one could glimpse the lights of a village. A steady, tranquil light. But for that matter, distant light is always steady and tranquil. The wind may blow, but if it does not blow it out the light remains like starlight: it shines with the tranquillity of a colour (if any colour were ever as bright). For the villagers itself, it might be blowing a hurricane; but distance is peace. (SSJ, 247)

The relationship with Borlini degenerates into one as tiresome as that he left behind. "Slavery," realizes Signor Aghios, "was not only a

fate, it was a habit" (SSJ, 253) . And as a habit, the bourgeois bur-
dens of responsibility are desired as well as resisted. The family at
this point seems infinitely preferable to Signor Borlini.

Liberated from his companion at Padua, Signor Aghios imposes
his prison image upon a couple working in the fields, viewed swiftly
from the window. The "sincerity of the flesh" is once again betrayed:

> They had formed an association, sexual in origin, which would
> degenerate into one of material interests, encompassing the field
> they worked in and the cottage . . . where they slept. What a
> colossal trick! Drawn by pleasure together, ensnared by their own
> natural warmth, they were loaded with chains without noticing it.
> (SSJ, 257)

But just as quickly, in the alternation between dream and waking
that dominates the rhythm of the story, he takes pride in his racial
distinction in Italy (like Bloom's in Dublin) :

> It's convenient . . . belonging to another race. It's as if one were
> perpetually on one's travels. One's thoughts are freer. And it's the
> same with the way one looks at things. I don't approve of the
> Italian way of seeing things, but neither do I approve of the Greek
> way. (SSJ, 263)

Obviously, the sense of Triestine citizenship which, because of its
estrangement from Italy, Svevo felt so keenly as both an advantage
and disadvantage, is projected upon his character. But what is important here is that such a sentimental rationalization leads him into
another trap of intimacy, another dream become a prison. The
young Bacis calls himself a displaced traveler too, doomed as well to
dialect despite some linguistic education. Once again, overwhelmed
with a desire to give and receive kindness, Aghios befriends the
treacherous Bacis and shows him Venice in his "barque of benevolence" (SSJ, 264) . But soon he marvels "how prolonged companion-
ship even with one man was enough to deprive him of the great
freedom of travel," a freedom felt only by its alternations, it appears,
with slavery: "Could there be a worse slavery than having to talk of
things one knew nothing about?" (SSJ, 266) . In a planetary fantasy
on the train entering Gorizia, Aghios extends his journey to Mars,
where boundless luminous space gives no resistance to his desire for
freedom: "To feel it, he needed to be able to boast of it" (SSJ, 293) .
No dream is free of the need for rhetorical witness. In an amusing

reminiscence of the dreams of Svevo's nice old man, Aghios blends paternalism, "kind and virtuous" (SSJ, 294), with sensual desire, as he protects the body of Anna, Bacis's willing victim of seduction, by lying on top of her. In such a dream "their posture together would last for all eternity" (SSJ, 295). This is the final taunt to dreams of intimacy, which must be dressed in psychic disguises. Upon awakening, Aghios experiences the human condition, a fatal mixture of shame and joy. The stealing of his money is almost an anticlimax in this level journey of alternations between the sentimentality of freedom and the cynicism of slavery, and this impression is aided by the suggestion that Aghios's subliminal shame over his stinginess had set him up to almost will the robbery. This is also Mother Nature's way of climaxing innocent dreams of freedom, intimacy, sincerity, and benevolence. What she gives to Mario, who doesn't want it, she takes from Aghios. The cleverest of all Mother Nature's plans to prevent the saint's abstractions from dominating reality is to place in the heart of man the compulsion to be a man, half slave and half free.

The thinning of personality gives a compensatory fluidity and casualness to the sixty-year-old reflection in these last stories; we lose the delightful surprises of Zeno's improvisations born of the spontaneous debate between coveting and prohibition. It is almost as if the fictional energy that goes into creating and keeping a consistent personality on the scene had slackened, allowing the association of an older and sensitive mind, one susceptible to general motions that entail the death of personality and literary disguise, a last yearning for freedom, sweeping benevolence, and the idea of intimacy, like pictures flashing by the train window, to spread across the scene. The old irritabilities remain, and the old affections, but in attenuated form. The reflexes of reaction are slower and the mind slides off the particular, like the two children—one imagined, one seen—whose faces immediately give way to sensations of victimization. Even the Venetian tour dissolves in the general movement toward death. But the Svevian humor is still busy setting up Mother Nature's contradictions through the fluctuations of images and feelings they evoke. There is still in the Svevian world no soul large enough to be independent of the disease of being human, and fantasy is checked by its own parasitic needs to live within a social frame. There is a strong suggestion that, with a finished manuscript, the journey away from the family would have become a journey toward it. The illusions fostered by the ageless traces of "senilità" assume a naturalness here, rather than a desperate defensiveness, because the mind is not old chronologically and, unlike the mind of Mario Samigli, domestically experienced. It carries with it, for each encounter, a hundred analogies from marriage that soften experience with generalization. That the state of reflection is never given the comfort of complacency is the sign of the Svevian temperament that has aged and tired but not grown old.

PART II:
THE CASE

Chapter 4
The Italian Identity

THE HISTORICAL AND CULTURAL SITUATION in which Svevo developed his fiction has, from our present perspective, all the melodrama Svevo persistently denied to his life. Fond of belittling his personal history, of muffling it in bourgeois comfort, the respectable business, ineffectual scribbling, and of humorously elevating his smoking habit to a lifelong obstacle more important than the obstacles to his literary acceptance, Svevo would have been amazed at the fascination of the "caso" Svevo, as he heard it called,[1] to modern literary historians. In his autobiographical pieces, Svevo modestly attenuates all his drama of frustration, neglect, and discovery, claiming for himself merely a life that does not appear so fine, but that was full of affections.[2] It must have seemed a life especially tame in comparison to the willed exile and aesthetic heroism of his friend Joyce. Typically, he races over accounts of his early education at the business school in Segnitz (1873–1878), poignantly examined in the incomplete sketch for a story "L'Avvenire dei ricordi," by admitting that he studied even less than what was offered.[3] His acquaintance with European literature, especially his passion for German literature, began and grew in a commercial school, and his Italian literary heritage had to be discovered in the public library while he studied at the Scuola Commerciale Superiore of Trieste. The bankruptcy and death of Svevo's father prevented even the possibility of expatriate study at Vienna, Prague, Florence, or Milan. The young Triestines associated

---

1. Svevo, "Profilo autobiografico," OO, 3: 810.
2. Letter to Benjamin Crémieux, 1927, OO, 1: 855.
3. Ibid., p. 854. In "Profilo antobiografico," OO, 3: 799, Svevo attributes his pen name to his German education rather than to his German heritage.

with the Florentine magazine *La Voce* had an entrée into Italian culture denied Svevo, yet even for them literary culture was gained at great effort and late because of the lack of any serious literary tradition in the commercial families of Trieste.[4] While the Stuparich brothers and the Triestine poet Saba grumbled about a Trieste so gravely in arrears of a general Hapsburg or Italian culture, Svevo, for all of his cultural inferiority complexes, refused himself vigorous complaint.

By nature not a writer attracted to group policies or schools, he preferred to see a Trieste well suited to the self-made dilettante:

> Trieste was then a place singularly adapted to intellectual cultivation. Located at the crossroads of many peoples, the Triestine literary ambience was permeated with the most varied cultures.[5]

Svevo's first two novels vividly expose his consciousness of Trieste's cultural provincialism. But where other Triestines resented it, Svevo, reading in the Biblioteca Civica, like Alfonso, nineteenth-century French novels and, guided by De Sanctis, sporadically catching up on the Italian masters, proudly saw at the "Gabinetti Minerva," Trieste's literary society, readers of French, Russian, German, Scandinavian, and English literature, who were also lovers of music and painting, and saw at the newspaper "l'Indipendente" irredentists who would solicit his literary criticism and publish his first fiction. Later, with the revision of *As a Man Grows Older,* he was to regret missing a chance to purify his language by a stay in Milan or Florence, but he never seriously regretted his Triestine life. Even when he traveled for the family business to England and France, or when he became an international hero in literature, he did not wave the flag of joyous cosmopolitanism. He did not, like Joyce, forge a place in history. He was simply discovered. And the delayed acceptance of this novelist has created problems for historians of Italian literature ever since.

The problem has been well diagnosed by A. Leone de Castris, who sets aside the question of pioneering consciousness on the part of Svevo, emphasizing instead the absence of an Italian tradition that could have tolerated and mothered his "uneasiness as a man and

4. See Carlo Stuparich, *Cose e ombre di uno,* ed. Giani Stuparich (Rome, 1968).
5. Svevo, "Profilo autobiografico," OO, 3: 801.

artist,"[6] that could have accepted his "novità morale," his moral originality. The anxious isolation has been somewhat eased by a European tradition quickly sketched after Svevo's adoption by the French, and by a search through the Italian narrative underbrush for compatible contemporary narrative tones and textures. But Svevo remains a man outside of his chosen culture, with no audacity of self-advertisement, who serves in a major way to bring Italian literature itself into a wider experimental atmosphere of modern European culture.

Many sophisticated readers of Italian literature confessed to certain difficulties in accustoming their literary tastes to Svevo's new language and direction. Montale's initial preference for *As a Man Grows Older* over *Confessions of Zeno* was a symptom of this difficulty, and the admission of G. B. Angioletti in the 1929 issue of *Solaria* devoted to Svevo is representative of a fairly common Italian reaction:

> It wasn't easy for me to approach Svevo's art: an art far from what was natural to my tastes, an art that did not take into account certain laws of style, certain sacrifices and subtleties that, perhaps wrongly, are dear to me. But right away I felt in Italo Svevo a man much superior to the common crowd of writers.[7]

The ultimate accommodation of Svevo's intimacy, irony, spontaneity of language, and thought in a history as aesthetically formal as that of Italian literature seemed to Emilio Cecchi possible, paradoxically, only *because* Svevo, "il barbaro triestino,"[8] was a man who came to literature as a nonprofessional exposed to so many cultural currents, adopting a language sometimes syntactically harsh and awkward, but uniquely disturbing and touching. To the young writers tired of worn-out conventions and academy expectations, Svevo, "a stranger,

6. de Castris, *Italo Svevo*, p. 16.
7. G. B. Angioletti, "Svevo," *Solaria* (Svevo issue, 1929): 11. See also Piero Gadda, "Lettura di *Senilità*," in the same issue, p. 42:

> I had then, and I still have with the reservations that the literature of Svevo has planted in my mind, a love of the sentence that soberly uncoils itself, with limpid cadence, with the formal precision and enamel quality of the flaubertian style. Svevo was thick, cluttered, apparently disordered, sometimes crude and rough; nevertheless, it [*Senilità*] took me in gradually with irresistible persuasion, as few books have been able to do.

8. Quoted in Bruno Maier, *Profilo della critica su Italo Svevo* (Trieste, 1951), p. 24.

mere flotsam,"[9] appears as a last-minute savior, bringing into Italy the European consciousness, the richness of its problems, man without his myths:

> With Svevo the "coscienza" of postromantic Europe entered, the ferment of a culture in which the contemporary soul manifested its destiny, the concrete shape of an historical drama that one could no longer shirk or disregard.[10]

As Giovanni Comisso testified in a note to Svevo's wife just after the novelist's death, this man assumed unexpectedly a role he had never dreamed of, that of "maestro" to the young.[11] This is an unusual development, to say the least, for one who had remained for so long a man "without a country and without a tradition,"[12] who wrote to Montale with tongue in cheek: "I am very curious to find out to what school I belong."[13]

In a literature that itself had only a sporadic narrative tradition, whose great modern representatives, Manzoni, Verga, Fogazzaro, and D'Annunzio, did not seem to exercise the least influence on him, Svevo's originality seems all the more evident. At a time in which a country of "orecchianti" was appreciating D'Annunzio's elaborate prose, the world of *A Life* and *As a Man Grows Older,* conjectures Francesco Flora, would have seemed gray, poor, regressive.[14] Yet D'Annunzio's antagonism to an exhausted naturalism might have prepared a place for Svevo, however antithetical the two writers were in their textures, however averse Svevo was to D'Annunzio's lack of spontaneity in characters and language, if he had enlisted himself in the battle of the "periodizzazioni della storia," the history of the "ismi."[15] The important point is that Svevo was indifferent, by choice and fate, to all literary schools and styles of the last two decades of the nineteenth century. Living in the midst of the heroic mysticism of Fogazzaro, the decadent lyricism of D'Annunzio, the

9. Elio Vittorini's phrase in *Diario in pubblico* (Milan, 1957) , p. 14.

10. de Castris, *Italo Svevo,* p. 11.

11. Letter dated September 1928 in *Saba/Svevo/Comisso* (lettere inedite) , a cura di Mario Sutor (Padua, 1968) , p. 79.

12. de Castris, *Italo Svevo,* p. 13.

13. Letter to Eugenio Montale, 22 June 1926, OO, 1: 796.

14. *Storia della letteratura italiana* (Milan, 1947) , 5: 742.

15. This phrase is Giacomo Debenedetti's in *Il romanzo del novecento* (Milan, 1971) , p. 693.

veristi, and divorced from the "imprecise polemic"[16] raging around him concerning "verismo" and false "verismo," "dannunzianismo" and false "dannunzianismo," Croce, *La Voce,* "crepuscolarismo," futurism, impressionists, and fragmentists, it seems astounding that Svevo could ever be considered a central representative of the modern age in literary Italy. Furthermore, as Mario Lunetta writes, borrowing some phrases from Giorgio Luti:

> The Triestine [Svevo] found himself beyond the romantic crisis, beyond that particular situation which had led to the extremely limited experiments of Italian naturalism, and for this reason, Svevo was involved in the rather vast and profound climate of European sensibility.[17]

The impossibility of characterizing Svevo by association with a school, a literary argument, or a program, has made any definition of his art in literary history seem almost always off the mark. In the absence of a neat tradition by which to define him, attempts to force upon Svevo a social or literary consciousness beyond his interest have that ring of inauthenticity I have previously noted. Luti insists, for example, that Svevo is not a man outside of his time. We can assume that his novels could not have been written if he had not been sensitive to social and political crises of his epoch. When, however, as proof of this sensitivity, Luti cites Svevo's aversion to D'Annunzio, by which one could presage how antifascistic Svevo would have been, the emphasis upon social consciousness loses its force.[18] What reader could ever believe Svevo to be anything but an enemy of fascism? Such apologies indicate embarrassment at the lack of genuinely interesting social and political material, in and out of the novels, by which to pin Svevo down to a social polemic if he cannot be attached to a literary one.

This effort to find a place for Svevo in Italian literature elicits, ultimately, a kind of inverse hypothesis that Italy was really exiled from Svevo rather than vice versa. It is not the purist, argues Raffaello Franchi, but writers of the race of Svevo who make a

---

16. This is the phrase of Sergio Antonielli, "Dal decadentismo al neorealismo," *Letteratura italiana* (Milan: Marzorati, 1956), "Le correnti," 2: 898.

17. Lunetta, *Invito alla lettura,* p. 52. See also Giorgio Luti, *Svevo* (Florence, 1961), p. 66.

18. Luti, *Svevo,* p. 61.

literary history progress.[19] The noted critic G. A. Borgese, whose novel *Rubé* pictures the depression of the war and postwar generation, diagnosed Italian literature as a sickness, whose major symptom was varieties of ciceronianism which, capturing the ear with brilliant persuasion, blocked the exploration of a more intimate psychological world.[20] This eloquence, in turn, led inevitably to varieties of literary decadence. Such a verdict, in terms less harsh, has been seconded by European critics concentrating on the flimsy relations of much of nineteenth-century Italian literature to bolder and more openly publicized continental currents. Benjamin Crémieux, looking at Italian literature from the French point of view, a view praised by Svevo himself for its independence,[21] describes the Italian habit of living on the margin of European literary movements, its own literature turned to the heroic.[22] With Verga and the more intimate literature of the first decades of the twentieth century, Italian letters at last puts forth a more realistic and delicate reflection of itself. D. H. Lawrence, an admirer of Verga, with typically obsessive emphasis nevertheless accuses him and other Italian writers of wearing borrowed identities, of "always acting up to somebody else's vision of life":

> The trouble with Verga, as with all Italians, is that he never seems quite to know where he is. When one reads Manzoni, one wonders if he is not more "Gothic" or Germanic, than Italian. And Verga, in the same way, seems to have a borrowed outlook on life: but this time, borrowed from the French. With D'Annunzio the same, it is hard to believe he is really being himself. He gives one the impression of "acting up." Pirandello goes on with the game to-day. The Italians are always that way: always acting up to somebody else's vision of life. Men like Hardy, Meredith, Dickens, they are just as sentimental and false as the Italians, in their own way. It only happens to be our own brand of falseness and sentimentality.[23]

The metaphors of borrowed identities, mirrors turned outward, diseases of eloquence, all forged by writers active in the shaping of modern literature, forcefully if carelessly describe in unison a sense

19. Rafaello Franchi, "Omaggio a Svevo," *Solaria* (Svevo issue, 1929), p. 41.
20. Antonio Rufiero, *La critica letteraria di G. A. Borgese* (Venice, 1969), pp. 80–1.
21. Svevo, "Mezzo secolo di letteratura italiana," OO, 3: 631.
22. Benjamin Crémieux, *La Littérature italienne* (Paris, 1928).
23. D. H. Lawrence, review of *Mastro-don Gesualdo, D. H. Lawrence: Selected Literary Criticism*, ed. Anthony Beal (London, 1956), p. 272.

of a literature in which the age-old separation between the art of the academy, of ideal poetry, of aristocratic Italy, and that of the people, regional, spontaneous, had never been healed. One of the most influential modern Italian critics of the novel, Giacomo Debenedetti, concurs in this impression, especially in relation to the novel as a genre. Svevo's historial importance for Italian literature hinges upon the fact that for him the novel was as natural a choice of form as it had been self-conscious to his predecessors: "I would say that in him the *taste* for the novel was innate."[24] In the work of D'Annunzio, Fogazzaro, and the veristi, whatever the quality of single pieces, the consciousness of an external model, argues Debenedetti, and the deliberate desire to create an Italian novel, betray themselves. In Svevo, by contrast, "the intention to write a novel never appears to be a conscious decision or the result of willful deliberation. It seems obvious that he could never write anything *but* a novel."[25]

In an interview in *The Paris Review*, Moravia, in the face of his denial of the Svevian influence (Svevo is a writer he didn't know at all well; he read him *after* he wrote *Gli indifferent*)[26] that critics impose upon him, talks of the reasons for the lack of general success of the Italian novel abroad. He conjectures that the lack of ideological and psychological dimension and the concentration on provincial life with its "moeurs restreintes" are not easily translatable in atmospheres almost antithetical to such a closed arena. Complementing the sentiment of Lawrence that the Italian novel seems to have borrowed itself, Moravia asserts:

> Most of the Italian novelists are not real novelists. Perhaps I exaggerate, but I repeat, there are only one or two novelists in Italy: Manzoni and Svevo.[27]

Debenedetti supports this judgment, not only by insisting on the genuine novelistic temper of Svevo, but also by analyzing his inevitable neglect in an Italy in which the very few good novels at the end of the nineteenth century had the characters of "delicate and uncertain transplants, paradoxical and unrenewable."[28] Montale participates too in this assessment:

24. Debenedetti, *Il romanzo*, p. 54.
25. Ibid., p. 56.
26. Conducted by Anna Maria de Dominicis and Ben Johnson, *Paris Review* 6 (Summer 1954) : 21.
27. Jean Duflot, "Entretiens avec Alberto Moravia" (Paris, 1970) , p. 90.
28. Debenedetti, "Svevo e Schmitz," *Saggi critici*, pp. 50–51.

We have had other novelists, we still have them, but Svevo will remain, with us, the novelist in person, the writer who gave to the genre a sense of categorical authenticity. An illusion, I know, but the fruit of a narrative genius to which we were not accustomed.[29]

And Elio Vittorini talks about the Svevian instinct, at a time still filled with the oldest of arguments about the duality of form and content, to use the art of the novel to explore and express thoughts and feelings "in one huge difficulty."[30] This sense of Svevo's difficulty of style and analysis is, in general, a judgment that has become familiar in Svevo studies. It was a style and an approach not easily appreciated in Italy, which had for so long remained the country of a highly stylized literature. Not until the postwar "memorialisti" and "neorealisti" arrived on the scene could, in Arnaldo Bocelli's opinion, Svevo's art of self-analysis and analysis, his interest in the humorous and anxious links between a personal past and the present, his insecure world, find an audience.[31] All these conjectures suggest that Svevo, however nonrevolutionary his nature, was, in relation to Italian literature, ahead of his time.

In attempts to square modern Italian literary history with that of Europe at large, we often discover the cultural inferiority complex so marked in American and Russian apologists for native strengths. Literary assessments are characteristically turned to defense. De Sanctis's seminal plea for a strong Italian literature closely binding the book and the being behind it is, in actuality, a plea against parasitism, the second-rate. The arguments assume the rhythm of compensation. If the Italian "scapigliatura" does not have the revolutionary coherence and firmness of the French symbolist movement, it softens the heroic with ironic and lyrical autobiography, opening the way to both European poetry and a healthy regionalism.[32] Literary Italy has no Poes, Baudelaires, and Wagners, and the provincialism of its narrative is the price paid for a long interest in the art of aristocratic ideals, both "fantastico ed astratto,"[33] but it

29. Montale, "Il vento è mutato," dal "Corriere della Sera," 30 December 1949, *Lettere,* p. 139.

30. Vittorini, *Diario in pubblico,* p. 14.

31. This opinion is quoted in the indispensable Bruno Maier, *Profila della critica su Italo Svevo,* p. 36, and is from an article entitled "L'ultimo Svevo," *Il Mondo,* 4 February 1950.

32. See, for example, Mario Marcazzan, "Dal romanticismo al decadentismo," *Letteratura italiana* (Marzorati) , "Le correnti," 2: 759.

33. Ibid.

has a truly nostalgic and lyrical adherence "to the animated and living reality of the natural and psychological landscape, felt as a recall of a distant civilization, as a spiritual and literary legacy unpublished and unexpressed, more than as an ingenuous and primitive given."[34] While French naturalism has the advantage of revolting against strong traditions of Romantic realism, the Italian "veristi" profit from their preference for a closeness to the earth, to elemental passions, over the dehumanizing scene of Paris.

It is no wonder then that Italian critics, taken by surprise, felt a combination of scorn and envy for the European discoverers of Svevo. They had not been ready for an Italian novelist turned toward a European atmosphere that was openly recognizing and publicizing the limitations of naturalism and moving beyond it to decadence and symbolism, to a kind of exacerbated aesthetic and psychological narcissism, an attribute of a self-conscious and superfluous bourgeoisie set adrift from political and social action. Svevo, "exemplary peripheral mediator" between naturalism and Freudianism, can accept of the former "only the widest aspects of its approach,"[35] in the first two novels rejecting and making rhetorical irony out of the narrow school theories of cause and effect. Unable by time and temperament to describe his examination of psychological man through romantic irony or a pitiless naturalism (though both of these perspectives leave traces in the early novels), Svevo uses the chaotic play of a secular consciousness in the face of the collapse of old faiths.[36] Because of the resulting vulnerability, critics are tempted to push him into one sphere of influence or the other. Thus, if he leaves the naturalism of Zola, he is automatically closer to Proust and Joyce. These kinds of compensatory juxtapositions are almost always unsatisfactory, for Svevo's originality is such that it rapidly overturns each attempt to make him an Italian Proust, Kafka, or Musil. As Antonio Testa reminds us, these mythical couplings that give us cultural security merely make the situation more incomprehensible, for "the young Svevo is as far from Zola as the old is from Proust."[37] The most helpful approach to the placing of Svevo in cultural history before isolating him with Pirandello as

34. Ibid.
35. Luti, *Italo Svevo*, p. 67.
36. See Pampaloni, "Italo Svevo," pp. 512–513.
37. Testa, *Italo Svevo*, p. 26.

the father of a new tradition, or Europeanizing him, is therefore the sensitive and subtle consideration of Debenedetti, who enlarges the question "Why was Svevo rediscovered?" to "Why, for so long, was Svevo undiscovered?"[38] He turns us to the problems and obstacles that blocked the modern novel in Italy, a stepchild in that country's hierarchy of forms.

In his lectures on the novel, Debenedetti contends that not yet in Italian critics and readers was *born* and stimulated that taste for the novel, that sense of it that was *inborn* in Svevo himself, that receptive capacity which would take its value for granted as a major literary genre.[39] Why, asks Debenedetti, is that appreciation so quiescent at the very time that Italians, including Svevo, were avidly reading French, Russian, and English novels? Even Verga had to wait until the early twenties to be reevaluated and fully appreciated, and it took Pirandello the dramatist to find an audience for his earlier fiction. The answer that Debenedetti posits with convincing emphasis, one supported by other critics,[40] lies in the attitude toward the novel of the two most influential literary magazines of pre-World War and post-World War Italy, *La Voce* and *La Ronda.* In an atmosphere of enthusiastic new literary directions and programs, in a country that still had never settled on distinctions between romanticism and classicism, the history of their contributors and polemics is confusing and complex, but the preference for the literature of fragments, "intimistic" prose, a postsymbolist religion of poetry clearly was not favorable for the modern novel. Furthermore, the confidence of their manifestos intimidated its practice and inhibited acceptance. In the second decade of the twentieth century, many young writers were attracted to the proclaimed purity of "frammentismo," a literary attitude characterized by a high regard for moments in prose of lyric transparency in preference to the diffuse and dense texture of the novel. The editor of the second *Voce* (1914–16), the young and polemical Giuseppe de Robertis, insisted on the "essenzialità" of the fragment, its unmediated and almost mystic power of penetration,

38. Debenedetti, *Il romanzo*, p. 12.
39. Ibid., pp. 12 ff.
40. See, for example, Spagnoletti, *Svevo*, p. 45. But some critics like Bruno Maier ("Virgilio Giotto," *Letteratura italiana*, "I contemporanei," [Marzorati]: 3–4) feel that the vocean favoring of autobiography, fragmentism, the confession, and the examination of "coscienza" was complementary to the Triestine habit of introspection found in Saba and Svevo.

and Arturo Onofri, in a piece that came to be seen as another vocean manifesto,[41] urged the liberation of poetry from the plotted social world. When De Robertis proposed, in his famous essay "Saper leggere," that the new reader must have the courage to use a second sight, to see beyond and through words, the visionary exercise quickly became a literary law. These are hardly recommendations favorable to the impurities of mixed time and language that mark the modern novel,[42] and, in fact, Debenedetti insists that such a program was not just indifferent, but hostile to the novel.[43] The founder of the first *La Voce*, Prezzolini, later attempted to "correct" the narrowness of the "frammentisti" philosophy of form, but his apology is, in Debenedetti's view, as nefarious to the novel as what he is qualifying.[44] Prezzolini claims to see beyond the taste for the fragment a more expansive and bolder purpose, to express a new truth through lyric autobiography. It is Debenedetti's contention that the "superior" truth of the autobiography tended to compete with and patronize fictional truth and, once again, the latter suffered demotion in the hierarchy of forms.

Svevo was far removed from this atmosphere of literary polemic, from "il gruppo fiorentino,"[45] yet it would be hard to deny that its prejudices seriously affected his fate. Before his Europeanization, the construction of a tradition for Svevo was a confusing enterprise. Debenedetti takes Bruno Maier, Svevo's conscientious editor, to task for his carelessness in his analysis of the problem of Svevo's neglect.[46] But Maier himself, reviewing general critical opinion through the years, recognizes that definitive categories applied to Svevo are al-

---

41. See the collection of articles from *La Voce*, ed. Angelo Romano, in the series *La cultura italiana del '900 attraverso le riviste* (Turin, 1960). The manifesto of Onofri appears on p. 523 of the second volume of vocean articles. "Saper leggere" is reprinted in the same volume, pp. 471–78. Onofri's manifesto is hardly favorable to the novel's impure texture, and especially one as harsh and analytical as Svevo's. Massimo Bontempelli ("Colloqui con Bontempelli," *Tempo*, September 1942, pp. 10–17, quoted in Maier, *Profilo*, pp. 34–5) goes so far as to identify Svevo, mistakenly, as belonging, with American novelists, to the "frammentisti" who, against the great tradition of Italian classicism, produced interesting parts, but not a coherent whole.

42. Debenedetti, *Il romanzo*, p. 25.

43. Ibid., p. 19.

44. Ibid., pp. 48 ff.

45. This is the title given to a letter of Renato Serra (*La Voce* 2: 482–86), De Robertis's idol and friend, a contributor to *La Voce* and an ally in the anti-Crocean battles as well as a model of the highly valued prose writer of sincerity and limpidity (all the rest, as De Robertis says, echoing Verlaine, is merely literature).

46. Debenedetti, *Il romanzo*, pp. 526 ff.

most always misleading. The term *analytic novelist* could not have the same meaning for Italians as it did for other Europeans, and the more specific term *psychoanalytic* tended to isolate his example. While the early critics of Svevo were struggling with ways to tie him to the "veristi," his new realism was gradually getting the atmosphere it needed to be evaluated, the European example of Joyce, Proust, Mann, and Kafka which, coming into Italy helped to place him in a new age—"the age of anxiety."[47] His early novels, from this perspective, could be seen as novels opened to a new world of fiction, but before their time. The fiction of the European experimentalists paved the way for the appreciation of Svevo by definitively preventing "the possibility of reading novels settled in an easy-chair, slippers on the feet and a blanket on the lap, with the tranquil and genial security of listening to a story. . . ."[48]

Paradoxically, from this expansion has emerged an Italian tradition in retrospect. Other novelists who were, like Svevo, later to be celebrated with the European giants by the young writers of *Solaria,* shared in the neglect and misunderstanding. The two most commonly mentioned comrades in exile are Federigo Tozzi and Luigi Pirandello. Debenedetti raises the early narratives of Tozzi to the status of pioneering importance in the resurrection of a novelistic tradition in Italy. Tozzi and Pirandello knew and liked each other, were thoroughly involved in experiencing the contemporary Italian literary tradition, especially Verga and D'Annunzio and, in these significant ways, were less divorced than Svevo from a self-conscious literary scene. In addition, Svevo could not take too much heart from the alliance that was to be traced by future historians since he complained that Pirandello had never acknowledged the work he had sent him.[49] All three writers have been linked with Verga and his muted world of victims, though the differences between their atmospheres and textures are as marked as their differences in temperament. A general verdict ties Tozzi to the "frammentisti" and vocean practitioners of "intimistic prose," to the Crepuscolari poets with their short-winded and gentle melancholy, though Debenedetti makes a strong case for signaling him out as a natural writer of

47. Ibid., p. 530.
48. Ibid., p. 529.
49. Letter to Maria Anne Comnène, 28 November 1925, OO, 1: 770.

narrative from the early *Bestie* on.[50] The early fiction of Tozzi, especially *Ricordi di un impiegato,* which was later rewritten and published posthumously by Borgese in 1920, and *Con gli occhi chiusi* (1919), one of his major novels, has been compared with *A Life* in terms of the physical and psychological atmospheres, yet beyond the most superficial resemblances, it is difficult to determine why. The hostile primitivism; the aggressive anger under the surface of all his characters; an impassive and tangential prose; a surly and depressive stinginess and cruelty that invade nature, itself narcissistically busy with its own mass of details; and vague states of mind grudgingly articulated by limited and distorted consciousness all send out from Tozzi's novels an emanation very different from that of Svevo's fiction, compelling and effective in its own right though it may be.

Actually, Tozzi's tone is quite antagonistic to Svevo's. To compare Oedipal strains in delayed adolescence of characters, to juxtapose Tozzi's Ghisola and Svevo's Angiolina, or the lives of petty clerks, or father-son relationships, turns out to be an arid exercise. The emphasis of Sandro Maxia on Tozzi's contribution, through his suspended atmosphere, to the "putting into crisis of narrative temporality," an effect that makes elliptical both time and motivation, is a more persuasive way of linking Tozzi to Svevo and Pirandello in the general opening of Italian narrative to the larger European experimentations.[51] Debenedetti too sees the three novelists as allies in the creating of a new vision for the novel, and censures the acerbic Russo for reading Tozzi as if he were reading Verga, by veristic standards.[52] Tozzi's work, claims Debenedetti, like Pirandello's, is busy destroying the naturalistic world of cause and effect, of ratios that guarantee the usual ethical securities:

> In him [Tozzi] there is the sorrow, the pain of no longer being able to look naturalistically at the world.[53]

This perspective helps us to bind Svevo to the two novelists by a larger effect, the subversion of the old novel. Svevo, we remember,

50. Debenedetti (*Il romanzo,* p. 89) censures Borgese's attempt to force this early work into the mold of the later "naturalist" *Tre croce* and his insensitivity to what was new in Tozzi's fiction.
51. Sandro Maxia, *Uomini e bestie nella narrativa di Federigo Tozzi* (Padua, 1971), p. 14.
52. See Luigi Russo, *I narratori* (Rome, 1923), and Debenedetti, *Il romanzo,* p. 244.
53. Debenedetti, *Il romanzo,* p. 256.

used naturalism as a target of irony, turning the volatility of Mother Nature's world against its social predictions, and his own humor against Darwinian and Freudian determinism. Debenedetti suggests that the seemingly unmotivated leaps and hops of successive mental states in Tozzi and the murky readings of his passively aggressive characters turn up a level of compulsive rather than conscious action that again might seem to lessen the distance between the worlds of Tozzi and Svevo. However, Tozzi's close and unconscious dramas of psychological and moral mutilation persistently veer away from social acceptance and courtship, impelling characters to an isolated ineptitude never sanctioned by Svevo.

The great value of Debenedetti's analysis lies in his stubborn insistence on the quiet revolution in favor of the novel and against the magazine culture, a revolution that pushes both Tozzi and Svevo beyond categories like "decadent" and "frammentisti." From this view, even Borgese's enthusiasm for Tozzi, misguided though it may be in Debenedetti's opinion, was a significant turning point in the battle against the hostility to fiction sustained by the voceans.[54] Borgese's own *Rubé* (1921), the reevaluation of Tozzi, the rereading of Verga, the discovery of Svevo, and the appearance of Moravia's fiction made of the twenties in Italy the watershed for a new post-naturalistic narrative. Rubé, a hyperconscious and depressed carrier of the disease of D'Annunzian decadence, an illness that could be readily recognized by the literary world, exhibits in and out of war an affective and ideological aridity blamed on the education of the bourgeois intellectual who destroys himself by the expectation of all or nothing. He goes through life, and to death, like an automaton, " 'always in a position,' " as Rubé's fiancée tells him, " 'in which the reason spies on the soul,' "[55] a favorite posture of European decadence. We might certainly imagine Svevo sympathetic to this picture of the bankruptcy of the idea of the superman that he found so vicious an infection. The envy that the sick Rubé has of health, his uselessness, his recognition that he tends to "slide over life without making contact,"[56] and the horror of making choices that might rouse hopes all link him to a host of postromantic anti-heroes. At the end of the novel Rubé reviews his modernity, his hypochondria, his

54. Ibid., p. 127.
55. Giuseppe Borgese, *Rubé* (Verona, 1938), p. 107.
56. Ibid., p. 109.

faithlessness, and his belief only in fortune, and he asks an apparently Svevian question: " 'Have I never been innocent?' "[57] Innocence is equated with a trust in instinct which, as a willed intellectual, he has lost. Ultimately Rubé suffers as meaningless a death as a life, shot in a mob scene between two modern rhetorics, those of Communism and Fascism. If Rubé at all reflects Alfonso, whose possibilities and education are a much more modest affair, whose small, provincial Napoleonic dreams of success are never tried on the wide fields of historical crisis or on the pages of Nietzsche and D'Annunzio, if he suffers like all Svevo's heroes from abulia and the desire for innocence, it is difficult to believe that this novel looks back to *A Life* or prepares for *Confessions of Zeno*. A humorless sarcasm, a pretentious tendency to moralize and metaphorize, the calling into question of an entire age and its ideals set us miles apart from the petty bank clerk exposed with such delicate irony, or from the playful Zeno who cannot conceive of a world other than the anxious one in which he restlessly lives. The Svevian hero is thoroughly modern, but he is not absorbed by his age. It is hard to imagine a Svevian character ever granted a consistent or immodest enough vision of his disease in the midst of racing after health to proclaim himself a representative of his times. Yet many critics continue to wonder why, after the excitement generated by Rubé, readers remained indifferent to *Confessions of Zeno*.

More cogent are the claims for pairing Svevo and Pirandello as creators in Italy of the new man, already wandering over Europe, experiencing psychological and existential invasions of bourgeois order. Renato Barilli has attempted to establish the pair as a tradition equal in importance and as legitimately native as other moments in the classical Italian narrative:

> There was the great moment of the Boccaccian *Decameron;* from there the development of the "novel," in the form of the heroic poem, from Boiardo to Ariosto to Tasso; finally, the powerful curve that reaches from Manzoni to "verismo" and to regionalism; and now the Svevo-Pirandello block can be added as the latest moment.[58]

A great appreciator of Tozzi's new way of seeing the world, Pirandello was also an admirer of Alberto Cantoni, whose novella

57. Ibid., p. 320.
58. Renato Barilli, *La linea Svevo-Pirandello* (Milan, 1972), p. 8.

"L'Altalena delle antipatie" (1887) has been called a forerunner of the Svevo-Pirandello humor. Pirandello's essay on Cantoni (1905), really an excuse to work out his celebrated definition of the humorist as "un critico fantastico," though applicable to many artists, is particularly useful in bringing Pirandello and Cantoni close to Svevo.[59] Pirandello singles out the novella "L'Altalena delle antipatie" in *Il Demonio dello stile*[60] as a fine example of the humorist's feelings complicated by criticism. The title novella deals with the importance of how one sees over what one sees and, through an unreliable narrator, slaps at the complacency of those naïfs who think that a clear vision uncluttered by distractions can achieve sincerity. But it is "L'Altalena" that is nearest to Svevo's temper for its alternations of humors and for the inventive rationalizations of its simultaneously attractive and repellent narrator who, like the underground man, wears honesty like a badge. The attempt to cure his automatic antipathies by marriage to a young orphaned girl whom he identifies with anonymous innocence certainly seems to look forward to *Confessions of Zeno,* but the cynical deliberateness of the act and the harsh consequences of the disease of self-analysis, the high price for "sincerity," and the growing indifference of the wife become mother, radiate a much rougher and more intellectual atmosphere, less spontaneous and improvised, than that which surrounds Zeno. Nevertheless, the hero's address to the baby,[61] in which he talks of the innocent life that it owes to the father's sick hostilities (for had he not been hostile he would not have married), the many witty metaphors applied to love and marriage, the recognition that a superior consciousness is a curse but also a dimension that raises one over healthy "normal" wives of the earth, make Cantoni, whose work is contemporaneous with Svevo's early novels, the closest to the Svevian vision of the Italian writers sharing Svevo's world.[62]

Pirandello's own novel of 1904, *Il fu Mattia Pascal,* has come to take a major place not only in line of the rebirth of the Italian novel, of its Europeanization, but also as a predecessor of *Confessions of Zeno,* though as Marziano Guglielminetti wisely reminds us,

59. Luigi Pirandello, *Saggi, poesie, scritti vari,* opere a cura di Manlio Lo Vecchio-Musti (Milan, 1960), 6: 363–87.
60. Alberto Cantoni, *Il demonio dello stile* (Florence, 1887).
61. Ibid., p. 123.
62. See Ferdinando Bernini, "Modernità di Alberto Cantoni," *Giornale storico della letteratura italiana* 160 (Turin, 1937).

Pirandello as novelist, unlike Svevo, did not succeed in broadening
the base of his existential examination sufficiently beyond its provincial beginnings to enter into the great tradition of the European
novel.[63] Giving new depth to the clichéd tag of "inetto" by which
the heroes of Svevo and Pirandello are so often joined, Renato Barilli
writes:

> It goes without saying that Mattia is presented to us as a "thorough
> inept," with amazing correspondence to the figure of Zeno Cosini;
> he is also a daddy's son, mildly interested in disobeying, but appear-
> ing on the outside full of respect and timidity: a major weapon of
> an actual disobedience, as the psychoanalyst was well aware, that of
> wishing oneself into an inept, doomed to fail in any "healthy"
> practical enterprise.[64]

The suggestion of Barilli that the new ineptitude, susceptible to
psychological examination, grafted in Pirandello's novel to the old
"veristic" provincial victimization and susceptible to sociological
analysis, points Pirandello's journey from Verga's shadow toward his
unique existential comedy is an interesting one but, in balance, the
existential emphasis upon the philosophical problem of identity
completely overwhelms the desperate provincial naturalism of the
beginning of the book. Dissipation of an inheritance, the insignif-
icance of the hero's job, and the grim household of a star-crossed
marriage might seem to justify the adventure of Mattia's fake
death and his subsequent experiment in freedom, but from the
moment Mattia wins the money at gambling that enables him to
undertake a new identity, our attention is entirely turned away from
cause and centered on the problem of the nature of being in the
modern world, a concentration that makes the novel's start appear
almost artificial. The central section, in which Mattia sets himself up
as Adriano Meis in the Paleari household in Rome, a household
suffering from varieties of material and psychological misfortunes, is
the real story. The terrible renunciation required of emotional in-
volvement with those who want and deserve it for the sake of staying
"free," the hangovers of guilt from the advertisement of false
premises, and the mistaken assumption that he could shake the moral
nature of the old identity, bankrupt the experiment. The novel has

63. Guglielminetti, *Struttura e sintassi*, p. 101.
64. Barilli, *La linea*, pp. 191–92.

perhaps more interest for students of Svevo when set beside "Short Sentimental Journey" than *Confessions of Zeno,* for here Svevo too examines the meaning of freedom and social identity, though in a higher level of bourgeois society. Instantly, with this juxtaposition, we see the enormous differences between the two authors. By this time, to be sure, Svevo was a mature narrator, but he gives us a far more spontaneous fiction, unpropped by the often forced intellectual premises with which Pirandello, here (and in the essays that sparked his conflict with Croce) feels he must fortify his new vision. Svevo would never conceive of pushing such an experiment beyond the confines of a short train ride *back* to Trieste. If Mattia, from his experience, understands the impossibility of living without reciprocal confirmations of social, emotional, and intellectual identity, he has already gone, with two deaths, too far beyond *his* Trieste to be successfully resurrected. The confinement of character and consciousness to the static atmosphere of the intellectual problem has destroyed any interest for the reader in a return to a familiar environment that was living death just as the traveled identity was death in life. Inevitably such a return has to be a serious anticlimax, for the questions raised have made readjustment an absurdity. When the premise is fantasized and played out with a half-hearted infantilism in Svevo's hero, the trip can gracefully come full circle without major jolts. This is not to say that Pirandello should not, in this early work, have taken the risk of letting the problem run away with the personality, which is paralyzed when it cannot define itself against social pressures. But the absurdist experiments of the humorist, meant to reflect the postnaturalistic vision of a world ruled by accident and chance, are subverted by the mechanical consistency of the intellectual inquiry, a consistency for which Svevo's self-appointed dilettantism would have had little patience or taste.

We see, in a piece like "Specifico di Dr. Menghi," and in many of Svevo's plays, how strained and stiff his humor is when it is forced to follow through a problem rather than a character or a volatile consciousness, whereas such tenacity is essential to Pirandello's drama. The deliberate nature of the hoax in *Il fu Mattia Pascal* eventually sucks out of the hero's responses all spontaneity, and all tone out of his recitation. A cynical recapitulation of situation must serve for climax when exploration grinds to a halt. In the novel the seriousness of the existential problem of freedom seems trivialized by the

absurdity of such a low-level exchange of lives. A less bold experi-
menter like Svevo would never have taken such a chance, would
never have pushed his characters beyond the social scene from which
their rationalizations draw sustenance, their fantasies security.

As shaky as the alliance may in fact have been among Tozzi,
Pirandello, and Svevo by 1930, it had given to the young writers
associated with the literary magazine *Solaria* enough of a new tradition to honor, even as they honored the great European novelists.
Pirandello and Svevo, with Kafka, point toward the future for Italian
fiction. Peter Bondanella is certainly justified in claiming:

> If Svevo is the father of the modern Italian psychological novel, he
> is also—with Kafka and Pirandello—the precursor of such recogniz-
> ably absurdist writers as Dino Buzzati, Italo Calvino, and Eduardo
> De Filippo.[65]

Not only did *Solaria* ("The Hoax" was published there in 1928) and
Il Convegno (which published "The Mother" in 1927) honor Svevo
as a modern, but they saw him as a master who had restored the great
tradition of narrative art to Italy. His recognition by the young
seemed to Svevo, as he testifies in his last letters, a particular joy
because of his rejection by the old literary Italy, and because it com-
pensated for the lost literary youth he had hoped for.

One of the most important obstacles to acceptance by the old
guard had been Svevo's language, and the debates about his syntax
and the dialectical impurities of his narrative diction were long at
the center of the Svevo case. But the issue of his language is encased
in a larger one, that of his role as a master who worked with an
antiliterary style and temper that had at last found its time. A long
history of reluctance on Svevo's part to call himself by profession a
literary man (his wife's biography is particularly touching on this
issue) is now a benefit, as the bona fide "curiosità antiletteraria"[66]
discovered by the French becomes an example to those tired of

65. Peter Bondanella, "'The Hoax,': Svevo on Art and Reality," *Studies in Short
Fiction* (Summer 1973), p. 264. See also Antonio Illiano, "A View of the Italian Absurd
from Pirandello to Edoardo De Filippo," *From Surrealism to the Absurd*, ed. W. Zyla,
Proceedings of the Comparative Literature Symposium 3 (Lubbock, Texas, 1970):
55–76.

66. This phrase appears as an insult in the harsh and ungenerous review of Giulio
Caprin in 1926, a review that greatly wounded Svevo. See Bruno Maier, *Profilo*, p. 20,
and Svevo's letter to Joyce, 15 February 1926, OO, 1: 777; to Montale, 17 February
1926, OO, 1: 780, and to Prezzolini in the same year, OO, 1: 778.

highly self-conscious literary traditions—a society, in spite of the voceans, still possessed of the flavor of anachronistic Dannunzians and purists, of failed Manzonians.[67] This recognition becomes standard, and is behind the early judgment of Sergio Solmi on the superiority of Svevo's reliance upon experience rather than tradition, on his contribution of a new "virginal power of representation."[68] It underlies the later one too of Francesco Flora, that Svevo the industrialist was spared the "perilous eloquence" of the "professional" writer.[69] This enthusiastic inversion of defect is paralleled by the oddity that, just as Svevo was greeted as the maker of a new novel, so was he after it paradoxically appreciated as a narrative *undoer*, whose relaxed diffusion of consciousness in the last stories, the presence of that "other imperious protagonist, his philosophy of life,"[70] seemed to open the door even wider to a modern style of sincerity. Those who prepared the way for the heroism of the antiliterary Svevo included, ironically, the group of Triestine writers associated with *La Voce,* writers like Scipio Slataper, Carlo and Giani Stuparich, and the poet Umberto Saba, a phenomenon that must qualify Debenedetti's contentions about the monolithic vocean crimes against the novel.

Giani Stuparich in particular, always politically sensitive, especially from the time of his student days in Prague, held as an ideal a kind of muscular introspection, an antiacademic grounding of literature in a life that was at once turned inward, morally serious, open, and engaged in the pre- and postwar worlds of vulnerable consciences.[71] The insistence upon plain speaking and firsthand observation, which had been anticipated by the "Crepuscolari" poets,[72] might have helped to clear the way for appreciation of Svevo. If we look at Giani Stuparich's criticism of D'Annunzio's prose, we can see

67. Pampaloni, "Italo Svevo," p. 500.
68. From *Il Convegno,* November 1927, quoted in Bruno Maier, *Profilo,* p. 56.
69. Francesco Flora, *Storia della letteratura italiana,* a cura di Attiglio Momigliani (Milan, 1947) 3: 603–4.
70. Pampaloni, "Italo Svevo," p. 517, and see A. Leone de Castris, *Decadentismo e Realismo* (Bari, 1958) , p. 262.
71. For an account of Triestine life and politics from a temperament markedly different from Svevo's, see his friend Giani Stuparich's *Trieste nei miei ricordi* (Milan, 1948) .
72. The poet Saba resisted the association with the "crepuscolari" often forced upon him, but he admitted that the group had been an important stimulus to the new sensibility. See Joseph Cary, *Three Modern Italian Poets: Saba, Ungaretti, Montale* (New York, 1969) , pp. 4–7.

an attitude emerging that would be sympathetic to Svevo's fiction.[73] The nice precision and delicacy of Stuparich's complaint that the major problem of D'Annunzio's prose is the "lack of interior pauses"[74] (those silences so often praised in Manzoni) lead him to claim that his prose was rich in external qualities of tone and color only at the price of being poor in internal qualities. A prose that is, on the contrary, to all appearances poor, may be rich in subtlety and substance. The question is then raised by Stuparich of the egocentricity of D'Annunzio's art, an art that refuses simplification and renunciation, and should assume a modesty disguising effort. D'Annunzio's refined sensibility and his acute attention to all the mutations and fluctuations of feeling become ends in themselves:

> Hence the disappointment; what we ask of great narrative art, the humanity of the story, is in D'Annunzio dried at the roots. The glorious vegetation of his prose springs from an arid ground; it is nourished and it prospers in an artificial atmosphere. One must regret that this great artist, a fine model of firmness and technical ability and an acute interpreter of the senses and of the mind that registers them, lacked faith in his heart.[75]

Stuparich's hostility to the Decadents led him to try to clear Svevo of their infection, so often imputed to him for want of a better disease, and to link him *retrogressively* to an older novel. In an article in *Solaria* just months after Svevo's death, Stuparich attempts as well to save Svevo from too limited a Freudian category by calling him "a simple, healthy man of the nineteenth century."[76] Such an exaggerated reversal of direction is Stuparich's way of sparing Svevo from false alliance with the new aesthetes, the empty skepticism, and "funambulist relativism" that characterized for Stuparich so much of modern Decadence. Here is quite a different Svevo from that celebrated by other *Solaria* admirers. When Stuparich identifies these modern Decadents as Proust, Joyce, and Kafka, he begins to sound almost as philistine as Max Nordau. But his view of Svevo as a conservative narrator in relation to experiments like the "stream of consciousness" and "intermittences of the heart," and as one for whom

73. Giani Stuparich, "Omaggio a D'Annunzio," ed. Giuseppe de Robertis e Enrico Falqui, *Letteratura* (March 1939) : 201.
74. Ibid.
75. Ibid., p. 203.
76. Renato Bertacchini, *Stuparich* (Florence, 1968) , p. 84.

analysis led to a philosophy of life rather than art,[77] is a good counterforce to overzealous claims for Svevo's revolutionary nature. All
we must remember is that if Svevo, like Stuparich, admires the De
Sanctis who looks for the whole man in his words,[78] he cannot really,
as a whole writer, stand as flat-footed as his friend against the risky
experiments in consciousness of contemporary practice.

A more sensitive reflection of Svevo's vision comes out of the comments of another vocean Triestine, the poet Saba. In an autobiographical piece in the third person, like Svevo's own profile, Saba
gives his famous "antiliterary" version of Verlaine's manifesto, that
for him "literature is to poetry as the lie is to the truth."[79] Anxious
to bring Svevo into close accord with the Triestine voceans, Maier
seizes upon Svevo's often quoted antiliterary pronouncements, his
claim to have definitively eliminated from his life that ridiculous and
nefarious thing called literature, and his statement that through the
diary and his scribblings he wants only to understand himself
better.[80] And certainly Saba and Svevo share a suspicion of the literature that calls too much attention to itself to be sincere.[81] Svevo
would be in sympathy with Saba's sense of contrast between the art of
D'Annunzio and that of Manzoni, between a dishonest and honest
art,[82] and with this comment:

> From a manzonian, even not of the highest genius, one can always
> expect something good, because he would have learned from the
> master not the necessity of being a great man, nor an original writer
> at any cost; but to be, in life as in literature, an honest man.[83]

In fact, Svevo went further in his antiliterary sentiments by claiming,
to his friend Montale and others, that poetry was, in the formality of
its disguises, a kind of dishonest literature in relation to prose, or
that he, unfortunately, was deaf to its charms.[84] There is a strong tie

77. Ibid., p. 85.
78. Letter to Montale, 10 March 1926, OO, 1: 786.
79. See Saba's account of the history of the *Canzoniere* in *Prose,* p. 412.
80. Svevo, "Pagine di diario e sparse," OO, 3: 816, 818. See discussion in Bruno Maier,
Saggi sulla letteratura triestina (Milan, 1972) , p. 5.
81. See letter of Svevo to Valéry Larbaud, 30 April 1926, OO, 1: 793:

Saba seems to me an interesting man and a great poet who draws from things words
that are truly his.

82. Saba, "Quello che resta da fare ai poeti," *Prose,* p. 751.
83. Ibid., p. 752.
84. See letter to his daughter, 10 April 1908, OO, 1: 473; to Montale, 1 December
1926, p. 817, and to Montale again, 6 December 1926, p. 820.

between Svevo's habitual self-examination and his unwillingness to release consciousness from the tense orders of morality, and the sentiments of the vocean Triestines. Yet once again, the particular temperament of Svevo that gets into his prose seems to suggest his differences more than his similarities with these late friends. For one thing, we cannot imagine Svevo issuing literary manifestos that are meant to accomplish anything but strengthen his own personal resolves, and even these are filled with the reticent ambivalence, so typical of Svevo's mind, that forces the most serious concerns to surface into play.

Never literarily secure enough to issue vocean manifestos, and tempermentally unsuited to such a role, he laughs with those benevolent critics who, unable to call him a great writer, call him a great industrialist, for he is, in his own eyes, neither.[85] His diaries are filled with the rhythm of his adjustment to a disappointed ambition. It is touching to read his resolution of 1902 that he will not publish what he writes, having eliminated literature from his life,[86] but it has often been taken too seriously by critics anxious to chart his life in terms of turning points and climaxes. The motives for his declaration of renunciation have been much discussed, and most would agree with Pampaloni's hypothesis that his long silence following the neglect of the first two novels was partly stoicism and partly a reaction to his rejection on the grounds that he was, in fact, antiliterary.[87] From the vantage of success, Svevo can tell Signora Bice Rusconi Besso:

> As for your demon of literature, I do not fear it. I remember that, even before the favor that fell upon me because of the fancy of a great man, I always loved it. I pushed it away, not because of resentment that it did not accord me fame. I feared that it would keep me from doing the duty that was thrust upon me, for my benefit, for the sake of my family and my associates. It was a question of integrity, because it didn't take much to make me realize that if I wrote or read one line, my work in practical life was ruined for an entire week.[88]

85. Svevo, "Soggiorno londinese," OO, 3: 689.
86. Ibid., p. 818.
87. Pampaloni, "Italo Svevo," p. 500.
88. Svevo, Letter to Signora Bice Rusconi Besso, 19 April 1928, OO, 1: 872.

If we cannot quite believe this to be the deepest cause, it is because we feel that Svevo's renunciation is accompanied by a psychological fear, noted early in his brother Elio's notebook, that relates the young Svevo's writer's block to the desire for his father's approval, a fear certainly reinforced by critical neglect.[89] Again and again we have seen Svevo take a negative attitude and turn it into a comfortable adjustment, but never convert it, by rationalization or justification, into a full-blown rebellion. For this reason, I think Pampaloni's distinction is valid, that the rejection of literature regards his lack of literary fortune, while his acceptance of it as the only salvation ("Outside of the pen there is no salvation") reflects his stubborn faithfulness to his work as an artist.[90] We have the assurances by those close to him that he never really stopped writing. Everything seems to point to a constant literary activity of comedies, fables, sketches, and stories in the years between *As a Man Grows Older* and *Confessions of Zeno,* and from this perspective the renunciation looks more like gestation. To accept the silence as a serious abandonment, like that of Valéry or Rimbaud, would be to attribute to Svevo an aesthetic purity or a clear Romantic rebellion of life against art that was totally uncharacteristic. A. Leone de Castris captures the texture of this intricate case when he writes:

> He thought he wrote only to understand himself better, and that was his literature. He spun invisible threads—and here and there very visible—between the work of his youth and that of his maturity. He wove his story as he could, hiding it from others, in order to live serenely, and from himself, in order to live honestly: he created, in substance, a literary offering of his whole life.[91]

A tenacious companion to discussions concerning Svevo's attitude toward the literary profession is the long and complicated debate

---

89. Livia Veneziani Svevo, *Vita di mio marito,* p. 27. It is interesting that Svevo's wife takes his reasoning as the whole story (p. 80). And we cannot overlook the fact that *Confessions of Zeno* was written at the end of the war when the factory was shut down and the world was "emptied of clients"; the only block left between Svevo and literature was "the violin, aided by the heaviness of the weather" ("Soggiorno londinese," OO, 3: 698).

90. Pampaloni, "Italo Svevo," p. 496.

91. de Castris, *Italo Svevo,* p. 181. Compare also Bruno Maier's statement in the introduction to OO. 3: 5:

. . . in reality he never abstained from writing and considered his literary activity, whether only in a private orbit, or "to understand himself better" (OO, 3: 818) and to "feel alive" (OO, 3: 136), the center and fixed point of his entire existence.

over the acceptability of his language. Here, most of all, Svevo found himself disadvantaged by the absence of an Italian literary background, and once again we see him extremely vulnerable to critical opinion, displaying the insecurity that starts up in his own mind, that familiar rhythm of compliance and adjustment. Neither the language of Manzoni nor that of Verga could be his, any more than their milieux. But as always, in evaluating Svevo's isolation by hindsight, we can surmise that ultimately, for all his linguistic discomfort, there was more to be gained than lost from this condition. It would be difficult to disagree with Renato Barilli's contention that one of the liberating contributions of Svevo and Pirandello was the example of overcoming "decisively the problem of dialect"[92] in spite of their regional roots, and in having discovered new languages that could interpret as well as describe their deracinated visions. For Pampaloni the fragmentation of the moral man that cannot be healed by poetic syntheses is reflected in a language and scene that "open[s] into the disintegration of reality as such,"[93] forcing the novel out of the nineteenth century into the twentieth. Though we have no sense at all in Svevo's style of a self-conscious experiment, as we do in Joyce's, such claims are most often made in analyzing the nature of Svevo's narrative language, "a language that, without the security of a tradition and the protection of a sure linquistic usage, had to *invent* for the first time in Italy new narrative procedures to accommodate itself to an analytic syntax without precedent."[94] For Giulio Marzot the "suggestive barbarity" of Svevo's style corresponds to the uncertain rhythms of the unconscious,[95] and for Umbro Apollonio it is "an instinctive method of clarifying the consciousness."[96] All true artists, reminds Apollonio, create their languages, which then must convince us of their inevitable correspondence with the creative origin of the fiction.[97] This kind of assumption is behind Pampaloni's description:

> The language of Svevo, with its bureaucratic detachment, its wriggling, talkative verve, its systolic and diastolic movement of de-

92. Barilli, *La linea Svevo-Pirandello*, p. 7.
93. Pampaloni, "Italo Svevo," p. 530.
94. de Castris, *Italo Svevo*, p. 321.
95. Giulio Marzot, *Il decadentismo italiano* (Bologna, 1970), p. 183.
96. Umbro Apollonio, preface to *Corto viaggio sentimentale e altre racconti inediti* (Milan, 1957), p. 9.
97. Ibid., p. 14.

scriptive accumulation and of the unburdening of them, always provisional in the diagnoses, corresponds exactly to the narrative necessity that moves it.[98]

The argument from necessity leads some critics to say that Svevo's style is not to be judged by standards that cannot account for it.[99] Svevo himself, especially in the confidence of his last period, registers a double attitude of resignation to the consciousnees of linguistic oddity and of humor that makes of his "defect" a part of his strength. Ingenuously delighted at comments about the improvement of his writing between *As a Man Grows Older* and *Confessions of Zeno,* he waggishly writes to Montale: "Now, if I had another twenty years of abstention, God only knows how I would write."[100] And, as if to support this contention, Silvio Benco, in a 1929 review of Svevo's last writing, notes that the language of *Confessions of Zeno* and of much of *Further Confessions of Zeno* is by far Svevo's best.[101] Ettore Bonora's fine essay climaxes with the contention that the last period exhibited a new "aristocratic ease."[102] The "Short Sentimental Journey," in which action is at a minimum, coincides, claims Bonora, with his most relaxed and masterful style.[103] Aside from the strengthening of authorial humor and confidence manifested by the modal changes,[104] the greatest gain is not in becoming more acceptably literary, but in walking away from the shadow of the Academy.[105] That is why Devoto is harsh on the half-hearted and inorganic corrections Svevo felt obliged to make for the second edition of *As a Man Grows Older,* for these corrections are, as Bonora puts it, "lessicale," whereas his blessed difficulty was "sintattico," a problem that Bonora defines as the consequence of a language that, "obliged to have all the fluidity and sinuosity necessary to analyze and to deal with psychological time, hits too frequently against the hardness of a

98. Pampaloni, "Italo Svevo," p. 529.
99. de Castris, *Svevo,* pp. 306–7.
100. Svevo, Letter to Montale, 3 April 1926, OO, 1: 791.
101. Review of *La novella del buon vecchio e della bella fanciulla ed altri scritti, Pegaso* 1, no. 2 (August 1929): 246.
102. Ettore Bonora, "Italo Svevo," *Gli ipocriti di malebolge* (Milan-Naples, 1953), p. 96.
103. Ibid., p. 110. Cf. Pampaloni, "Italo Svevo," p. 529.
104. These are sensitively charted by Marziano Guglielminetti in *Struttura e sintassi.*
105. This gain is well explored by the classic studies of both Bonora and Devoto. See Giacomo Devoto, "Decenni per Svevo," *Studi di stilistica* (Florence, 1950), pp. 175–192.

concrete exterior."[106] Devoto distinguishes Svevo from those writers in whom the separation between the word and the heart is the sign of bad writing.[107] That this in itself was a conviction of Svevo, however evident his linguistic inferiority complex, is amply evidenced by his defenses, both in the irony of his fiction (Alfonso's philosophical treatise, Alfio's fashionable causes, Emilio's dead literary life of fantasy, even in the sparring of Zeno against the psychoanalyst) and in his humor turned against himself. Svevo's language has found many defenders, but his own reactions reflect the gradual course of public acceptance.

The difficulties of measuring his unorthodox language against a more traditional literary one, with its teutonisms, its tags of Triestine dialect, its archaisms—a language, as he calls that of *A Life,* "stuffed with solecisms and dialectical formations"[108]—are fully recognized by Svevo, but he counters the criticism with the claim made later in his behalf by almost all his defenders: "He well knew that his language could not adorn itself with words he did not feel."[109] Only a living tongue is worth writing in, and for him that tongue is, for better or for worse, "Triestine speech which shouldn't have had to wait until 1918 to be heard as Italian."[110] His early style was more susceptible to linguistic pressures, what Bonora calls "concessions to the poetics of the traditional novel,"[111] but even if confidence came late, finding its best instrument of expression in the attractive rationalizations of Zeno, an instrument capable of expressing that double direction of admission and defense, Svevo always knew the hopelessness of writing in a language not his own. In a letter to Giuseppe

---

106. Bonora, "Italo Svevo," p. 101. Devoto sees the major weakness as one affecting the formal links between images (*Studi di stilistica,* p. 191) . Svevo writes:

Entrò vestita semplicemente di una vestaglia nera, la capigliatura nel grande disordine di cappelli sconvolti e forse anche strappati da una mano che s'accanisce a trovar da fare qualche cosa, quando non può altrimenti lenire.

Devoto would have preferred:

Entrò vestita semplicemente di una vestaglia nera con i capelli disordinati, sconvolti; forse anche strappati da una mano che, non potendo lenire, si era accanita nella ricerca di qualche cosa da fare.

107. Ibid., pp. 190–91.
108. Svevo, "Profilo autobiografico," OO, 3: 803.
109. Ibid., p. 806.
110. Ibid.
111. Bonora, "Italo Svevo," p. 101.

Prezzolini concerning his reception by the French, he reveals his
typical mature defense:

> I don't deny that I thought (without false modesty) that perhaps
> such a judgment was facilitated by the fact that the [French] feeling
> for our language is less delicate. For me, growing up in a country
> where, until seven years ago, our dialect was our true language, my
> prose could not have been other, unfortunately, than what it is and
> now there is no time to straighten out my crooked legs.[112]

The same humor is well displayed in his comments on his first two
novels. In a letter to Enrico Rocca in 1927, he writes in retrospect of
A Life:

> It was written at a time in which other novelists wrote in a manner
> different from me, but not better, when they didn't write too
> well.[113]

After speaking in the same letter of his corrections of *Senilità* he
notes: "Perhaps it is obvious that I have written only one novel in
my whole life. All the less pardonable that I wrote it always poorly."
Svevo delighted in the discovery that Dostoevski's narrative diction
was also censured by Russian critics and, in a letter to his French
friend and codiscoverer Valéry Larbaud full of good humor about
language and praising Saba's courage to write in words that are really
his, he speaks of the Italian vice of pleasure in finding novels that are
badly written.[114]

If Svevo cannot, in view of the literary Triestines who wrote
"good" Italian, ascribe to his city his "brand of Italian Esperanto,"[115]
it is to his love of Trieste and its atmosphere that Montale ascribes
his style's strength. In an imaginative coupling that marries words to
the weather, the poet writes:

> The men and women of Svevo speak the language of the Tergesteo,
> the language of old triestine merchants; this is the music—together
> with that incessant "bora"—that underlines the sombre *cafard,* the
> assiduous inner monologue, the courageous self-auscultation of his
> characters.[116]

---

112. Svevo, letter to Giuseppe Prezzolini, 21 November 1925, OO, 1: 769.
113. Svevo, OO, 1: 846.
114. Svevo, 30 April 1926, OO, 1: 793.
115. Renato Poggioli, "A Note on Italo Svevo," *The Spirit of the Letter* (Cambridge,
Mass., 1965) , p. 173.
116. Svevo, "Il vento è mutato," *Lettere,* p. 139.

It would take, says Montale, a professor to complain of Carla's canzonetta and to wish for another language; the time has come to recognize that "among all the possible languages for an Italian novelist, Svevo's also has full right to citizenship." The theory that the younger Svevo was more susceptible to the lure of literary Italian because it represented a patriotic link with Italy has been put forward[117] and certainly the cultural situation of Trieste, hosting the Austrian and Slavic, as well as the Italian presence, is an important part of the story of Svevo's language. Writing in good Italian in a city "seething with repressed Italian patriotic feeling"[118] was an act of faith. But Svevo was philosophical about his early education in Germany instead of Italy. Other Triestines, despite the difficulties of having to be educated elsewhere, did not have to wait until the age of fifty to go to Florence. Because he was a cosmopolitan before an Italian, when Italy came to him at the liberation, he writes *Confessions of Zeno* now with a legitimate right to belong to Italy's literature.[119] The truth is that Svevo could never really interest himself in the nationalistic rhetoric of irredentist Trieste, so unsuited to receive a novel like *A Life*. His authentic interests were freed from political Trieste by the war itself.

The most crucial European influence for Svevo came, of course, from Austria. Saba and Svevo, with other intellectual Triestine Jews in an atmosphere free from prejudice (while Vienna was becoming more and more anti-Semitic), were particularly receptive to Freud and to thinkers like the controversial Weininger, whose theories on women show up in the mouth of Guido in *Confessions of Zeno*. And this was at a time in which the rest of Italy was closed to such currents.[120] The reasons behind the Italian resistance to Freud have been well traced in Michel David's classic study:[121] the long tradition of literary idealism and Catholicism, unfriendly to the irrational and to scientific determinism; a new tendency to fascism hostile to the Jewish pessimism in Freud; the absence of a leftist political force

117. Domenico Cernecca, "Dialectical Element and Linguistic Complex in Italo Svevo," trans. Renata Treitel, *Modern Fiction Studies*, Svevo issue, p. 84.

118. Stanislaus Joyce, *The Meeting of Svevo and Joyce*, p. 8.

119. See letter to Attilio Frecura, mistakenly identified as a letter to Benjamin Crémieux by Bruno Maier, OO, 1: 825. The letter has been traced by A. Meoni as one dating from 10 January 1923. See Maier, *Saggi*, p. 74n. for text.

120. Bouissy, "Les Fondements idéologiques," 2: 367.

121. Michel David, *La psicanalisi nella cultura italiana* (Turin, 1966).

that fathered the strange anticlerical alliance of Marx and Freud in other countries; the presence of the jealous guardians of Italian cultural superiority; and an Academy that tended to stifle intellectual curiosity. *Confessions of Zeno,* which Svevo hoped had introduced psychoanalysis into Italian literature, did not have an easy road to reception. We remember that Aghios in "Short Sentimental Journey," after he hears a young man talk of psychoanalysis and watches him get off the train at a small station, imagines drolly that psychoanalytic theory entered with him into the countryside. After the war, Svevo's Triestine friends—the poet Saba, Scipio Slataper, Giani Stuparich, and his young admirers—shared with him the culture that had produced this novel. Saba particularly, whom Svevo admired though he was cautious about his difficult personality,[122] was even more involved than Svevo with the world of psychoanalysis, and he appreciated Svevo's defensive humor, which he identified as "his supreme form of kindness."[123] The desire to bring literature into intimate contact with life at the risk of being called antiliterary, the neurasthenic nature, an obsession with forms of psychological senility, and late fame, also linked the two writers. It was as if suddenly a genuine and original Triestine culture had been established out of the realization that all the city's writers had, whatever their contacts, moved, from birth, on the outskirts of literature. And in fact, that the great tradition of Triestine literature now took shape with Svevo as its father has been convincingly established by Bruno Maier.[124] It is one marked by autobiographical mediation to the world, by the *esame di coscienza,*[125] a term so dear to the voceans, though Quarantotti Gambine, a figure in the new tradition, cautioned against too easy an assumption of a common tradition among writers as divergent as Svevo, Silvio Benco, Umberto Saba, Slataper, and Stuparich.[126]

What is most interesting about Svevo's Trieste is the sense, attested to by all his readers, of a place loved and lived in by its author that suffuses his fiction, yet, except for some spot lyrical descriptions, all

122. See letter to Montale, 30 June 1926, 00, 1: 797.
123. Saba, "Italo Svevo all'ammiragliato britannico," *Prose,* p. 154.
124. Maier, *Saggi,* p. 30.
125. Ibid., p. 12.
126. See interview with Quarantotti Gambini, "Fiera letteraria," 15 November 1964, cited in Riccardo Scrivano, "Pier Antonio Quarantotti Gambini," *Letteratura italiana* (Marzorati), 3: 610.

in a mediating mind and difficult to establish physically. As an atmosphere rather than a city, it is pervasive. One reader asks us to imagine Svevo's major fiction under any other sky than that of Trieste, and it is indeed difficult to conceive, yet it is more a state of mind than a place.[127] As a place, it is too provincial to hide victims of a public hoax from derision (H, 120–21). It is a city whose commercial business sent poets to their shelters to dream of literary fame. When Musil's Count Leinsdorf has qualms about the disloyalty of Trieste to Austria and delivers a speech against social assimilation of classes (especially in regard to the Jewish question) that, coming as it does at the point of collapse of the Hapsburg Empire, has a highly ironic ring to it, he speaks of Trieste as "the Hapsburg of the Mediterranean."[128] And it is this city—in which the bourgeois keepers of culture in a commercial port, like the aristocratic Jews of Hamburg, absorbed the influence of Vienna—that turned provincial dreamers like Italo Svevo to a Hapsburg world wider than that entertained by a jealous Mother Italy.

127. Spagnoletti, *Svevo*, pp. 11–12.
128. Robert Musil, *The Man Without Qualities*, trans. Eithne Wilkins and Ernst Kaiser (London, 1960), 3: 205–6.

Chapter 5

The European Identity

BECAUSE OF ITS PERSUASIVE INSISTENCE, Edouard Roditi's attempt in an early essay to place Svevo in a European rather than an Italian fraternity permanently widened the Svevo case.[1] Aligning him with European narrative masters like Schnitzler, Musil, and Kafka, and to less well known Czech and Hungarian novelists, Roditi based the connection largely on an elusive assimilation of an atmosphere of decadent bourgeoisie at the decline of the Hapsburg Empire that was alien to the Italian climate. This is a relation unanimously agreed upon by students of the Svevo case. Renato Poggioli, for example, identifies Svevo's "senility" as an attribute of a bourgeoisie that existed in Italian literature[2] neither as a sociological condition nor a state of mind, but that certainly could be felt in Trieste. Roditi's argument in detail seems at times forced, as when he juxtaposes the jargon of Schnitzler's "Leutnant Gustl" with that of *A Life,* the first a conscious literary device and the second not, to indicate that they both reflect the language of a declining bourgeoisie that has cobbled up a parodic version of an older aristocratic language. Grounding his conviction of literary affinity in the historical situation of the last decades of the Austrian empire, he refuses to accept a theory like Debenedetti's about Svevo's Jewish legacy and his identification with

1. Edouard Roditi, "Novelist-Philosopher: Italo Svevo," *Horizon* 10 no. 59 (November 1944) : 342–59. See also François Bondy: "Italo Svevo and Ripe Old Age," *Hudson Review* 20 (Winter 1967–8): 575–98: "Today Svevo takes his place quite naturally in that literature of 'Cacania,' along with the Croat Krleža, the Hungarian Karinthy, the Pole Bruno Schulz. His German translator, Piero Rismondo, and Edouard Roditi, among others, have sufficiently demonstrated it" (p. 569) ; see also G. Cattaneo, "Italo Svevo e la psicanalisi," *Belfagor,* 31 July 1959, p. 460.
2. Poggioli, "A Note on Italo Svevo," p. 172.

199

Weininger's thesis of the Jew as a hereditary neurotic, claiming instead that if Svevo reveals Jewish traits in his fictional attitudes, he is manifesting the environmental influence of an Austrian society, an influence that can be traced in other Jewish writers like Kafka and Schnitzler, or in the Jewish characters of writers like Musil.[3] The Svevian "inetto" is now pictured as a natural inhabitant of the European scene of a bourgeoisie without enough reasons to live, without enough faith to survive amidst crumbling old social and economic structures. Svevo is from these perspectives seen not as a mediator, but rather as "an isolated outpost," a part of the Hebraic-Christian literary family that flourished in the Hapsburg Empire of Schnitzler, Rilke, Kafka, and Musil and in the Paris of Proust, all directly or indirectly touched by Freud.[4] (This is one reason that *Confessions of Zeno* was always favored in the European countries over *As a Man Grows Older,* while, for a long time, the reverse was true in Italy.)

That the Austrian bourgeoisie, especially in its Jewish element, desired assimilation into the aristocracy without achieving it, the fact that it did not succeed either in destroying or in fully fusing with it, that it felt the social movements of the laboring classes from below as a threat rather than a hope, made it "inetto" as a class,[5] stranded in social and political irrelevance, dependent upon the Emperor as a protector. Svevo could receive this feeling from the Hapsburg climate, even if he was a mere stepchild to the paternal protector of a multiracial Empire, emanating a pseudo-security that sponsored gay and lively Vienna on the eve of disaster and that later spawned nostalgic odes to its golden age. Every historian of the Hapsburg Empire has heard the Viennese music of gaiety and abandoned melancholy as a desperate compensation for the lack of political participation and responsibility. It is a tone carried by the secret

3. Roditi, "Novelist-Philosopher," pp. 348–49.

4. Pampaloni, "Italo Svevo," p. 499.

5. See Claudio Magris, *Il mito absburgico nella letteratura austriaca moderna* (Turin, 1963), p. 31, and Carl Schorske, "Politics and the Psyche in 'Fin de siècle' Vienna," *The American Historical Review* (July 1961), p. 933. See also Schorske, "The Transformation of the Garden: Ideal and Society in Austrian Literature," *American Historical Review* 72: 1304–5:

The Austrian aesthetes were neither as alienated from their society as their French soulmates, nor as engaged in it as their English ones. They lacked the bitter anti-bourgeois spirit of the first, and the warm melioristic thrust of the second. Neither *dégagé* nor *engagé*, the Austrian aesthetes were alienated not from their class, but with it from a society that defeated its expectations and rejected its values.

melancholy of an operetta world, both capricious and sensuous in the face of impending extinction.[6] Blocked from the possibility of social meaning in a country, as a character in Schnitzler's *Der Weg ins Freie* puts it, of "social shams," where there "existed wild disputes without a touch of hate and a kind of tender love without the need of fidelity," in a country that could not hope for gradual insertion into the modern political world, the sensitive Hapsburg writers registered frustration in patterns that reflect their distinctively different temperaments. Besides their political and social instabilities, a linguistic instability, brought on by the multitude of languages in an Empire writing in German and holding together disparate nationalities, has been hypothesized, and this triple uneasiness is one that certainly could be absorbed by a Triestine novelist, himself an exile in his own country. Freud's enthusiasm for Schnitzler's descriptions of the war between morality and the instincts, and for his perception in the creation of the dilettante of feeling, was one that Svevo might have envied. It is tempting, too, to find a link between Svevo's defensive irony and that of the Hapsburg Jew who found himself in a situation of choice, in Schnitzler's view, between "being counted as insensitive, obtrusive and fresh, or of being oversensitive, shy and suffering from feelings of persecution,"[7] a representative of "a tired and sad humanity."[8] The patriarchal structure at the heart of the Empire, from Franz Josef down to the father of the family whose authority, as it moved from a social to a psychological emphasis, pervaded the worlds of both Freud and Kafka, is one experienced by Svevo and described in touching and humorous ambivalence in *Confessions of Zeno*.[9] In addition, the short-winded cultivation of personal feelings practiced by the feuilletonists, the café flâneurs writing of an anecdotal and random world, and the breaking up of the sustained

6. Schorske, "Politics and the Psyche," p. 188.

7. Arthur Schnitzler, *The Road to the Open*, trans. Horace Samuel (London, 1922), p. 371.

8. Arthur Schnitzler, *My Youth in Vienna*, trans. Catherine Hutter (New York, 1970), pp. 6–7. See Allan Janik and Stephen Toulmin, *Wittgenstein's Vienna* (New York, 1973), p. 273. The authors are speaking of the causes of Vienna's sickness and its symptoms:

anti-semitism, suicide, rigid sexual conventions, artistic sentimentality, political "double think," the rise of an underground press, divisive nationalisms, and the alienation of serious-minded intellectuals—all of these . . . either sprang from, or were enhanced by, the basic divorce of political and social realities from the appearances which were acceptable in the eyes of the Hapsburg autocracy.

9. Magris, *Il mito absburgico*, p. 288.

narrative action peaking in traditional climaxes of plot might well find their place in Svevo's story as a structural symptom parallel to the strain of intimate diary prose of the voceans.

But there is finally something unsatisfying about seeing Svevo as a peripheral Hapsburg citizen. For one thing, the persuasive and well-known thesis of Carl Schorske, that "in Vienna, it was political frustration that spurred the discovery of [the] now all-pervasive psychological man,"[10] we find in its literature; that it was political frustration that stimulated a change in the consideration of art "from an expression of value to a source of value,"[11] when applied to Svevo, overwhelms him with a historical situation that touched him only tangentially. There is no question that Svevo shared the fin-de-siècle condition, and it is understandable that critics might make this kind of association between Schnitzler's "Anatol" and Svevo's *Confessions of Zeno:*

> In this first theatrical work of Schnitzler the character seems to dissolve and his personality appears to break into sensations and corrosive analyses; a pattern that will find in Hofmannsthal and then in Musil a more complete expression and that is one of the peculiar characteristics of middleeuropean literature, from which will issue the Svevian *Confessions of Zeno.*[12]

But the more one tries to sweep Svevo into the arena of the Hapsburg man without qualities, the more his temperament seems to

10. Schorske, "Politics and the Psyche," p. 931.
11. Ibid., p. 936. Earlier in this essay, Schorske makes this distinction:
While traditional bourgeois culture saw nature as a sphere to be mastered by imposed order under divine law, Austrian aristocratic culture viewed nature as a scene of joy, a manifestation of divine grace to be glorified in art. Traditional Austrian culture was not, like that of the German north, moral, philosophical, and scientific, but primarily aesthetic. Its greatest achievements were in the applied and performing arts. The Austrian bourgeoisie, rooted in the liberal culture of reason and law, thus confronted an older aristocratic culture of sensuous feeling and grace. The two elements . . . could only form a most unstable compound. (pp. 933–34) .
And see Janik and Toulmin, *Wittgenstein's Vienna*, p. 44:
Once inside his castle, the paterfamilias could devote himself to enjoying the fruit of his labors—to the art, the music and the literature which were at once the "natural" humanizing outlet for all of his passions and the source for him of metaphysical truth.
Here, the bourgeois businessman could emulate the aesthetic cultivation of the ancient Catholic aristocracy. The sons, like Stefan Zweig, brought the cultivation outside the house. See his autobiography, *The World of Yesteryear*, trans anon. (Lincoln, Neb., 1964) , in which he vividly describes the aesthetic mania of the Austrian sons of the middle class at the turn of the century.
12. Magris, *Il mito absburgico*, p. 223.

resist, almost by a childish ingenuousness and independence, an atmosphere so heavy with historical consequence. For one thing, Svevo instinctively turns from the dissolution of consciousness and moral purpose, even as he is tempted to it, by accepting the value of bourgeois order and conscience on faith, rebelling against its constrictions only by opening around it a comic and "original" universe. Never would he feel cornered into accepting art as "a source of value" rather than as "an expression of value," and we have seen how persistently he used his fin-de-siècle traits as a means of combating this conversion rather than sanctioning it. The link between "devotion to art and the concern with the psyche," which Schorske sees as the result of the bourgeois sense of a world slipping away,[13] was a real but tenuous one for Svevo, constantly subject to his sociable irony and to his constant refusal to let the aesthetic accomplishment or desire extricate itself from the bourgeois scene, its given host. When we look at particular fictions and their experimental structures that translate disintegrated man, like "Leutnant Gustl" (1900) and "Fräulein Elsa" (1924) and try to relate the stream-of-consciousness technique not only to a general change in narrative rendering but specifically to Svevo's structure and approach, we cannot achieve a substantial sense of affinity. Schnitzler, Hofmannsthal, Kafka, and Musil shared with Svevo a Hapsburg world beset by anxiety and yearning for unity, a world that had to be described by new kinds of prose and character, but Svevo's directions and tendencies only hover uncomfortably at the edge of its rich compensatory art. It is impossible to ignore the bourgeois boundaries of conventional moral attitudes with which Zeno willingly rings himself, the hard-edged analytical word, the social wit, and the intimate irony by which the stream of consciousness is bridged.

The view from the eyes of the man without qualities, high enough in Musil to neutralize murder and sexual taboos, is a view that quite easily penetrates the screens behind which Svevo prefers to live. The aggressive and primordial power and energy of thought, of universal

---

13. Schorske, "Politics and the Psyche," p. 935:
The bourgeois, whether as fop, artist, or politician, could not rid himself of his individual heritage. As his sense of what Hofmannsthal called *das Gleitende*, the slipping away of the world, increased, the bourgeois turned his appropriated aesthetic culture inward to the cultivation of the self, of his personal uniqueness. This tendency inevitably led to preoccupation with one's own psychic life. It provides the link between the devotion to art and the concern with the psyche.

irony loosed from character: "If mankind could dream collectively, it would dream Moosbrugger,"[14] the scorn of that secure sociability for the "human something floating about in a universal culture-medium"[15] and of the intimacy that prescribes moderation, are luxuries of explosive relief never dreamed of in Svevo's philosophy. While the presence of historical contemplation in Musil's novel is stirred to a high allegorical pitch, Zeno, still bound by his sociability and his psychology, lives in historical comfort, despite all that rages around him. War is no match for the domestic dramas of desire and guilt. Zeno's vision expanded to the range of Mother Nature is regulated by bourgeois parents. As the first mother plots a zigzag route from desire to effect, the second helps to turn accident into intention. Meanwhile Musil's Ulrich says to Arnheim:

> In the old days people felt as it were deductively, starting from certain definite assumptions. That time is past. Nowadays we live without any guiding idea, but also without any method of conscious induction. We go on trying things as haphazardly as an ape does.[16]

Zeno knows what he wants; spared guiding theories, he will not miss the truth by taking a deliberate direction. He rises by analysis to a wise and sane induction about life which, taking account of the absurdity of its logic, does not diminish its worth.

Because of some biographical resemblances, some striking parallels of scene in the fiction, and the late enthusiasm of Svevo for his work,[17] Kafka has often been compared with Svevo. The Jew no longer practicing his religion but not fitting into the Christian world, a German-speaking Czech, a writer forced into a business clerkship, and a man with a poignant sense of alienation from his father's commercial world[18]—being all these tends to give to Kafka that sense of internal as well as external exile that is such a special

14. Robert Musil, *The Man Without Qualities,* trans. Eithne and Ernst Kaiser (New York, 1953), 1: 85.
15. Ibid., p. 257.
16. Ibid., 2: 418.
17. See Livia Veneziani Svevo, *Vita,* pp. 144–45: "L'ultimo suo amore letterario fu Kafka."
18. See Günther Anders, *Franz Kafka,* trans. A. Steer and A. K. Thorlby (London, 1960), p. 18, and Peter Bondanella, "Franz Kafka and Italo Svevo," *Comparative Literature Symposium: "Franz Kafka: His Place in World Literature,"* ed. W. T. Zyla, *Proceedings of the Comparative Literature Symposium* 4 (Lubbock, Tex., 1971): 17–34.

mark of Svevo as a literary man. While it is difficult to imagine Kafka as a man who would think disease the best part of us, still, a simultaneous skepticism about psychoanalytic therapy and fascination with its theory can be put beside Svevo's attitude, even if Kafka's evaluation is viewed as a desperate justification of the martyrdom of the artist. In a letter to Milena he writes:

> I consider the therapeutic part of psychoanalysis to be a hopeless error. All these so-called illnesses, sad as they may appear, are matters of faith, efforts of souls in distress to find moorings in some maternal soil; thus psychoanalysis also considers the origin of religions to be nothing but what (in its opinion) causes the "illnesses" of the individual. Nowadays, of course, we generally lack a sense of religious community; the sects are countless and confined to single individuals—though perhaps it only appears so to the eye colored by the present.
>
> Such moorings, however, which really take hold of solid ground, are after all not an isolated, interchangeable property of man, rather they are pre-existing in his nature and continue to form his nature (as well as his body) in this direction. And it's here they hope to cure?[19]

We can certainly picture Svevo's delight and amazement in reading a story like "Das Urteil" (Peter Bondanella conjectures that Svevo probably read Kafka before or during the writing of *Confessions of Zeno*[20]), in noting the guilt-ridden relationship between a sick father, who accuses his son of covering him up, and the similarity to the comparable scene in *Confessions of Zeno,* which climaxes with a slap in the face, a less fearful version of Bendemann père's sentencing.[21] The question of competitive strength, which is so movingly treated in "Das Urteil" (as well as in "Brief an den Vater," which Svevo could not have known), is a major structure in Svevo's chapter, though Kafka's characteristic unsettling primordial atmosphere of the dream unresponsive to a social world, of a fierce and literal submission of the adult view to the child's fantasy, is not the

19. Kafka, *Letters to Milena,* trans. Tania and James Stern (New York, 1962), p. 217.
20. Anders, *Franz Kafka,* p. 20. Bondanella's article examines interesting analogies between the writers and their works.
21. The raised hand appears in Kafka's *Brief an den Vater* (New York, 1966), Schocken bi-lingual edition, p. 32:
> Du hast mir aber schon früh das Wort verboten, Deine Drohung: "Kein Wort der Widerrede! und die dazu erhobene Hand begleiten mich schon seit jeher."

Svevian texture. It is impossible to suppose Svevo ever capable of writing Kafka's letter to his father, for he would claim no privilege of reproach for his neurosis. The reply allowed the father begins to resemble Svevo's self-irony. Even in this fruitful comparison, the conservative nature of Svevo's narrative vision emerges. The tripartite world that Kafka and his hero inhabit as it is described in "Brief an den Vater,"[22] one in which he is the slave living under laws not understood and invented only for him, laws that he could not completely comply with, for some reason; the second world infinitely remote from that in which the father resides, issuing orders and demanding obedience; and the third, in which everyone else lives happily and free from the duties of obedience, is finally a much more radical melodrama of pathos than is Svevo's zoned universe. In the Svevian world there are adjustments and compromises, persuasions and special bargainings, humorings and unforeseen long-range fortune, marriages of sons, and new patriarchs of self-irony. The double time of high consciousness may separate Zeno from Augusta, the "parental" laws may force his ineptitude and set him apart from Guido, but these boundaries are constantly crossed and, in fact, turn out to be illusory when they are seen from opposite sides. So too, Kafka's separation of the bourgeois family's happiness and normality from celibate and death-intoxicated art, is absolutely anxious and compulsive, while Svevo's is playful and never seriously allowed. Svevo links the two worlds by daydreams, while Kafka forges art from his bachelor nightmares. That is why Kafka's art dominates our imagination in a way that Svevo's cannot. No Flaubertian saint, Svevo could reconcile art and marriage.

For all their differences, a winning defensive humor that marks the temperaments of both Kafka and Svevo brings them much closer in our minds than Svevo to Mann, the last of the writers in German to whom Svevo is most often compared.[23] It is a discouraging enterprise to get the wide-ranging and intellectual irony and play of *Der Zauberberg* under the same roof with the domestic and anecdotal humor of Svevo, yet, of course, the juggling with two times—the cutting through of burgher morality, of the good and bad, by psycho-

22. Ibid., pp. 27–8.
23. See Lilian R. Furst, "Italo Svevo's *La coscienza di Zeno* and Thomas Mann's *Der Zauberberg*," *Contemporary Literature* 9 (1968) : 492–506.

analytic categories of sickness and health; the fascinating power of disease and its relation to art and "coscienza"; the simultaneous envy and scorn of bourgeois health; the echoes of an absurd war in the background—all attract consideration, as does a shared enthusiasm for Schopenhauer and Freud.[24] But while *Der Zauberberg* plays and develops variations on the great themes of Goethe and German philosophy, on an entire culture, within dialectical battles that almost dwarf the hero, the *Confessions of Zeno* is relentlessly personal and particular in its examination of Zeno's disease. That disease itself, which merely sticks its head into a sanatorium, for all its adequacy to represent the cultural neurosis of the fin-de-siècle bourgeoisie, is experienced as one that refuses to make symbolic claims that would raise it above the air of sustained distraction in the world of business and marriage. Every intellectual question is spontaneously broken by desire before it gets beyond the bounds of immediate analysis, and even at the end of Zeno's novel, the philosophical spanning of psychological breaches is just modest enough to stay within the range of Zeno himself. The kinds of questions raised by the highly deliberated coincidence of the collapse of the Buddenbrook firm and the musical genius of Hanno could have no parallel in Svevo, but the crossing of the lines of strong and weak, sick and healthy are suggestive in helping to bridge the enormous gap between the two writers. The structure, if not the texture of a humor that easily passes over conventional boundaries of moral and psychological time and "coscienza," and that lets no system or life stand unattended by irony, is a sign of analogous intelligences.

The relationship between Svevo and Joyce, so exciting a chapter in the history of literary friendship, is a much less exciting one in the history of influence. Svevo's lecture on Joyce, an act of gratitude, is not without its insights ("Joyce loves to impose chains on his own inspiration"[25]), but one always feels, in this and in his references to Joyce in letters, the strain of having to deal with Joyce's literature, awed as he was by it, rather than the great man himself, his savior. He seems more comfortable speaking of him, in the preface to the second edition of *Senilità* (Morreale), as one who repeated the

---

24. The attraction of both Alfonso and Thomas Buddenbrook to false versions of Schopenhauer has been mentioned by Svevo critics.

25. Svevo, "Scritti su Joyce," OO, 3: 717.

miracle of Lazarus. The two were so different in temperament that
we think of the relationship as a lucky one for both writers instead of
an intimate one. Joyce's brother, Stanislaus, corroborates this sense:

> The literary friendship between Svevo and Joyce was spontaneous
> and genuine, but the men were different temperamentally and in
> education. Joyce was the product of a Catholic, national education;
> Svevo of a Jewish and somewhat cosmopolitan education. Joyce was
> a born believer; he was impelled by nature to believe fervently in
> something, and in spite of poverty and continual disappointments,
> he was optimistic, almost truculently optimistic, about his work,
> with bursts of wild gaiety. Svevo was a skeptic with that vein of
> amiable pessimism that seems inseparable from the skeptical tem-
> perament. Even his belief in psychoanalysis was detached and ex-
> perimental, though he did try to make a convert of my brother.[26]

In a touching defense of Svevo against accusations of critics like
Heyse that his characters were weak and inept, Stanislaus Joyce
grants a weakness, but of another kind—"the weakness to allow the
obtuseness of critics and a life of material prosperity to frustrate his
life as an artist for so many years."[27] If this weakness was propped by
Joyce's confidence, Joyce, who is supposed to have used some of
Svevo in Bloom, might have found a father as well as discovered a
pupil in his transposed Dublin, Trieste. Perhaps, conjectures Harry
Levin: "In knowledge of human nature, particularly the nature of
l'homme moyen sensuel, James Joyce had much to learn from Italo
Svevo,"[28] and if Svevo could repay Joyce's generosity as a fellow
artist, it might be by imparting to him a "new tolerance for the
ineffectuality and mediocrity of ordinary lives."[29] All of this must, of
course, remain mere supposition, and attempts to force more out of
the history, like the reviewer who hypothesized that Joyce's greatest
work might have been the discovery of Svevo, or out of the relation

26. S. Joyce, *The Meeting of Svevo and Joyce,* p. 14. Stanislaus Joyce makes an
interesting, even if careless, ascription to *Confessions of Zeno* of "an egocentric outlook
on life and the seemingly uncontrolled outpouring of the all but subconscious mind in
a series of loosely connected episodes" (p. 15), and calls it "a rebirth under a new
form of the Protean spirit," which contrasts with the classical belief in form of his
brother.
27. Ibid., p. 17.
28. Harry Levin, "Carteggio inedito: Italo Svevo–James Joyce," *Inventario* 2 (1949):
112.
29. Ibid., p. 116.

between Joyce's stream-of-consciousness techniques and Zeno's analyses, are absurd fantasies.

The persistent attempts by French critics in Svevo's own lifetime to absorb him into their great tradition by calling him the Italian Proust surprised Svevo, for he had not read the French master before *Confessions of Zeno* and talked of the cultural blackout he experienced during the war,[30] just before he began the novel. When he did read Proust, he could not have had the same sense of recognition he must have had on reading Kafka, for here was a novelist almost antithetical to him in every important way. The superficial rapports noted between Swann and Odette on the one hand and Emilio and Angiolina on the other, the habit of analysis, a few salon scenes of social satire that might have seemed to touch the violin competition of Guido and Zeno, the meditations on time and consciousness, the hours spent in French beds and those spent in Triestine smoking and, most of all, the feeling that Svevo was more European than Italian, all these tempted the comparison. But Svevo himself anticipated the deceptive nature of the alliance and vigorously supported the protest of Marcel Thièbaut who, in speaking of Proust's dominating philosophical and psychological reflections, described a novelist "who was a thinker placed so clearly and comfortably above all genres, that it seemed arbitrary to compare to him, no matter how excellent, a writer [Svevo] whose intellectual activity exercised itself in an area less extensive."[31] Like Stuparich, Thièbaut would like to spare Svevo these comparisons to the Decadent tradition, to novelists for whom art itself could be a salvation from time, by ferrying him out of this century and pushing him back into the eighteenth for his dryness of style and into the nineteenth for his richness of character and atmosphere. Whatever distortions this escape might in turn promote, Svevo was relieved to be detached from Proust. He wrote to Valerio Jahier in 1927:

> Don't think I regret seeing myself detached from Proust. They were two entirely different destinines. His much more fine than mine, and it is not possible that a man as unpolished as I am could resemble the most perfect product of a civilization so refined.[32]

30. Svevo, Letter in French to Valéry Larbaud, 16 March 1925, OO, 1: 760.
31. The article which appeared in the *Revue de Paris* (15 November 1927), is referred to in Svevo, "Profilo autobiografico," OO, 3: 804.
32. Svevo, 2 December 1927, OO, 1: 857.

We are aware of his habitual defense, his recall of his antiliterary nature, and it was, in fact, in the elaborate Proustian style that he saw the greatest contrast with his own work:

> It's necessary also to remember that the Proustian sentence, with its engraved brilliance and its erudite complications that call to mind German syntax, finds no correspondence in the short, brusque, and untidy sentences of Svevo.[33]

With his usual delight in identifying with masters of literature censured for writing badly, he wryly greets Proust as an ally in critical scoldings. Some Italian critics—unwilling to accept Svevo's novel, finding it difficult to pin him down long enough to punish him, and already jealous of the French discovery—maliciously referred to his comparison to Proust as his greatest merit.[34] But with recognition came support for Svevo's desire to be unhooked from a writer who bore so little resemblance to him. Mario Lunetta pits the "bourgeois layman's common sense"[35] of Svevo against the aestheticism of Proust's style and thought. In the 1929 Svevo edition of *Solaria,* André Thérive distinguished the vulnerability of Svevo's moral generalizations from those closed aphoristic summations that join Proust to the great French tradition of maxim writers[36] and Giacomo Debenedetti succinctly contrasts the two: "Where Proust divines the soul in things, Svevo discovers the kernel in them."[37] Even the old Zeno finds it difficult to wallow in the past, for the need to live in the present is for Svevo imperative, and if the present can, as in Proust, stub its toe on the past, what is evoked cannot in any sustained way be captured in the net of the one great Time of Art.[38]

However misleading the analogies, the practice of comparing Svevo to European masters of narrative who emerged between 1915 and 1927 greatly enriched critical perception of his work. It pointed Svevo toward a new brotherhood that included such writers as Gide, whom Svevo mentions in a letter,[39] much closer to Svevo than

33. Svevo, "Profilo autobiografico," OO, 3: 804.
34. See Maier, *Profilo,* p. 21.
35. Lunetta, *Invito alla lettura di Svevo,* p. 104.
36. André Thérive, "Sur Zeno," p. 80.
37. Debenedetti, *Il romanzo,* p. 530.
38. See also Guido Almansi, "The Italian Proust," *Adam International Review,* nos. 310–12 (1966), pp. 115–18.
39. Svevo, to Montale, 5 July 1926, OO, 1: 798.

Proust, but who would not be brought into his orbit were it not for the French appropriation of Svevo's literature. Despite Gide's self-conscious literary experiments, his resistance to attitudes of aesthetic decadence and his predilection for the humor of the open temperament are examples that help to free Svevo from conventional literary descriptions, especially those associated with Decadence. Svevo himself, we remember, in his "Diario per la fidanzata" playfully termed himself a fin-de-siècle decadent who cannot be expected to know how to love well[40] and elsewhere, moved by the love between him and the young Livia, he wonders how he could have been so fortunate, he who was "the last product of the fermentation of a century."[41] We realize that, as always with Svevo, these epithets are being used to describe a temperament loosely thrown into a period of historical decline, but one that, as a state of mind, appeared constantly and periodically at the imagined end of all ages. The emphasis is only ironically historical, to give pseudo-magnitude to the personal case of "senilità." But critics have pressed upon these terms and looked in Svevo's subjects and motifs for the Russian hyperbolic consciousness, oblomovism,[42] the Hapsburg malady, the Flaubertian fatigue of sentimental educations in an age of spiritual mediocrity. The historical category of Decadence, as distinguished from temperamental ascriptions, encases his attitudes in the dignity of a period. As with the major ideological currents, the novelist only plays with these identities and is overcome by none of them.

The issue of literary designation is complicated by the problem of an Italian Decadence predictably in arrears of that of France, Austria, and England, its parent Romanticism having already been out of step. Walter Binni's classic study of Italian Decadence, which attempts to counter the Nietzschian sense of it as a recurrent temper by giving it the muscle of a specific literary movement, emphasizes the lack in Italian Romanticism of those mystical and sensual elements that evolved into the Decadent period in European literature.[43] If the Scapigliati are the first post-Romantics in Italy to display the "equilibrio morale" of the decadent spirit, they are, by

40. Svevo, "Diario per la fidanzata," entry of 26 January 1896, OO, 3: 780.
41. Svevo, to Livia Veneziani, 23 December 1895, OO, 1: 39.
42. See Giuliano Manacorda, "Oblomovismo italiano? La fortuna letteraria di Italo Svevo," *Rinascita 6* (6 June 1949) : 276–80.
43. Walter Binni, *La poetica del decadentismo* (Florence, 1949) , p. 321.

comparison to Lautréamont or Rimbaud, greenhorns of unsustained rebellion:

> The scapigliati are abnormal souls who do not have a deep-rooted and solid base for their liberty.[44]

The momentum necessary for a new program equivalent to those of the French schools was never generated. Post-Romantic literary Italy is caught between the desire and difficulty of renewing itself and the fear of being behind time, caught "with its clothes out of fashion"[45] in the mirror of European modernity. As one historian observes:

> In the manner of verismo, also decadence is with us a simpler and more modest affair, still anchored, even in its social make-up, to the provinces.[46]

One would not assume this simplicity from the over-elaborate and all-embracing categories of Giulio Marzot, who makes of Italian Decadence virtually the equivalent of modern literature.[47] Any individual writer suffers when stuffed into descriptive pockets meant to hold others as well as himself, but no one seems more awkwardly placed than Svevo in this panorama. He is banked on one side by the "Crepuscolari," fathered by Pascoli and living a daily life of journeys into the self, recording the poetry of the earth, a group Marzot calls "neoprovinciali." Passive and private rather than political and active, divorced from a large social reality, acutely sensitive, favoring their sickness, their fragility, and curbing self-pity with irony, Gozzano, Corazzini, Moretti, F. M. Marini, the early Saba, Palazzeschi, and Valeri correspond somewhat with the French poets who were so influential in twentieth-century American poetry, Laforgue, Corbière, Jammes. The "spiritualisti" (Tommaseo, Fogazzaro), the aesthetic and experimental "Erotici" (D'Annunzio, "who gathers in himself all the 'ismi' of Decadence, both foreign and indigenous"[48]), the "Dionisiaci" (D'Annunzio, voluptuary of war, disciples of Nietzsche and Wagner, Papini, the Futurists), "ermetismo" (the Mallarmé-Valéry school of Italian decadence un-

44. Ibid., p. 40.
45. Ibid., p. 51.
46. Mario Marcazzan, "Dal romanticismo al decadentismo," *Letteratura italiana* 2: 888.
47. See Marzot, *Il decadentismo italiano.*
48. Ibid., p. 159.

der which are listed Onofri, Ungaretti, early Quasimodo) —all these surround Svevo's category, "tragic analysts," which he shares with Pirandello[49] and Borgese, shapers of soliloquy, of modern man fractured in himself and from society. The disequilibrium of stress and the disintegration of classical notions of social and stylistic unity are the common denominators between these varieties of decadence, and such a disjunctive rhythm and scene would seem to apply to the incomplete sketches Alfonso, Emilio, and Zeno. But the peculiar nature of Svevo's irony that refuses any aesthetic neutralization of morality (nothing could be more offensive to him than the Decadent slogan: art a morality and morality an art) is one that treats this condition as an affliction to be humored, not to be taken advantage of. His vision runs past Decadence both temperamentally and historically.

Svevo would have been familiar with the diagnosis of Paul Bourget of the age in which he lived, as one of moral exhaustion, German pessimism, Slavic nihilism, bizarre Latin neurosis, nausea, hysteria, egoism,[50] as with the definitions of decadence of Nietzsche and Max Nordau described in those familiar metaphors of parts stubbornly rebelling against the whole, petty tyrants of stylistic exaggeration, scornful of moral and political integration. For Nietzsche, decadence is characterized

> by the fact that in it life no longer animates the whole. Words become predominant and leap right out of the sentence to which they belong, the sentences themselves trespass beyond their bounds, and obscure the sense of the whole page, and the page in its turn gains in vigor at the cost of the whole—the whole is no longer a whole.[51]

For Max Nordau, whom Svevo identified with Molière's Alceste,[52] all of modern literature is decadent, degenerate, and the fall occurs when the aesthetic prevails over the useful and rises to orgiastic mysticism:

49. Luigi Ferrante writes in "Rosso di San secondo," *Letteratura italiana: I contemporanei* (Marzorati), 3: 108: "Svevo and Pirandello [are] the greatest examples of the Decadent period."

50. Paul Bourget, "Théorie de la décadence," *Essais de psychologie contemporaine* (Paris, 1901), 1: 258.

51. Friedrich Nietzsche, "The Case of Wagner," *The Philosophy of Nietzsche*, p. 269.

52. Svevo, "Il vero paese de' miliardi," review of Nordau's *Studi e schizzi parigini*, OO, 3: 563.

However dissimilar such individualities as Wagner and Tolstoi, Rossetti and Verlaine, may at first sight appear, we have, never the less, encountered in all of them certain common traits, to wit, vague and incoherent thought, the tyranny of the association of ideas, the presence of obsessions, erotic excitability, religious enthusiasm, by which we may recognize them as members of one and the same intellectual family, and justify their union into one single group—that of mystics.[53]

This kind of escape by self-denial into salvation leaves Nietzsche's Christianity as the highest form of decadence.[54] Bourget prefers the biological image in describing the decadent rebellion of cells against the whole organism. Society becomes decadent when individual life is exaggerated and language when the page becomes superior to the piece.[55] The disproportion of parts to the whole is precisely that aspect of naturalism which Heyse had deplored when he wrote in his letter to Svevo:

It would delight me to meet you soon again in cleaner air, instead of in that dank atmosphere of Decadence.[56]

Yet this is to assume an identity of Svevo's subject with his vision. In a man falling short of the transcendence of Schopenhauer and the transvaluation of Nietzsche, in a man amused by the energetic misanthropy of Nordau, it might be difficult to spot this distinction.

If, from about 1880 until the beginning of the twentieth century, the European world sent down to Trieste the image of a modern man who was a victim of "refined appetite, sensations, tastes, of luxuries and pleasures, neurosis, hysteria, hypnotism, morphinomania, scientific charlatanism, excessive schopenhauerism,"[57] it was an image that touched the fiction of Svevo without finding a comfortable place within it. To display sickness like a badge of distinction and to transvaluate it in the D'Annunzian manner are attitudes that seem possible to a man who asks: "And why wish to cure ourselves of our

53. Nordau, *Degeneration*, trans. from 2d ed. of German work, ed. G. Mosse (New York, 1968), p. 16.

54. Nietzsche, "Case of Wagner," p. 287.

55. Bourget, "Théorie de la décadence," p. 49.

56. Ferdinando Pasini, "Italo Svevo con due lettere inedite di Paul Heyse," *Annali triestini* 1 (1929): 183.

57. From an article in "The Decadent," 10 April 1886, quoted in Mario Praz, *The Romantic Agony*, trans. Angus Davidson (New York, 1956), p. 382.

sickness? Should we really take from humanity what is best about it?"[58] Yet it is precisely the harboring and humoring of such sickness that becomes the best protection against complacent and antisocial resignation, the cures of ecstatic supermen:

> We are a living protest against that ridiculous conception of super-man that has been foisted off on us, especially on us Italians.[59]

An age that made use of "every kind of exoticism and eclecticism to distract the restlessness of its exasperated senses and to make up for its lack both of profound faith and of an authentic style"[60] is not an age exemplified or exploited by Zeno's psychic explosions and improvisations. Svevo's irony spans the distance between sickness and health in a constant effort to keep the two on talking terms. His presence in the early novels would not allow the victory to neurotic rationalizations, pseudo-"schopenhauerisme à outrance," but it also provided another kind of sensibility in authorial qualification and ironic sympathy that keeps the egoism of the "normal" world in its place. Even the uniqueness of Zeno's personality is appreciated by a world of less acute consciousness, and no Svevian character is permitted to revel underground. Cures are more dangerous than disease, and solutions must give way to tones that keep us modest parasites on the earth.

Svevo's early admiration for Turgenev's narrative policy of hands-off, his attraction to an irony that sustains the greatest degree of unsentimental tolerance, were never to change.[61] If he could not achieve Turgenev's narrative poise and assurance, the Russian master helped him to realize a narrative philosophy. Leone de Castris convincingly argues, if too tendentiously, for an evaluation that would put Svevo in the line of those who, while fully experiencing the problems of fin-de-siècle decadence, achieve a new realism by assiduously examining its "coscienza": "It is a realism *as* critical 'coscienza' of the man of the age of Decadence."[62] As a correction to the identification of Svevo with a passive decadence, the argument is valuable. To speak of Svevo as one of those twentieth-century literary heroes who searched for a new reality to replace ones that social and

58. Svevo, Letter to Valerio Jahier, 27 December 1927, OO, 1: 859.
59. Ibid., pp. 859–60.
60. Praz, *The Romantic Agony*, p. 389.
61. Svevo, "Poesie in prosa di Ivan Turgenieff," 1884, OO, 3: 572.
62. Quoted in Bouissy, "Les Fondements," 1: 211.

literary Decadence had consumed strains our notions of his determination and intention. This is probably why André Bouissy refuses to accept De Castris's designation of "decadent" at all for Svevo,[63] who separated himself from his weaker characters by an irony that, even when it blossomed into the full and sympathetic humor of Zeno, weighed civilization's discontents on Mother Nature's volatile and provincial scales.

63. Bouissy, "Les Fondements," 1: 211.

Epilogue

"I MUST GO THE SAME WAY with my pen as with my feet,"[1] writes Montaigne in one of his many formulas that indicate the closeness of the life and the art. Ettore Schmitz gave himself no such commandment and, indeed, published himself as "Italo Svevo." His country certainly did not point the way. For twenty-five years, while she was opening doors for the businessman Schmitz, Mother Italy was slamming them in Svevo's face. Yet, the blind "imperious will preparing the way for the future" (FCZ 109) or that maniac Mother Nature, which Zeno pictures leading men and their works on curious and surprising journeys across fields and pages, has a habit of bringing them safely home together. Svevo's daughter movingly writes of Schmitz's ability to "give to the young that confidence in life which he himself lacked."[2] As we might expect of a true son of Mother Nature, Italo Svevo also gave to the young a cultural revolution because he had no idea he was doing it.

One of his best short stories, the often-anthologized fable "The Mother," has been read in the way one might read Mario Samigli's fables, as merely a slap at Svevo's cold-hearted and scornful country for not accepting his pen. Such a reading, however gratifying it may be for Svevo to settle the score at last, fails to do justice to the philosophic scope of the comic vision of both the man and the writer, a vision that will not and cannot capture at the same time both cause and effect, though their relationship is obsessively pondered.

The chicken Curra, hatched in an incubator, begins to long for a

1. Montaigne, *Essays,* 3: 9, 758.
2. Letizia Svevo Fonda Savio, "A Daughter's Tribute," *Modern Fiction Studies,* Svevo issue, p. 4.

natural mother as soon as he hears that such a person exists. The chick might be Freud's modern technical man, described in *Civilization and Its Discontents* as one who thought he could be happy mastering Nature, but still cannot overcome the tragic struggle, both within him and without, between the forces of life (Eros) and those of destruction (Thanatos) :

> it is this battle of the giants that our nursemaids try to appease with their lullaby about Heaven.[3]

When Curra, a comic second Adam, naïvely asserts: "What is more, it will be easy for me to obey her because I already love her" (p. 19) ,[4] he has forgotten that in Svevo's universe the Mother is always the mother of someone else. At the climax of the fable, when Curra eagerly insinuates himself into the mother hen's search for worms to feed her own chicks, the mother cruelly turns on poor Curra and excludes him with the cosmic pronouncement: " 'I am the Mother!' "

Curra does not have the heart to face this rejection without masking it with illusion. Like Mario Samigli, he palliates the attack by appropriating it. " 'My mother,' " he says to the chicks when he gets back to the yard, " 'unlike yours, was a revolting creature, and it would have been better if I had never met her' " (p. 21) . To see himself as the victim of a heartless mother leaves intact the myth of a universe ordered by Motherhood.

We have witnessed Schmitz's taking Svevo and Svevo's taking Zeno beyond barnyard rationalizations into a wider consciousness. If this space is not so secure as we want it, still it gives us many advantages. The ugly duckling, the incomplete biological and psychological sketch that represents modern man, achieves, on this stage, a kind of bittersweet dignity. If he can accept his humiliations with grace, if he can humor but not indulge the illusions without which he cannot live, his subdued heroism is ageless, beyond history, though it is particularly poignant in an age of anxiety. When his fables open him to play with the paradoxes of life and refuse to soundproof him from the noisy battle of the giants, he wins, if not her protection, the respect of Mother Nature.

3. Freud, "Civilization and Its Discontents," Standard ed., 21: 122.
4. I use the translation of Edwina Vittorini in *Italian Short Stories*, vol 2, ed. Dimitri Vittorini, Penguin Parallel Text (Harmondsworth, Middlesex, England, 1972) .

Bibliography

Anthologies of critical articles and views on Svevo:

In Italian:

La critica e Svevo. Edited by Sandro Briosi. Bologna, 1975.

Leggere Svevo. Edited by Luciano Nanni. Bologna, 1974.

Maier, Bruno. *Profilo della critica su Italo Svevo.* Trieste, 1951.

'Omaggio a Italo Svevo' in *Il Convegno* 10 nos. 1–2, gennaio-febbraio 1929.
    Contains articles by G. Debenedetti, C. Linati, G. Stuparich and A. Rossi.

'Omaggio a Italo Svevo,' in *Solaria* 4 nos. 3–4, marzo-aprile 1929.
    Contains articles and views by G. B. Angioletti, J. Boulanger, M. Brion, J. Chabas, A. Consiglio, B. Crémieux, G. Debenedetti, Ilya Ehrenburg, G. Ferrata, L. Ferrero, R. Franchi, P. Gadda, Ivan Goll, F. Hellens, James Joyce, Valéry Larbaud, C. V. Lodovici, Paul-Henri Michel, Adrienne Monnier, Eugenio Montale, A. Palazzeschi, G. Raimondi, A. Rossi, Umberto Saba, E. Schwenk, Sergio Solmi, Philippe Soupault, G. Stuparich, B. Tecchi, André Thérive, A. van Schendel.

In English:

Essays on Italo Svevo. Edited by Thomas F. Staley, University of Tulsa Monograph Series, no. 6. Tulsa, Okla., 1969. Includes articles by Thomas F. Staley, John Gatt-Rutter, Jan Paul Malocsay, Brian Moloney, Bruno Maier, R. S. Baker, Jan Paul Ragusa, Maralee Frampton.

Modern Fiction Studies. Svevo Issue, 18 no. 1 (Spring 1972). Includes articles by Thomas F. Staley, Gian-Paolo Biasin, Paula Robison, Beno Weiss, Renata M. Treitel, Domenica Cernecca, Teresa de Lauretis, Niny Rocco-Bergera, Lina Galli, and a bibliographical checklist.

Works cited in text:

Almansi, Guido. "The Italian Proust." *Adam International Review,* nos. 310–312 (1966) : 115–118.

Apollonio, Umbro. Preface to *Corto viaggio sentimentale e altri racconti inediti.* Milan, 1954, pp. 7–15.

Barilli, Renato. *La linea Svevo-Pirandello.* Milan, 1972.

Battaglia, Salvatore. "Coscienza della realtà nei romanzi di Svevo." *Filologia e letteratura* 10 (1964) : 225–48.

Benco, Silvio. "Italo Svevo." *Pegaso* 1 (January 1929) : 48–56. Reprinted in *Umana* 20 (May-September 1971) : 64–68.

———. Review of *Novella del buon vecchio e della bella fanciulla ed altri scritti* (Milan, 1920). *Pegaso* 1, no. 8 (August 1929) : 244–49.

Biasin, Gian-Paolo. "Zeno's Last Bomb." In *Literary Diseases: Theme and Metaphor in the Italian Novel. Austin, Tex.,* 1975. pp. 63–99.

Binni, Walter. *La poetica del decadentismo.* Florence, 1949.

Bondanella, Peter E. "Franz Kafka and Italo Svevo," *Franz Kafka: His Place in World Literature.* Proceedings of the Comparative Literature Symposium, ed. W. T. Zyla. Lubbock, Tex., 1971, 4: 17–34.

———. " 'The Hoax': Svevo on Art and Reality." *Studies in Short Fiction* 10, no. 3 (Summer 1973) : 263–79.

———. "The Reception of Italo Svevo." *Italian Quarterly* 12 (Winter-Spring 1969) : 63–89.

Bondy, François. "Italo Svevo and Ripe Old Age." *Hudson Review* 20, no. 4 (Winter 1967–68) : 575–98.

Bonora, Ettore. "Italo Svevo." In *Gli ipocriti di malebolge.* Milan and Naples, 1953. pp. 86–105.

Bontempelli, Massimo. "Confessionale." *Tempo* (September 1942) : 10–17.

Bouissy, André. "Les Fondements idéologiques de l'oeuvre d'Italo Svevo." *Revue des études italiennes* 12, no. 3 (July-September 1966) : 209–45; pt. 2, 12, no. 4 (October-December 1966) : 350–73; pt. 3, 13, no. 1 (January-March 1967) : 23–50.

Boulanger, Jacques. "Sur Zeno," *Solaria* 4 nos. 3–4 (March-April 1929).

Brion, Marcel. "Une oeuvre nouvelle d'Italo Svevo: 'Una burla riusita'." *Nouvelles littéraires, artistiques et scientifiques* (24 March 1928).

Camerino, Giuseppe A. *Italo Svevo e la crisi della Mitteleuropa.* Florence, 1974.

Cattaneo, Giulio. "Svevo e la psicoanalisi." *Belfagor* (31 July 1959) : 454–60.

Cernecca, Domenica. "Dialectical Element and Linguistic Complex in Italo Svevo." Translated by Renata Treitel. In *Modern Fiction Studies* 18, no. 1 (Svevo Issue) (Spring 1972) : 81–90.

Citati, Pietro. "Il violino di Svevo." In *Il tè del capellaio matto*. Milan, 1972. pp. 158–63.

Consiglio, Alberto. *Studi di poesia*. Florence, 1934, pp. 83–113.

Crémieux, Benjamin. *La Littérature italienne*. Paris. 1928.

———. "Italo Svevo." *Le Navire d'argent*, 1 February 1926, pp. 23–26.

David, Michel. *La psicoanalisi nella cultura italiana*. Turin, 1966.

Debenedetti, Giacomo. *Il romanzo del Novecento*. Milan, 1971.

———. "Svevo e Schmitz." *Saggi critici*, n.s. (Milan, 1955) . pp. 49–94.

———. "Lettera a Carocci intorno a 'Svevo e Schmitz.'" *Saggi critici*, n.s. (Milan, 1955) , pp. 99–101.

———. "*L'ultimo Svevo*." *Saggi critici*, n.s. (Milan, 1955) , pp. 102–16.

De Castris, A. Leone. *Italo Svevo*. Pisa, 1959.

———. "La coscienza di Svevo." In *Il decadentismo italiano*. Bari, 1974, pp. 83–134.

Devoto, Giacomo. "Decenni per Svevo." In *Studi di stilistica,* Florence, 1950, pp. 175–93.

Flora, Francesco. "Italo Svevo." In *Storia della letteratura italiana*, 5. Milan: Mondadori, 1947, pp. 741–42.

Forti, Marco. *Svevo romanziere*. Milan, 1966.

Franchi, Rafaello. "Ommaggio a Svevo." *Solaria* (Svevo Issue) 4 nos. 3–4 (March-April 1929) .

Freccero, John. "Zeno's Last Cigarette," *Modern Language Notes* 77 (1962) : 3–23. Reprinted in *From Verismo to Experimentalism: Essays on the Modern Italian Novel*. Edited by Sergio Pacifici. Bloomington, Ind., 1969, pp. 35–60.

Furbank, P. N. *Italo Svevo, The Man and the Writer*. Berkeley and Los Angeles, Calif., 1966.

Furst, Lilian R., "Italo Svevo's *La coscienza di Zeno* and Thomas Mann's *Der Zauberberg*." *Contemporary Literature* 9 (1968) : 492–506.

Gadda, Piero. "Lettura di *Senilità*." *Solaria* (Svevo Issue) 4 nos. 3–4 (March-April 1929) .

Guglielminetti, Marziano. *Strutturra e sintassi del romanzo italiano del primo Novecento*. Milan, 1964.

Heyse, Paul. In F. Pasini. "Italo Svevo con due lettere inedite di Paul Heyse." *Annali triestino* 1 (1929) .

Illiano, Antonio. "A View of the Italian Absurd from Pirandello to Eduardo De Filippi." *From Surrealism to the Absurd,* edited by W. T. Zyla, Proceedings of the Comparative Literature Symposium 3 (Lubbock, Tex., 1970) : 55–76.

Jacobs, Lee. "Zeno's Sickness Unto Death." *Italian Quarterly* 11, no. 44 (Spring 1968) : 51–66.

Jonard, Norbert. *Italo Svevo et la crise de la bourgeoisie européenne.* Paris, 1969.

Joyce, Stanislaus. *The Meeting of Svevo and Joyce.* Edited by Sergio Perosa, Trieste, 1965.

Levin, Harry, ed. "Carteggio inedito: Italo Svevo–James Joyce." *Inventario* 2 (1949) : 106–138.

Lunetta, Mario. *Invito alla lettura di Italo Svevo.* Milan, 1972.

Luti, Giorgio. *Svevo.* Florence, 1967.

Magris, Claudio. *Il mito absburgico nella letteratura austriaca moderna.* Turin, 1963.

Maier, Bruno. *Profilo della critica su Italo Svevo.* Trieste, 1951.

———. *Saggi sulla letteratura triestina.* Milan, 1972.

———. *Italo Svevo.* 4th ed. Milan, 1975.

Manacorda, Giuliano. "Oblomovismo italiano? La fortuna letteraria di Italo Svevo." *Rinascita* 6, no. 6 (June 1949) : 276–80.

Marcazzan, Mario. "Dal romanticismo al decadentismo." In *La letteratura italiana* "Le correnti." 2 Milan: Marzorati, 1957.

Marzot, Giulio. *Il decadentismo italiano.* Bologna, 1970.

Maxia, Sandro. *Lettura di Italo Svevo.* Padua, 1965.

Moloney, Brian. *Italo Svevo: A Critical Introduction.* Edinburgh, 1974.

Montale, Eugenio. *Lettere Italo Svevo: con gli scritti di Montale su Italo Svevo.* Bari, 1966.

———.*Interview with Moravia.* Conducted by Anna Maria de Dominicis and Ben Johnson. *Paris Review* 6 (Summer 1954) .

Moravia, Alberto. *Entretiens avec A. Moravia.* Edited by Jean Duflot. Paris, 1970.

Nelson, Lowry, Jr. "A Survey of Svevo." *Italian Quarterly* 2, no. 10 (Summer 1959) : 3–33.

Pacifici, Sergio. *The Modern Italian Novel: From Manzoni to Svevo.* Carbondale, Ill., 1967.

Pampaloni, Geno. "Italo Svevo." In *Storia della letteratura italiana: Il Novecento.* Edited by Emilio Cecchi and Natalino Sapegno. Milan, 1969, pp. 493–532.

Pasini, Ferdinando. "Italo Svevo." *Annali dell'Università degli Studi Economici e Commerciale di Trieste* 1, fasc. 1 (1929) : 161–83.

Pfohl, Russell. "Imagery as Disease in *Senilità.*" *Modern Language Notes* 76, no. 2 (1961) : 143–50.

Poggioli, Renato. "A Note on Italo Svevo." *Spirit of the Letter.* Cambridge, Mass., 1965) , pp. 171–79.

Ricciardi, Mario. *L'educazione del personaggio nella narrativa di Italo Svevo.* Palermo, 1972.

Robbe-Grillet, Alain. "Zeno's Sick Conscience." In *For a New Novel,* translated by Richard Howard (New York, 1965) , pp. 89–94.

Robison, Paula. "Svevo: Secrets of the Confessional." *Literature and Psychology* 20, no. 3 (1970) : 101–14.

———. "*Senilità:* The Secret of Svevo's Weeping Madonna." *Italian Quarterly* 14, no. 55 (1971) : 61–84.

———. " 'Una burla riuscita': Irony as Hoax in Svevo." *Modern Fiction Studies* (Svevo Issue) 18, no. 1 (Spring 1972) : 65–80.

———. "*Una vita* and the Family Romance." *Modern Fiction Studies* (Svevo Issue) 18, no. 1 (Spring 1972) : 33–44.

Roditi, Edouard. "Novelist-Philosopher: Italo Svevo." *Horizon* 10, no. 59 (1944) : 342–59

Rosowski, Giuditta. "Théorie pratique psychoanalitique dans l'oeuvre d'Italo Svevo." *Revue des études italiennes* 1 (1970) : 66–70.

Saba, Umberto. "Italo Svevo all'ammiragliato brittanico." In *Prose.* Milan, 1964, pp. 152–55 and *passim.*

Saccone, Eduardo. "*Senilità* di Italo Svevo: dalla 'impotenza del privato' alla 'ansiosa speranza.' " *Modern Language Notes* 82, no. 1 (January 1967) : 1–55.

———. "Svevo, Zeno et la psicanalisi." *Modern Language Notes* 85, no. 1 (January 1970) : 67–109.

———. *Commento a Zeno.* Bologna, 1973.

Solmi, Sergio. "Ricordi di Svevo." *Solaria* (Svevo Issue) 4, nos. 3–4 (March-April 1929) .

Sutor, Mario, ed. *Saba/Svevo/Comisso.* Padua, 1968.

Spagnoletti, Giacinto. *Svevo.* Milan, 1972.

Svevo, Livia Veneziani. With Galli, Lina. *Vita di mio marito.* Edited by A. Pittoni. Trieste, 1958.

Tancredi, Marida. *"Una vita* di Svevo." *Angelus Novus,* no. 21 (1971), pp. 55–84.

Testa, Antonio. *Italo Svevo.* Ravenna, 1968.

Vittorini, Elio. Review of 2nd. ed. of *Una vita. Solaria* 5, no. 12 (December 1930) : 47–58.

———. *Diario in publico.* Milan, 1957. *passim.*

Wilden, Anthony. "Death, Desire and Repetition in Svevo's Zeno." *Modern Language Notes* 84, no. 1 (January 1969) : 98–119.

Index